UNION WITH CHRIST

"Everyone seems to agree that union with Christ is a biblical teaching crucial to understanding and communicating the gospel, but preachers today do not give it the same emphasis that the New Testament does. One reason is that, unlike the new birth, justification, and adoption, it requires multiple metaphors to draw out its rich meaning. Rankin does so clearly and compellingly. This is simply the best book for laypeople on this subject. It is grounded in exegesis and theology and yet is lucid and supremely practical. While not unaware of the recent controversies about union and justification, which are briefly sketched in the endnotes, Rankin's whole concern is to make the biblical teaching accessible and applicable to the reader. He does this with excellence."

Tim Keller, senior pastor of Redeemer
Presbyterian Church, New York City

UNION WITH CHRIST

RANKIN
WILBOURNE

UNION
WITH
CHRIST

The Way to Know and Enjoy God

David C Cook®
transforming lives together

UNION WITH CHRIST
Published by David C Cook
4050 Lee Vance Drive
Colorado Springs, CO 80918 U.S.A.

David C Cook U.K., Kingsway Communications
Eastbourne, East Sussex BN23 6NT, England

The graphic circle C logo is a registered trademark of David C Cook.

The website addresses recommended throughout this book are offered as a
resource to you. These websites are not intended in any way to be or imply an
endorsement on the part of David C Cook, nor do we vouch for their content.

Unless otherwise noted, all Scripture quotations are taken from the ESV® Bible (The
Holy Bible, English Standard Version®), copyright © 2001 by Crossway, a publishing
ministry of Good News Publishers. Used by permission. All rights reserved. Scripture
quotations marked KJV are taken from King James Version of the Bible. (Public
Domain); NET are taken from NET Bible® copyright ©1996–2006 by Biblical Studies
Press, LLC. http://netbible.com All rights reserved; NIV are taken from the Holy Bible,
NEW INTERNATIONAL VERSION®, NIV®. Copyright © 1973, 2011 by Biblica,
Inc.® Used by permission. All rights reserved worldwide. NEW INTERNATIONAL
VERSION® and NIV® are registered trademarks of Biblica, Inc. Use of either trademark
for the offering of goods or services requires the prior written consent of Biblica, Inc.;
NLT are taken from the *Holy Bible*, New Living Translation, copyright © 1996, 2007 by
Tyndale House Foundation. Used by permission of Tyndale House Publishers, Inc., Carol
Stream, Illinois 60188. All rights reserved; and NRSV are taken from the New Revised
Standard Version Bible, copyright 1989, Division of Christian Education of the National
Council of the Churches of Christ in the United States of America. Used by permission.
All rights reserved. The author has added italics to Scripture quotations for emphasis.

LCCN 2016938482
ISBN 978-1-4347-0938-7
eISBN 978-1-4347-1087-1

© 2016 J. Rankin Wilbourne

The Team: Tim Peterson, Keith Jones, Amy Konyndyk, Jack Campbell, Susan Murdock
Cover Design: Nick Lee

Printed in the United States of America

First Edition 2016

5 6 7 8 9 10 11 12 13 14

101717

To Morgen, my Beatrice

I now see clearly that our intellect
cannot be satisfied until that truth enlighten it
beyond whose boundary no further truth extends.

In that truth, like a wild beast in its den, it rests
once it has made its way there—and it can do that,
or else its every wish would be in vain.

Dante, *Paradiso* IV:124–129

CONTENTS

FOREWORD

I'm trying to remember the last time I was more excited about a new book or a new author.

Rankin Wilbourne brings a remarkable flair for writing, and a great breadth and depth of learning, and a passionate heart, to the most important subject in the world: What is the true and sufficient destiny for human life?

Those of us who call ourselves Christians know that the answer to this question, somehow, is wrapped up in the gospel. But the word *gospel* itself has become fuzzy and debated and truncated and partially buried under the distortions and misreadings that are an inevitable part of human history.

One clue to recovering the gospel lies in comparing the way we describe ourselves with the language of the New Testament itself. The word *Christian* is found only three times. However, the New Testament letters associated with the apostle Paul use the phrase *in Christ* around 165 times.

Perhaps one of the greatest barriers to faith is not the things we don't know but the things we think we know yet we're wrong about.

We think of heaven as the pleasure factory rather than life with God. We think of salvation as being able to avoid pain rather than being made right. We think of the gospel as the minimal entrance requirements for getting into heaven rather than the announcement that life with God is now possible on earth through Jesus. We think of faith as what we're supposed to believe rather than the mental map about how things are that we carry with us and inevitably live from. We think of Christians as people who have got the heaven job done, while we think of discipleship as optional extra-credit work for spiritual overachievers.

All of this is what Rankin addresses so clearly and compellingly in this book. He combines a rich knowledge and appreciation of historical theology with a penetrating analysis of how God brings about transformation in embodied and largely habit-driven creatures. He does this by unearthing a notion that was central to the early followers of Jesus but has become largely lost in our day: union with Christ.

Life consists in the ability to connect with and draw nourishment from its surroundings. A seed is planted in the ground and would otherwise die except that something whispers to the seed to put out roots and give birth to a stalk, and life happens. A branch is alive only when it is united to a vine.

Human beings were created to live in what Dallas Willard called "reciprocal rootedness." We are made to be alive spiritually. This is evident to any objective observer regardless of what they think about God or religion. But it means we require a transcendent connection through which the inner unseen person—mind and will—can be nourished and sustained. Apart from this we wither. With this we flourish.

And this is Christ.

This is union with Christ.

It is our salvation. Salvation is not mostly a matter of relocation; it is a matter of transformation. It does not consist primarily of ending up in the right place, but being made into the right person. And this happens when we are immersed in Jesus the way a dolphin is immersed in the ocean, when we are united to Jesus (though more deeply and more profoundly) like a bride is united to her groom.

With this understanding of union with Christ, discipleship suddenly takes its proper place. It's not extra-credit work to earn something. It's the means by which we experience union with Christ more fully and deeply. If we want Christ, we will want to be disciples. If we don't want discipleship, then we might desire to avoid pain, but that's not the same object as desiring Christ.

All of this unfolds with clarity and grace in the pages to follow. Rankin does a masterful job of articulating what union with Christ consists of, how central it was to the writers of Scripture and to great thinkers through the centuries, why it has been lost in our day, and most importantly how to pursue it as a concrete reality in daily life for ordinary people.

So that's why I'm excited for you to meet Rankin and enter a new world. Enough overture. Time to get to the good stuff.

John Ortberg

INTRODUCTION

The soul never thinks without an image.

Aristotle

"Once upon a time, Tommy opened a door."[1] This is all a three-year-old needs to be drawn in, G. K. Chesterton claims. A very young child's imagination is so strong he doesn't need much of a story to be engaged.

But as we get older, we require more details and more action to ignite our imaginations ("Tommy opened a door and saw a dragon" might work for a seven-year-old, Chesterton suggests).[2] The younger we are, the less we need in order to be captivated. Our imaginations were stronger when we were children.

Storytellers and poets have long known that imagination touches something deeper than our thoughts. "God loves you as you are, not as you should be"—as consoling and true as that might be—won't reach us in the same way as a story that begins, "A certain man had two sons ..." (Luke 15:11 KJV).

This book will require you to use your imagination because union with Christ is an enchanted reality. And we live in a disenchanted world.

IMAGINATION RECONSIDERED

But before you set this book aside as something for "creative types" or someone not you, we need to talk about this word *imagination*. Because as much as we prize it, we often clip its wings. We hear "imagination" and think it's about fiction and fairy tales, a child's business, or things not real. Hence our phrase, "Oh, that's just your imagination."

But I'm using the word in a larger, more human sense. Imagination is that distinctly human capacity by which we *image* anything and everything that is not immediately visible to our eyes. Where did you last set down your keys? What would you like to have for dinner tonight? What color are your mother's eyes? (This requires imagination unless you're looking at her.) Whether you're aware of it or not, you use your imagination all the time.

Imagination is also an integral part of science. Isaac Newton saw the apple fall, as many had before him, but he used his imagination to discover the fact of gravity. Any invisible force, anything conceptual, requires us to use our imaginations to engage with and understand. This might explain why Albert Einstein said, "Imagination is more important than knowledge."[3] More than merely seeing what is unreal or fantastic, imagination is used to *image* anything that is real but not visible. It's not *just* your imagination; it's your imagination!

Most important, imagination is necessary to know and enjoy God. How else can we relate to the true God, "whom no one has ever seen or can see" (1 Tim. 6:16), than by using our God-given imaging capacities—our imaginations? We must use our imaginations if we want to fully inhabit and experience the Christian life.

If language like this makes you nervous, please notice that the Bible, from beginning to end, calls to our imagination. When Moses tells the people to say from generation to generation, "It is because of what the LORD did for *me* when *I* came out of Egypt" (Exod. 13:8), he is calling them to use their imaginations—to put themselves in the Exodus story and to make it their own. When you read a parable of Jesus and try to tease out what it might mean for you, you are using your imagination.

When the New Testament writers ask us, "Set your minds on things that are above" (Col. 3:2), it's not a command to crane our necks and look at the skies, but to look for a reality beyond what we can naturally see. When they tell us to "fix our eyes … on what is unseen" (2 Cor. 4:18 NIV), it is our imagination that must respond.

Or, take that most frequent biblical command to "remember." "Do this in remembrance of me" (Luke 22:19). You can't remember without engaging your imagination. And that tragic refrain "But they forgot" (Judg. 3:7; 1 Sam. 12:9; etc.) can be diagnosed as a failure to call to mind, that is, a failure of the imagination.

In this book, we will excavate a forgotten treasure, the reality of union with Christ. Why would something so valuable need to be excavated? In a later chapter, I'll offer several suggestions as to why, on the whole, we have lost union with Christ as a controlling lens for how we think about the gospel and salvation; but here I'll offer just one.

The biblical scholar Walter Brueggemann claims, "The key pathology of our time, which seduces us all, is the reduction of the imagination, so that we are too numbed, satiated and co-opted to do serious imaginative work."[4] I think he might be right. And if Chesterton is right as well, and you are older than three (highly likely if you are reading this), then your imagination is already somewhat diminished, or at the very least, out of shape.

One way to think about the Christian life—not the only way, but a powerful and too-little-used way—is that believing the gospel means having your imagination taken captive and reshaped by a new story. And perhaps this is a child's business, and at least part of what Jesus meant when he said, "Unless you turn and become like children, you will never enter the kingdom of heaven" (Matt. 18:3). So let's do some imaginative work together.

IMAGINE A NEW STORY

Most of us have wondered, at one time or another, if we were switched at birth. "Are those *really* my parents?"

Now, imagine your parents are mean and critical, that you have always been a disappointment to them and they to you. But then, one day, you find a dusty trunk in the attic. You quietly pick the lock and open the trunk and discover papers that prove you had, in fact, been abducted as a baby. These aren't your parents after all—why, they're criminals!

You discover that your real mom was a painter at the Sorbonne in Paris and your real dad was a Nobel Prize–winning scientist *and* a professional baseball player. And you say to yourself, "Of course, this explains everything! I *am* extraordinary! I knew it all along." You also read that they are fabulously wealthy and have a lavish inheritance waiting for you.

It's a fantastic story, but you get it. Such a discovery would cause you to reinterpret everything about your life: where you came from, your true identity, your capacities and capabilities, the resources available to you, your future, and your destiny. After that day, your life would never be the same. You would come down from that attic with new eyes for everything and everyone. Your whole life would feel new, changed, and invigorated.

But here's the thing—it had always been true. It was the truth underlying your life even before you discovered it. It was rooted in history, and you had the DNA to prove it. It was true while it was hidden from your sight. But it didn't change your life until your eyes were opened to it.[5]

This book is like opening that trunk.

Union with Christ tells you a new story about who you are. If you are "in Christ," you too have been given a new identity. God has called you into a new life, rooted in a history that predates you, anchored in the life, death, and resurrection of Jesus. You discover who you are "in Christ," and you are given the DNA to prove it, the Holy Spirit. You once were lost, but now you are "found in him" (Phil. 3:9).

This truth can change everything for you, but living in this new reality will require your imagination. The Christian message is simple enough for a child to understand. At the same time, the Bible says that because of the new life you have been given in Christ, "from now on, therefore, we regard no one from a human point of view" (2 Cor. 5:16 NRSV). Coming to see your union with Christ is like finally putting on a pair of desperately needed glasses—Wow! Look at that! We see ourselves, and everything else, with new eyes.

IMAGINATION REQUIRED

I'm starting this book on union with Christ by talking about imagination because you will need yours, even to answer the question, what *is* union with Christ?

Jesus says your relationship with him is like that of branches to a vine (John 15). It's living and organic, dependent on a source outside of you to sustain you. Grafted into the vine, your very nature begins to change. The lifeblood of another flows within you and gives you life.

The apostle Paul says your relationship with Christ is like the most intimate of human relationships, marriage (Eph. 5). You no longer belong only to yourself. Your identity now includes another; it is broadened from "me" to "us."

Or, it's like the relationship between the parts of a body with their head (1 Cor. 12), which if you think about it, is the most essential relationship there is. You can get away from your spouse, even your arm for that matter. But if you get separated from your head, that's it. Life's not possible.

The apostle Peter takes a different angle and calls us living stones being built together into a temple (1 Pet. 2). Peter uses this image to describe how, when we are united to Christ, we become integrally connected to everyone else who is united to him, as together we house the very presence of God in this world.

It is revealing that the writers of Scripture, even Jesus himself, resort to word pictures, similes, and metaphors to capture the mystery of union with Christ. The *number* of metaphors employed tells us that this is important; the *variety* of metaphors tells us that it is far reaching. But the fact that similes and metaphors—the language of poetry—must be used at all tells us there is no way to get at this truth directly. Images are necessary. Your imagination *must* be engaged for you to lay hold of your new life in Christ.

IMAGINATION REWARDED

Perhaps you are thinking, *But why do I need to think this hard about union with Christ? I've gotten this far in my Christian life without really considering it—is it really necessary?*

If that's what you're thinking, let me ask you a few questions. Have you ever wondered, *Isn't there more to it than this?* Or have you ever had difficulty connecting what you know to be true about God with how you feel or how you live each day? Have you ever longed to change but just felt stuck?

One of the major arguments of this book is that union with Christ was once considered to be at the very heart of why the gospel is good news. Nothing is more basic or more central to the Christian life than union with Christ.

And yet for many of us, union with Christ might feel vague and shadowy, not central or basic. This has very real consequences for our everyday life with God. As our understanding and appreciation of union with Christ has diminished, so too has our sense of what salvation means. We may know what God has saved us *from*, but have we lost sight of what God has saved us *for*?

Becoming a Christian is not simply coming to believe certain things about a God who remains outside of you. And being a Christian is not simply about what you do or don't do. Christianity is a life of *faith*, but it's a *life* of faith. You have been grafted into God's own life, invited in to participate in the fellowship of God. "God is faithful, by whom you were called into the fellowship of his Son, Jesus Christ our Lord" (1 Cor. 1:9).

Could anything about the Christian life be more precious than this? This is what God has saved you for—communion, relationship, and intimacy with himself. This is what Christ suffered for, "that he might bring us to God" (1 Pet. 3:18). As J. I. Packer put it in his classic *Knowing God*:

> What will make heaven to be heaven is the presence of
> Jesus, and of a reconciled divine father who loves us for
> Jesus' sake no less than He loves Jesus Himself. To see,
> and know, and love, and be loved by, the Father and
> the Son, in company with the rest of God's vast family,
> is the whole essence of the Christian hope.... If you
> are a believer ... this prospect satisfies you completely.[6]

If the presence of Jesus is what makes heaven, heaven, and if union with Christ means that you can have the presence of Jesus dwelling within you now, then do you see what this means? Union with Christ means the reality of knowing God and living in communion with him doesn't begin when you die. Eternal life begins *in this life* when Christ joins his life to yours (John 17:3). We can have fellowship with God through Christ (1 John 1:3). We can begin to experience heaven in our lives here and now.

If you are united to Christ, you *are* a citizen of heaven (Phil. 3:20). Present tense. You *have* "every spiritual blessing" (Eph. 1:3). You participate in heavenly realities *even as* you walk around with both feet on the ground. Today we do this by faith in what is unseen. It requires our imagination. But one day it will be by sight, when we see him face to face (1 Cor. 13:12).

Of all the good news the gospel brings, the greatest—and indeed the door to all the rest—is that you can be united to Christ. It's really possible. Union with Christ is not an abstract idea. It is a powerful reality. And if Jesus has joined his life to yours, then you have been given everything you need for life and godliness (2 Pet. 1:3). But unless you are united to him, all that he has done for you remains useless and of no value to you.[7]

LOOKING AHEAD

This book is divided into four parts. In part 1, we'll look at what union with Christ is and why we need to recover it. Already I've made some pretty substantial claims, including that union with Christ is central to the Christian life but largely misunderstood or overlooked today. So in part 2, I'll aim to substantiate these claims and offer some ideas as to why union with Christ may be only vaguely familiar to many of us today.

Part 3 addresses how union with Christ gets applied to our lives. You can see in the table of contents how this will play out, but we're going to frame our discussion around four fundamental questions: Who am I? Where am I headed? How will I get there? What can I hope for? Union with Christ answers each in a surprising way. It gives you a new identity, a new purpose, a new destiny, and renewed hope along the way.

Of course, it's one thing to have our questions answered, but another to integrate these truths into our lives day by day. That's part 4 of this book—how to live in union with Christ each day, more and more. Just as our loss of union with Christ as a controlling lens has had real negative repercussions, so its recovery holds such potential for hope and healing. We'll look at some of the possibilities this recovery holds, specifically how it can help us hold together things that often seem divergent: grace and obedience, cross and kingdom, mercy and justice, the personal Christ and the cosmic Christ.

C. S. Lewis famously said that before he was a Christian, reading the novels of George MacDonald "baptized" his imagination and made it feasible for him to envision a different way of looking at the world.[8] My hope for this book is that it will, in some small measure, do that for you as well—that you will be awakened to your union with Christ and it will ignite your imagination, and alter your vision, until you see yourself and others, God and this world, very differently.

The apostle Paul prays that "the eyes of your heart [would be] enlightened, that you may know what is the hope to which he has called you, what are the riches of his glorious inheritance" (Eph. 1:18). Paul prays for the *eyes of your heart*—what are they if not your imagination? My hope, then, is that with them you would see what is true, so that you may know God, and enjoy him, and be filled with hope. This glorious adventure begins in union with Christ.

Chapter 1

LIVING IN THE GAP

If Christianity is true in its promise of a new life, then why don't I feel more … new?

The 1983 film *Tender Mercies* won Academy Awards for screenwriter Horton Foote and lead actor Robert Duvall. Duvall plays a once-famous but now washed-up country music singer-songwriter named Mac Sledge, who is stringing dead-end jobs together and battling the bottle. A young widow named Rosa Lee, and her little boy, Sonny, befriend Mac. Late in the movie, Mac and the boy both get baptized at the local church and are driving home in a pickup truck.

Sonny: "Well, we've done it, Mac. We're baptized."

Mac: "Yeah, we are."

Sonny: "Everybody said I was going to feel like a changed person. I guess I do feel a little different. But I don't feel a whole lot different. Do you?"

Mac: "Not yet."

Sonny: "You don't look any different." (Sonny sits up to look at himself in the rearview mirror.) "Do you think I look any different?"

Mac: "Not yet."[1]

NOT YET

What am I missing? This was the question I asked myself as I stood, deflated, in front of the list on the wall. It was Monday morning. My name was three slots lower than it had been the month before. Just yesterday I had heard the preacher say, "The race is over. You are accepted. Your identity is not in what you do or have done but in what Jesus does and has done. You can rest." That sounded like such *good news*.

But here at the corporate bank where I worked, the race was far from over, and this week I was falling behind.

Each month the company would post a ranked list of everyone's performance—how much money we had earned the company year to date. No matter what the preacher said my value was, here it was by another measure, in black and white, posted on the wall for all to see.

I was like one of those giant inflatable Gumby-men you see at the used-car lot. My heart would rise and fall depending on how many deals I had closed. When I was successful or applauded, my heart would swell. When I was criticized or failed at something, I would deflate in disappointment.

I didn't want this list to bother me. I wanted to have peace, peace like a river. Hadn't Jesus promised, "Whoever believes in me, as the Scripture has said, 'Out of his heart will flow rivers of living water'" (John 7:38)? I read this and wanted to take Jesus at his word. But when I looked at my life, I wondered, *Rivers? Really? Maybe a trickle here and there on my best days. But I don't see any rivers flowing out of my life.* Hadn't Jesus said, "I will give you rest" (Matt. 11:28)? Then why was I still so restless?

I felt like that man in the gospel of Mark (8:22–26). Maybe you've read the story too. He was blind and his friends brought him to Jesus. Jesus "spit on his eyes and laid his hands on him, [and] he asked him, 'Do you see anything?'" The man said, "I see people, but they look like trees, walking." The man was no longer blind, but he could not yet see clearly. He was stuck. He was in between.

This is the only partial healing in the Gospels. What happened? Was there a power shortage? Did the one who calmed the stormy seas with a word need a second chance? Did the one who raised the dead need a do-over? Or did Jesus intend this man to serve as a sort of living parable, to say it's possible to *see*, but not yet see *clearly*?

I felt like that man. Stuck.

THE GAP

What was wrong with me? Why wasn't the gospel doing its deep work in my heart? The gap loomed large between what the gospel said was true of me (I'm forgiven, accepted, and secure) and how I saw myself. There was a chasm between what I said I believed and what I was experiencing. I felt discouraged by my lack of spiritual progress and exhausted by my efforts.

I had seen enough of Jesus to spoil my enjoyment of the world but not enough to be content with Jesus alone. And I didn't know how to move forward.

I became frustrated, then cynical. I wondered if other people were reading the same Bible and sensed the same disconnect. I felt alone. I felt like a fraud.

You may find it odd, then, that a few years later God called me to be a pastor. But this question of how to close the gap between our faith and our real lives remains one of which I'm always mindful. How can we connect the grand, high promises of God to the gritty details of our daily lives? How can we get the beautiful truths we hear on Sunday to sustain us on Wednesday afternoon at 4:00 p.m., so we don't rise and fall like inflatable Gumby-men? I'm writing this book to answer those questions, because I've learned I'm not the only one who asks them.

Melissa is in her twenties. She's tough, smart, and independent, a New Yorker transplanted to LA. She has a lot of friends because she's kind, and most of them aren't Christians because she just became one. But like so many other skeptical minds, Melissa has found herself captivated by the person of Jesus. Yet she doesn't want to become what she'd always assumed Christians were: people who claim to believe in love, forgiveness, and new life but instead live lives of fear, judgment, and smallness. She wants to experience this new life Jesus has promised, yet she doesn't feel her life changing as much or as quickly as she had hoped. And so she asks, "I *hear* what you're saying about the grace of God, but how do I get these truths from my head to drip down into my heart?"

Bill is in his sixties and has been around church since he was a boy. He's a business executive, hardworking, competitive, and driven. His face always looks tired. He's heard all the sermons and knows all the verses and can sing all the old hymns by heart. After one Sunday service I asked Bill how he felt about the sermon. His response was memorable: "Cynical as hell," he replied, and smiled that tired smile. He's been hearing for years how abundant and full life in Christ is supposed to be, but he knows how dry and empty he feels inside, and he's felt this way for so long.

Thom is young, single, and talented. He got an agent his first year in LA and thought things were going to take off. But he's getting fewer and fewer callbacks these days, and his confidence is flagging. Thom's not a Christian. He doesn't see how believing in someone who lived two thousand years ago could make much of a difference in his life today. It's not that Thom is hostile. He's just indifferent.

I'm writing this book for Lucy. She has made resolution after resolution and kept many of them. She's tried new jobs, a new haircut, a new city. But she's tired of herself and the way she does things. All she wants to do is change, but she doesn't know how to make that happen.

But it's not just Melissa, Bill, Thom, Lucy, and me who have felt that gap. John Newton was a pastor in Olney, England, in the eighteenth century, and he wrote what is probably the most famous hymn of all time, "Amazing Grace." Its theme of redemption is one Newton knew quite well. As a young man, he was a sailor, and even among this rough bunch he had earned renown, in one captain's words, as the most profane man he had ever met. After deserting the Royal Navy, Newton got into the slave trade. During a violent storm at sea in 1748, Newton cried out to God, and not for the first time found religion. But this time something real had happened in his heart, and Newton's life began to change. He stopped drinking and gambling, and began to pray and read the Bible. Yet he continued in the slave trade for several more years.[2]

His song can make it sound like the work of God's amazing grace in our hearts is deep and immediate:

I once was lost, but now am found
Was blind, but now I see.

But in Newton's own life, it was a long journey between "now I
see" and seeing clearly. As a pastor and in his letters, he openly shared
his struggles with sin and temptation—his own deep acquaintance with
the gap—which is why his letters of spiritual comfort are still treasured
today as masterpieces of devotional literature. It wasn't until 1788, forty
years after God's grace found a wretch like him, that Newton would
write, "I hope it will always be a subject of humiliating reflection to me,
that I was, once, an active instrument, in a business at which my heart
now shudders."[3] There were forty years between his conversion and his
conviction regarding the slave trade, forty years for the gospel to do its
deep work in his heart. The grace was amazing that first day, but it took
years to take root and blossom. And this for the man whose name is
synonymous with amazing grace. Forty years—that's quite a gap.

It's been said, "The longest journey a man will ever make is the
journey from his head to his heart." This book is about that journey
and the unparalleled power of our union with Christ to help us along
the way.

MIND THE GAP

Today, I'm a pastor of a church in Los Angeles, full of people who
come from many different walks of life and from all over our city.
They have questions similar to the ones I was asking in that banking
office not so many years ago: How do I connect God to my daily life?

A skeptical friend once asked me, "If the gospel is supernatural,
as you say, then why doesn't it seem to make more of a difference in

the lives of so many who claim to believe it?" That's a great question and not just for skeptics. Because the gap between what Christians claim is true about themselves and what we often see when we look in the mirror—that gap is real. Melissa knows it, and John Newton knew it. And I'm writing this book because I'll tell you a secret. In my job I've learned there are a lot of people out there who feel alone and afraid, who feel like a fraud.

Do you feel the gap? Having the courage to recognize it and admit it is the first step in this gap being closed. You must mind the gap.

But it's certainly possible to ignore, or not be bothered by, the gap. I'll never forget the first sermon I ever preached. As I stood at the door afterward, greeting people on their way out, one older man patted me on the shoulder as if I were a young Cub Scout and said, "Well, that was a *nice* sermon. Now, back to the real world."

If, like that man, you never try to connect the truths of God to your everyday life; if you construct a wall to divide the sacred "nice sermons" from the secular "real world"; if you keep Jesus and his authority safely tucked away in heaven where he can't threaten your way of doing things, then this gap won't concern you. It won't even occur to you that it should.

Nor will this gap concern you if you believe that the gospel means you have a ticket to heaven when you die and that grace means you don't need to strive to obey Christ while you live. If you believe "It is finished" means there's nothing then left for you to do; if you consider Jesus's call to discipleship to be optional, reserved for the cloistered few or supercommitted, then you won't be bothered by the gap either.

And sadly, many Christians have lived with this gap for so long that they no longer mind it. Ernest Hemingway ended his novel *The*

Sun Also Rises with the line "Isn't it pretty to think so?"[4] And isn't that how many of us feel, in the quiet of our hearts, about these grand, high promises in the Bible: "Rivers of living water" or "Whoever drinks of the water that I will give him will never be thirsty again" (John 7:37–38; 4:14)? *Wouldn't it be pretty to think so? Now, back to the real world.*

OUR ONLY HEALTH IS THE DISEASE

I'll admit this has been an odd way to begin a book about the best news you'll ever hear. It's discomforting. But feeling the discomfort of this gap is actually a sign that you want to take Jesus at his word, a sign that you want to be healed. "Our only health is the disease," wrote T. S. Eliot in one of his poems, "to be restored, our sickness must grow worse."[5]

While there are several responses on offer today concerning what to do with this gap (and many of them are good and helpful), there is one, it seems, that very few people are talking about.

It's all over the Bible and was prominent for the first seventeen hundred years of Christian thought. But on the whole, we've lost our grasp of it. It might be the most important aspect of the Christian life you've never heard of. And nothing is more needed today than a fresh appreciation of this very old reality. This book makes no claim to be original; it seeks only to excavate a treasure that has been buried for far too long. We need to rediscover our union with Christ.

UNION WITH CHRIST

The seeds of this book were planted almost twenty years ago. Reading the old theologians, I kept stumbling across the idea of *union with Christ*. The term sounded vaguely familiar. But the way these writers talked about it made me realize I must not really know what it meant. For example:

> First, we must understand that as long as Christ remains outside of us, and we are separated from him, all that he has suffered and done for the salvation of the human race remains useless and of no value to us. Therefore … he had to become ours and to dwell within us.[6]

I was much more accustomed to thinking of Christ as a savior *outside* of me than as one who dwells *within* and has united his life to mine. Yes, I had heard the popular refrain "Jesus in your heart," but my primary understanding of the gospel was that Jesus had accomplished something *for* me, once, long ago. However, these writers spoke of Christ uniting himself to me, here and now. I didn't see myself as one in whom the Son of God now dwells. I didn't go through my day mindful of the indwelling presence of Christ. And I certainly didn't see this as the heart of the gospel. All that Christ has done for us remains "useless and of no value to us," unless we are united to him? That's some strong language!

Over and over again, I found writers from across the centuries who defined salvation and the Christian life in terms of being united to Christ. For example:

- "That indwelling of Christ in our hearts … that mystical union [is] accorded by us the highest degree of importance."[7]

- "By virtue of the believer's union with Christ, he doth really possess all things."[8]
- "Being in Christ, and united to him, is the fundamental constitution of a Christian."[9]
- "Union with Christ is right at the center of the Christian doctrine of salvation."[10]
- "There are no benefits of the gospel apart from union with Christ."[11]
- "Union with Christ is the fountainhead from which flows the Christian's every spiritual blessing."[12]
- "Union with Christ is theological shorthand for the gospel itself."[13]

I hope you'll forgive my heaping up these quotes like endorsements on a movie poster. But listing them out helps us see the central importance union with Christ has consistently been given throughout history. Some of these voices are contemporary writers. And indeed, in academic circles, union with Christ has become a hot topic. But the one place union with Christ is not prominent today is the one place it most needs to be—the local church.

Union with Christ is not some dusty relic of history or ivory tower pursuit. It takes us to the very heart of the gospel. It's what makes the gospel good news.

How much should we make of our union with Christ? Writer J. I. Packer says that it is not possible to make too much of it and the communion with God it allows:

> Communion between God and man is the end
> to which both creation and redemption are the
> means; it is the goal to which both theology
> and preaching must ever point; it is the essence
> of true religion; it is, indeed, the definition of
> Christianity.[14]

Is this the definition of Christianity to you? Is this what you think of when you think of being saved? That "to be saved means to be united to the Savior"?[15]

The greatest treasure of the gospel, greater than any other benefit the gospel brings, is the gift of God himself. Is it any wonder, then, that twentieth-century writer John Murray concluded, "Nothing is more central or more basic than union with Christ … it is the central truth of the whole doctrine of salvation."[16]

NOTHING IS MORE CENTRAL OR MORE BASIC?

If it's true that nothing is more central or basic than union with Christ, and this book aims to show that it is, then it is fair to ask this: Why is union with Christ neither central nor basic to so many of us? Why, rather, is union with Christ, if it's talked about at all, reduced to some vague or optional aspect of Christian living, perhaps something reserved for theologians, as opposed to being seen as the central truth of salvation *for everyone*? Why, when asked, "What is the gospel?" would union with Christ not spring to our minds or come to our lips?

My initial interest began with this riddle: Whatever happened to union with Christ? How did something so central become so marginalized?

But my primary interest is not to solve a riddle or right a historical wrong, but rather to help us connect God to our daily lives. Union with Christ is the good news we need to hear today. It is good news for Melissa and Bill, Thom and Lucy, me and you. If you too have felt this gap and wondered how it can be closed, union with Christ might be what you are missing.

Our neglect of union with Christ explains the gaps between our faith and our lives. When the *work* of Christ *for* us becomes abstracted from the *person* of Christ *within* us, is it any wonder there is a chasm between our heads and our hearts or between our beliefs and our experiences? Is it surprising that we feel frustrated and cynical or tossed to and fro?

Union with Christ tells you that you don't have to be stuck, or resigned to "wouldn't it be pretty to think so?" Jesus's promises about rivers of living water—these are not hollow words. For he is that living water, and if you belong to him, he has joined his life to yours.

Union with Christ needs to become again what it once was, "of highest importance."[17] Because just as our neglect of this reality has had real and harmful consequences, so its recovery will have real and lasting benefits. If you have ever asked of the Christian life, "Isn't there more to it than this?" the answer is yes—union with Christ is the "more to it."

THE GREATEST, MOST HONORABLE, AND GLORIOUS OF GRACES

John Owen may not be widely known today, but he is considered one of the greatest theologians ever to have written in the English language. His collected works, still in print, run to twenty-four volumes, and he wrote more and thought as deeply about communion with God as anyone ever has.

"How few of [us]," Owen wrote, "are experimentally acquainted with this privilege of holding immediate communion with the Father in love."[18] We may pray to *Our Father*, Owen is saying in seventeenth-century language, but so few of us actually experience loving communion with him.

Owen is onto something here. When he writes "how few of us," he's lamenting the gap and acknowledging how very real it is for so many of us. He's also saying we shouldn't feel this way. It's a problem. We've addressed this gap in a variety of ways in this chapter, but perhaps they all boil down to what Owen so eloquently describes here: we find it so difficult to enjoy God.

John Owen was also a pastor, and when he wrote "how few of us," he was including himself. Elsewhere he wrote, "I myself preached Christ some years, when I had but very little, if any, experimental acquaintance with access to God through Christ; until the Lord was pleased to visit me with sore affliction."[19]

Owen was confessing that he, great theologian that he was, had been telling others about the riches of knowing Christ while he himself was not experiencing them. And this, he said, went on for "some years." Until by a strange remedy, the way of affliction, he was brought to the end of himself and into the light and solace of God's care and presence.

I'm writing this book for you because I know John Owen was right when he acknowledged, despite what we may say, how few of us are truly walking in the confidence that God, our Father, looks after us and is pleased with us.

I'm also writing this book because I believe Owen was right when he wrote elsewhere, "Union with Christ is the greatest, most honourable, and glorious of all graces that we are made partakers of."[20] For Owen, union with Christ is the missing link that connects the grace Christ offers with our experience of God's love.[21] Union with Christ is the thread that holds it all together.

The man in the gospel of Mark who saw men as trees walking didn't remain stuck in that dreaded in between. But it took the *presence* of Christ to heal him. "Then Jesus laid his hands on his eyes again; and he opened his eyes, his sight was restored, and he saw everything clearly" (Mark 8:25).

It might seem like healing is far away. "Not that I have already obtained all this, or have already arrived at my goal," Paul wrote, acknowledging the gap in his own life, "but I press on to take hold of that for which Christ Jesus took hold of me" (Phil. 3:12 NIV). Union with Christ enables you, like Paul, to face the gap with ruthless honesty, but also with unfettered hope, optimism, and energy. I want you to know that union with Christ is really possible. For you. You can press on, "further up and further in,"[22] to what is already yours in Christ.

Apart from him you can do nothing (John 15:5). But united to him, you can drink the sweet waters of the far country, even as you wander in a dry and thirsty land. For Christ will "make it a place of springs" (Ps. 84:6), even rivers of living water.

Chapter 2

UNION WITH CHRIST: WHAT IS IT?

When I was in junior high school, I played football on an organized team for the first time. And my size gave our team a distinct advantage. I was the smallest player on the field. I was so small, in fact, that when I had the ball, the opposing team had a difficult time tackling me because they could hardly see me.

In crucial situations when we had to have the yards, our go-to play was called "Refrigerator Right" (in honor of Chicago Bears defensive-lineman-turned-running-back, William "The Refrigerator" Perry). Coach Junior set Andrew, the biggest guy on our team, in front of me as a blocker, and the quarterback handed me the ball. With Andrew leading the way, one man made a way for another. I was completely obscured by his strength and powerful work, but running to freedom. Everything that was supposed to hit me hit Andrew. He blazed a path for me against hostile forces. He made a way to glory. I was hidden in him.

The Bible says that those who belong to Christ are so intertwined with his life that when he died, we died with him. "For you have died," Paul wrote to his very living audience, "and your life is hidden with Christ in God" (Col. 3:3). Everything that was supposed to hit us, even the judgment of God for our sins, hit Jesus. He blazed a path against hostile forces, seen and unseen. He made a way to glory. One man made a way for all to live (1 Cor. 15:22). We are hidden in Christ. That's one picture of union with Christ.

You may be thinking, okay, okay, you've given me several pictures now. Vine and branches, stones in a temple, marriage even, and now junior high football. But what exactly *is* union with Christ?

The Bible calls God's plan to restore humanity to himself "the mystery that was kept secret for long ages but has now been disclosed" (Rom. 16:25–26). Even in being disclosed, it remains a mystery. "This mystery *is* profound," the Bible says, talking about the union between Christ and the church (Eph. 5:32).

Explaining a mystery is like explaining a joke. If you do that, you kill it. So here we have a tension. I want to be as clear as I can while still holding on to the fact that this is a mysterious reality.

There are other mysteries essential to the Christian faith—how Jesus could be fully God and fully man, how God could be one and yet exist in three persons. Even though we don't fully comprehend these mysteries, we are still compelled to speak of them in wonder. It is the same with our union with Christ. John Calvin wrote:

> For my own part, I am overwhelmed by the depth
> of this mystery, and am not ashamed to join Paul
> in acknowledging at once my ignorance and my

admiration … whatever is supernatural is clearly beyond our own comprehension. Let us therefore labor more to feel Christ living in us, than to discover the nature of that intercourse.[1]

It makes sense that our human understanding could never fully encompass our union with Christ. But the fact that we can't get to the bottom of this ocean doesn't mean we shouldn't put our feet in, or even swim. So let us strive to understand and experience, taste and enjoy, all we can of this union while remembering that the Christ we experience is always better and more beautiful than our own personal experience of him.

Since union with Christ is irreducibly mysterious, I hesitate even to try to describe it simply. But because it is biblically so prominent, yet only vaguely familiar to most of us, we need to take a few steps back and define our terms. We must begin somewhere. So, to consider the question *what exactly is union with Christ?* let's start here: union with Christ means that you are in Christ and Christ is in you.

UNION WITH CHRIST MEANS YOU ARE IN CHRIST

In all his letters, the apostle Paul never once uses the word "Christian." Rather, his most common descriptor for those who follow Christ is that they are "in Christ." It can be easy to read over that little phrase. Yet it is impossible to overstate its significance for Paul. One New Testament scholar says, "Being 'in Christ' is the essence of Christian proclamation and experience … Without treating the 'in Christ' motif we miss the heart of the Christian message."[2]

What does it mean to be "in Christ"?

To be "in Christ" means that Christ represents his people. Scholars sometimes refer to this under the heading of a "corporate personality,"[3] a leader who represents a people or a group. As part of a representative democracy, Americans appreciate how representation works. Our elected leaders represent us; their actions speak for us. Or we can think of a sports team. When the forward on a soccer team scores the winning goal, that goal and the victory are credited to the entire team, even to the players sitting on the bench, even to the fans sitting in the stands or sitting on their sofas at home—even to those fans who didn't see the game (*You mean we won?*). They all participate in another's triumph.

Or take the story of David and Goliath. Have you ever wondered why only two warriors fought that day when the entire armies were gathered there against each other? The giant Goliath was chosen to represent the Philistines, Israel's enemy. He issued a challenge: "Choose a man for yourselves, and let him come down to me. If he is able to fight with me and kill me, then we will be your servants. But if I prevail against him and kill him, then you shall be our servants and serve us" (1 Sam. 17:8–9).

So, young David represented all of Israel. In what should sound like a familiar story, the young shepherd boy from Bethlehem, who would be king, fought as a champion on behalf of all the people. He was their representative. And David's victory was credited—it was imputed—to those he represented. All of Israel, we could say, was "in David," even though they themselves were not active participants in the battle.

In the same way, Christ represents those who place their faith in him. If we are united to Christ, then we are united to him in all that he has done for us. Christ represents those who come to be his so thoroughly that we are said to have been "crucified with Christ" (Gal. 2:20), "buried ... with him" (Rom. 6:4), and "raised with Christ" (Col. 3:1). We are even "seated ... with him in the heavenly places" (Eph. 2:6) now as we walk about with both feet on the ground.

Paul actually invented new words to describe this new reality. The phrases "crucified with," "raised with," "buried with," and "seated with" are each a single word in Greek beginning with the prefix *syn*, meaning "with." Those words didn't exist before Paul coined them. But something so unique had happened that there were no words for it! A new vocabulary was necessary. It was the only way he could describe who he had become because of Jesus.

When we are in Christ, *every* part of Christ's life, not only his death, has significance for us. We share in his life and obedience, his death and his resurrection, even his ascension! We participate in another's victory. All that is his becomes ours.[4] How can such things be? God in Christ assumed our full humanity to heal our full humanity. He came all the way down to blaze a trail all the way back—for us to live in the presence of God. This means our union with Christ is rooted and grounded in Christ's union with us in the incarnation. And so Charles Wesley's words in the old hymn may now come into sharp focus: "Made like him, like him we rise; ours the cross, the grave, the skies!"[5] Alleluia!

HIDDEN IN CHRIST

There is no place in the Bible that captures union with Christ more succinctly than Galatians 2:20. Listen closely to what Paul says of himself here, because if you are in Christ, you too can say with him:

"I have been crucified with Christ."

Notice the verb tense "have been" is present perfect—something that happened in the past with continuing present effect. If you are in Christ, then you are united to him in his death and crucifixion. When he died, you now share in that death.

"It is no longer I who live."

The person I was before I knew Christ is no longer the person that I am. The Christian life is not a self-improvement project. It's not about reforming the old self. We are talking about a new self. "If anyone is in Christ, he is a new creation" (2 Cor. 5:17).

"It is no longer I who live, but Christ who lives in me."

In a moment, we will get to what it means that Christ now lives in you.

"And the life I now live in the flesh."

Legend has it that Paul was a short man. When he says, "The life I now live in the flesh," he knows that he's still uniquely himself, diminutive and bold. His body and his personality have not changed. But in another sense, his person has been changed fundamentally.

"The life I now live in the flesh I live by faith in the
Son of God."

Faith is how union with Christ becomes operative and powerful in your life. Faith is a God-given gift that allows you to take hold of God's having taken hold of you. If you are in Christ, this is now the defining truth of who you are. Your life, your story, becomes enfolded by another story—Another's story. That's one way to define faith: faith means finding your identity in Christ.

> "I live by faith in the Son of God, who loved me
> and gave himself for me."

Paul is unusually personal here because he wants it to be utterly personal for *you*. He wants you too to be able to say, "I live by faith in the Son of God, who loved me and gave himself for me."

I have a friend who used to be Mickey Mouse. She was the person inside the costume at Disneyland. Reflecting on her time "in Mickey," she said, "Growing up, I thrived on behavior modification. I thought: If I'm good, I will be loved. If I'm bad, I will be rejected. I learned to wear a mask—not to show what was really going on. My core beliefs were that I was not worthy, accepted, or loved, so I would clamor and manufacture ways to elicit the positive responses I wanted from people. When I put on Mickey's costume, I got that positive response times a hundred." She felt safe and loved, covered in Mickey's "righteousness." But she also gained a new sense of what it means to be in Christ. She recalled praying, "Lord, is this what it's like to have masses of people run towards you with joy, excitement, and eagerness?"

This is another way to picture what it means for you to be in Christ. You are completely safe, hidden in him. He represents you before the Father. He covers you—your sin, your shame, your weakness. But he covers you in a very real way, not as a temporary fiction. Being "in Mickey" (or any other mask we hide behind) is to masquerade in a false identity. But being in Christ is to discover our true, God-given identity. You are alive in him, moving with him through this world, clothed in all his benefits and blessings. You are *in Christ*.

To be found in Christ means you don't have to prove yourself anymore. Your frantic attempts to find or craft an acceptable identity, or your tireless work to manage your own reputation—these are over and done. You can rest. In Christ. You don't have to be intimidated by anyone, ever. Who are you? You are in Christ! And you no longer need to fear the judgment of God (1 John 4:18). When God looks at you, he sees you hidden in Christ. This is freedom. This is confidence. This is good, good news.

UNION WITH CHRIST MEANS CHRIST IS IN YOU

My oldest son is six years old. The other day in the car, he must have been thinking about union with Christ, because he asked my wife, "So, Mommy. It's like this—Jesus lives inside me, and God lives inside my sister, and the Holy Spirit lives inside my little brother, right? But then who lives inside you and Daddy?"

It's not an unreasonable question. What does the Bible mean when it says Christ is in us? How can a person who lived two thousand years ago live inside another person now, much less live inside millions of people who follow him?

Jesus lives on in his followers in a way different from any other religious figure. Buddha, for example, lives on in the lives of his followers today through his teachings. That's how he is connected to them. But Christians believe that Christ is alive today, radically affecting his followers beyond merely the example of his perfect life or his impressive teachings. How, exactly, are Christ's followers connected to the Christ of history? The Bible teaches us that not only are you in Christ, but also Christ is in you.

In the gospel of John, as Jesus prepared his disciples for his departure, he called this bunch of grown men "little children." "Little children, yet a little while I am with you ... 'Where I am going you cannot come'" (John 13:33). This would be shattering news to these men who had left everything to obey Jesus's call to "follow me," now to be told that they could follow him no further. Yet Jesus continued, "Let not your hearts be troubled" (John 14:1). How could their hearts not be troubled when Jesus had just told them he would be going away?

A few verses later, Jesus picked up the children metaphor again and surely confused his friends: "I will not leave you as orphans" (John 14:18). And "orphans" must have felt like the appropriate word to them, the epitome of one alone. *If you leave us now, Jesus, who else do we have? And what are you saying? Are you leaving us, or will you never leave?*

Even more baffling, in this same conversation Jesus said, "Nevertheless, I tell you the truth: it is to your advantage that I go away" (John 16:7). How could this be true? What could possibly be better than having Christ beside them, day after day?

Jesus told them, "I will ask the Father, and he will give you another Helper, to be with you forever, even the Spirit of truth ... You know him, for he dwells with you and will be in you" (John 14:16–17). Much ink has been spilled attempting to translate the Greek word here translated "Helper." It is variously translated "Comforter," "Counselor," "Advocate," and "Friend." In fact, so much attention has been placed on this word that the word just before it can be easily overlooked. "Another"?

Up to this point, who has been their constant comforter, counselor, advocate, and friend? Could there be "another" like Jesus?

Yes. The Holy Spirit. Jesus promised that when he went away the Holy Spirit would come. And the Spirit would come in such a way that Jesus said, "It is to your *advantage* … for if I do not go away, the Helper will not come to you. But if I go, I will send him to you" (John 16:7). Why was it to their advantage?

The only thing that could be better than having Jesus with you, beside you, would be having Jesus within you, wherever you are and wherever you go. And that is what we have, those of us who are united to Christ. You have "Christ in you, the hope of glory" (Col. 1:27). This was how Jesus could truthfully promise his disciples, "I am with you always" (Matt. 28:20) right before he ascended to heaven and disappeared from their sight. It was why he could tell them, "Let not your hearts be troubled.… I will not leave you as orphans" (John 14:1, 18) on the very night he announced his departure.

It was also how Jesus could promise what might seem impossible, "Whoever believes in me will do the works I have been doing, and they will do even greater things than these, because I am going to the Father" (John 14:12 NIV). During his earthly life, Jesus's presence was localized to his physical body. He experienced our frustration of being only in one place at one time. But now that he dwells within his disciples by his Spirit, his ministry—his power through his people—is multiplied exponentially.

To be united to Christ is to have the Spirit of Christ within you. The Spirit is the real, living bond between Jesus and us. If you do not have the Spirit, then you do not have Christ (Rom. 8:9). But if the Spirit dwells within you, consider what you do have. "Having the Spirit," Sinclair Ferguson wrote, "is the equivalent, indeed the very mode, of having the incarnate, obedient, crucified, resurrected and exalted Christ indwelling us so that we are united to him as he is united to the Father."[6]

When Paul asked, "Do you not know that you are God's temple and that God's Spirit dwells in you?" (1 Cor. 3:16), you can be assured that his first readers were even more baffled than you might be. For them, the temple was the unique dwelling place of the one God, the meeting place of heaven and earth, kept protected behind curtains and approachable only through elaborate sacrifices, only once a year, and only by the high priest. The idea that God would—or could—dwell inside his people was, and is, difficult to grasp, even mind bending.

No wonder Paul ended one of his letters by asking, "Do you not realize this about yourselves, that Jesus Christ is in you?" (2 Cor. 13:5). I'm suggesting that no, we don't realize this about ourselves. This is "mysticism on the highest plane,"[7] as one writer called it. "That mystical union,"[8] said another. And by definition, what is mystical is hard to fathom. But it is true—Christ Jesus now dwells within his followers. Christ's power and life enter into our lives to transform us, not only to deal with (atone for) our past, but also now to liberate us with a strength and power and dignity unlike any other.

CHRIST IN YOU, THE HOPE OF GLORY

Christ dwelling in us by his Spirit is a guarantee that we can and will change. We are adopted into God's family, and not in name only.

The Spirit in us now guides and forms us more and more into the family likeness. The same Christ who overcame every temptation and was perfectly obedient—that Jesus is in you now. The Jesus who had compassion on the crowds and who healed the sick—that Jesus is in you. The humble Jesus who led as a servant, who washed his disciples' feet—he's in you. The Jesus who repeatedly shattered racial barriers with his teachings and in his life—that Jesus is in you. The Jesus who suffered and loved to the end—he dwells in you. And the Jesus who was raised to new life—that Jesus is living in you right now!

Do you realize what resources you carry around with you? Do you realize that you are never again alone to face whatever you are facing? This is why Paul prays for us, "that the eyes of your heart may be enlightened in order that you may know the hope to which he has called you, the riches of his glorious inheritance in his holy people, and his incomparably great power for us who believe" (Eph. 1:18–19 NIV).

Jesus was the perfect human. He was fully human, subject to all our temptations and indignities, but he lived the perfect human life. He is what *human* is supposed to look like. We often think of *human* as inherently flawed, as an excuse for our shortcomings: "I'm only human, you know." But the man Jesus Christ was the truest human, perfectly dependent on his Father, perfectly humble, obedient, strong, and kind. Christ in us now labors to make us more human, not less, and that's a good thing. Something has changed, and is changing, *in* us.

With that in mind, consider two superheroes, Batman and Spider-Man. Batman is a rich and strong man with lots of cool gadgets. His superpowers stem from his external possessions. Spider-Man has a few accessories as well, but he is a superhero because of the spider powers he obtained when he was bitten by a radioactive spider. His nature has been changed. He now has a new power accessible to him, within him.[9]

Christ in you makes you more like Spider-Man than Batman. Something alien to you, from outside of you, has entered into you and changed your nature. You now have power that you did not have before. The trouble with this analogy is that Spider-Man became something more than human, while we instead are being restored to our full humanity. We are becoming more like Christ.

So that's what union with Christ means. You are in Christ and Christ is in you. Simple, right?

I don't think it's preacherly hyperbole to say that you will never hear something more amazing in your entire life. Union with Christ touches on the highest and most profound truths of the gospel and at the same time reaches down into the depths of the human heart to fill us with more joy and hope, more comfort and strength than anything else ever could. Is there any truth we more need to lay hold of today than our union with Christ?

In Christ, like in that Mickey costume, you are hidden and secure. Christ in you, by his Spirit, dwells and gives you new life and power to change. And all this happens without obliterating you as you. You are precious and unique—God dreamed up the one and only you and knit you together himself—but he created you to be united to him. You are more and most yourself when united to Christ. He covers you, he shields you, he represents you before the Father. He also fills you, illuminates you, and animates you, making you more yourself and more human than you could ever be on your own.

NOT IDEAS, BUT REALITY

This is a stunning reality. We have spent some time thus far defining union with Christ, but I've done so at the risk of misleading you. Being a Christian is not about absorbing certain doctrines about God. Nor is it about being a better or different kind of person. The goal is having a personal, vital, profoundly real relationship with God through Christ by the Holy Spirit. The goal is enjoying communion with God himself. Union with Christ is not an idea to be understood, but a new reality to be lived, through faith.

And the reality will always be greater than our experience or understanding of it. C. S. Lewis said it well (of course):

> The presence of God is not the same as the *sense* of the presence of God. The latter may be due to imagination; the former may be attended with no "sensible consolation" … The act which engenders a child ought to be, and usually is attended by pleasure. But it is not the pleasure that produces the child. Where there is pleasure there may be sterility: where there is no pleasure the act may be fertile. And in the spiritual marriage of God and the soul it is the same. It is the actual presence, not the *sensation* of the presence, of the Holy Ghost which begets Christ in us. The *sense* of the presence is a super-added gift for which we give thanks when it comes.[10]

I want you to experience the living presence of Christ as integral to your salvation. But your experience is not primary. What is primary, Lewis is saying, is the reality of Christ's presence, sometimes in spite of our experience.

To put it another way, the faithfulness of God is not dependent on the strength of your faith. In one of her letters, Flannery O'Connor wrote that her faith "rises and falls like the tides of an invisible sea."[11] Our faith is indeed fickle and wavering, but God's love is constant and steadfast. When I base my Christian life on my Christian experience, I become locked in the labyrinth of my own performance. I am only as sure of God as my current emotions and obedience allow. My eyes are fixed on myself.

The gospel, the good news, is the way the Holy Spirit turns our eyes away from ourselves and onto Christ. The gospel brings you into union with Christ. Christ enters your heart and gives you faith. By that faith, you receive Christ and all his fullness. Faith fixes your eyes on Christ and rests in him.

The wonder of our union with Christ is not reducible to our experience or understanding of it. And isn't this wonderful news considering what O'Connor and Lewis are saying? It is not the quality or degree of our faith that matters as much as our being united to the object of our faith, the perfect Christ. It is the perfect Christ who saves us, not our imperfect faith or our imperfect obedience.[12]

We must be relentless about this. Otherwise, we run the risk of reducing the glory of our salvation in Christ to the smallness of our individual experience of him. So, as we explore the wonder and mystery of union with Christ together, let us always remember that the Christ we experience is always greater and more marvelous than our experience of him.[13]

A REALITY TO GROW INTO

My grandparents both died in recent years. They were married for seventy years. I called them Dear and Hacko—"Hacko" was my childish mispronunciation of my grandfather's middle name, and "Dear" because Hacko said that his wife was too pretty to be called anyone's grandmother. They were so close to each other that I can hardly speak one of their names without the other's.

Dear and Hacko were deeply in love. After so many decades together, they could finish each other's sentences. Dear could probably tell you, verbatim, all of Hacko's many stories. And boy, was he a storyteller! It's an inherent part of being a southern man, but Hacko was uniquely gifted in this capacity. Hacko could no doubt tell by the tone of Dear's voice or the tilt of her head what she was about to say to him as well. They felt each other's joys and pains, successes and failures. They always turned to each other, included the other. It would be foreign to one of them to make a plan that didn't include the other. They had lived life together for so long that they truly became one.

Now, objectively, they were no more married on the last day of their life together than on their wedding day, seventy years before. When the minister first pronounced them "man and wife," they were fully and completely married. Legally, they became a new entity, a married couple. They shared a family name. Their most significant possessions were no longer "his" or "hers," but "ours." They began to be "one."

But subjectively, their experience of this new identity grew over time. The sentence finishing, mind reading, need anticipating, thinking of the other before themselves—that grew with the years. And just as in a long marriage, your *experience* of being found in Christ is something that will grow over time.

Christ has wed himself to you. This is not just a declaration to agree with. It is an objective reality to live into. He has fully atoned for you, and he is now with you, assuring you that with him, you have the resources to overcome anything that threatens to overwhelm you.

THE GREAT PRAYERS OF THE BIBLE

I've noticed, over the years, that when I say, "You are in Christ and Christ is in you," people are still scratching their heads and asking, "Yes, but what does that mean, practically speaking?"

Jesus knows it can be hard to believe that *you are in Christ*. Perhaps that's why he prays for us in John 17, that "just as you, Father, are in me, and I in you, that they also may be in us … I in them and you in me … so that the world may know that you sent me and loved them *even as* you loved me" (John 17:21–23).

The Father loves you "even as" he loves his own son because all that belongs to the son he now shares with all those who are united to him. Whatever is true of Jesus in God's eyes is now true of you. That's union with Christ. Union with Christ means you are in Christ. And Christ himself prays for us to know we are hidden in him—and promises that he "will continue to make it known" (John 17:26).

It can also be hard to believe that *Christ is in you*. So that's why Paul prays for us in this way in Ephesians 3: "[I pray] that according to the riches of his glory he may grant you to be strengthened with power through his Spirit in your inner being, so that Christ may dwell in your hearts through faith—that you … may have strength to comprehend … and to know the love of Christ that surpasses knowledge, that you may be filled with all the fullness of God" (vv. 16–19).

You might find it strange that Paul prays for something that is already true—"that Christ may dwell in your hearts through faith"—since he is writing to Christians, who by definition are those in whom Christ dwells. We understand, however, that it's one thing to know something and another thing to *know* it. This is a prayer for what can be called *experiential knowledge*, "to know ... that [which] surpasses knowledge" (v. 19).

Here are two of the greatest prayers of the Bible, John 17 and Ephesians 3, and what are they about? Union with Christ! They are prayers that we would know—beyond mere intellectual comprehension—and experience our union with Christ. Thanks be to God!

I've tried to say as clearly as I can what union with Christ entails. And yet, we will never move beyond the need for images and imagination. So I'll conclude this chapter with my favorite image for union with Christ. It's from Ephesians 4, where Paul says our union with Christ is a reality we grow up into. We are to grow up "to mature manhood, to the measure of the stature of the fullness of Christ, so that we may no longer be children ... We are to grow up in every way into [Christ]" (vv. 13–15). The metaphor makes clear that we are already in Christ, definitively and objectively. And now, we are to grow up into him, experientially and subjectively.

Imagine a little boy wearing his father's dress shirt. He is already fully clothed, you could say, but he's still just a little boy. He'll have to grow up into this new covering until it fits him. In the same way, we are already completely clothed in Christ and his righteousness, but life in Christ is one of growing up into this new reality until it fits us. You are not striving to attain it. You are striving to lay hold of what is already yours. You are growing up into it.

Chapter 3

WHY WE NEED IT: TWO SONGS PLAYING IN OUR HEADS

The changes in our life must come from the impossibility to live otherwise than according to the demands of our conscience, not from our mental resolution to try a new form of life.

Leo Tolstoy

How do you know that you are ready to change? The famed novelist Leo Tolstoy says that what really propels people to change, more than our mental resolution (I need to change) is a firm conviction that our lives can't go on as they have before (I must change or I will die).

And yet this man who wrote so beautifully about the development of his characters and the possibility of change came face to face in his own life with a soul-wrenching collision, one in which the determined optimism of "I can change" collided with, and finally yielded to, the defeated resignation of his inability to do so. Tolstoy, remembered today as one of the world's greatest writers, spent his last year wracked in inner turmoil, torn between his high ideals and the harsh realities of his own home life.[1]

Learning more about his personal struggles, I appreciate Tolstoy's novels and stories even more, because he was wrestling so intensely with something deeply human: all you want to do is change, but you don't know how to make that happen. It's easy enough to change your circumstances, but the question often rumbling underneath is, *But do people really change? Can I? How?*

The Bible makes it sound as though this change is not only possible but inevitable. It says we can "be transformed" (Rom. 12:2) and be given "a new heart" (Ezek. 36:26), a new mind (1 Cor. 2:16), and even a "new self" (Eph. 4:24), one with the ability to see the world through new eyes (2 Cor. 5:16). It says we can "shine like stars" in the midst of this world (Phil. 2:15 NRSV).

We have our own experience, however, and the empirical data to match, that many who claim to have Christ in their lives don't seem to *shine*. Christians are supposed to be set apart by their love for one another and the world, but it's fair to say that's not what Christians are known for today (1 John 3:14).[2]

So what's the problem? Back to the gap with which this book began: Why does the life the Bible describes look so different from the lives many professing Christians are living? What are we missing? What do we need to hear?

TWO SONGS PLAYING IN OUR HEADS

Wise spiritual counselors give us conflicting advice about the root of the problem and the way to move forward. In the main, there are two dominant voices on offer today—one we will call *the way of extravagant grace*, "just believe," and the other we'll call *the way of radical discipleship*, "just obey."

Not that anyone wants to pit these voices against each other, but we often can't help but hear them as two different songs playing in our heads.

Imagine each of these songs with its own volume knob. As we turn *up* the volume on one, we often instinctively turn *down* the volume on the other. Or, if we try to hear them both simultaneously, we may think we have to listen to each at half-volume. We seek some balance and wonder how to hold these melodies together in harmony.

This isn't an academic question. It has everything to do with how we live, how we pray, what we think of when we think about God, and therefore how (and how often) we approach him.

BELIEVE THE GOSPEL ... MORE

In my own life, I first heard the song of extravagant grace in my early twenties through the writings of Brennan Manning and Henri Nouwen. In *The Ragamuffin Gospel*, Manning referred to the gap I've been talking about as the difference between what he called our "true self" and our "false self."

The true self is beloved by God and has done nothing to earn or deserve it. The false self draws its identity from past achievements and the adulation of others. Manning named this false self "the Imposter," which resonated with me because that's exactly how I felt. Manning's words were a watershed for me:

> My message, unchanged for more than fifty years,
> is this: *God loves you unconditionally, as you are and*

*not as you should be, because nobody is as they should
be.* It is the message of grace ... A grace that pays
the eager beaver who works all day long the same
wages as the grinning drunk who shows up at ten
till five. A grace that hikes up the robe and runs
breakneck toward the prodigal reeking of sin and
wraps him up and decides to throw a party no
ifs, ands, or *buts* ... [This] grace is indiscriminate
compassion. It works without asking anything of
us ... Grace is sufficient ... Grace is enough.[3]

About that same time someone handed me Henri Nouwen's *The
Return of the Prodigal Son,* in which Nouwen dwelled on the theme
of receiving God's love and resting in God's grace.[4] The book's cover
shows Rembrandt's painting of the same name, and the book consists
of an extended study of Jesus's most famous parable (from Luke 15),
accompanied by a running commentary on Rembrandt's painting.

The painting itself undid me. When the boy returns to his father,
one foot is bare and the remaining shoe is tattered. The son has literally worn himself ragged running from his father, before whom he
now kneels in weariness, burying his face in the father's bosom. The
father's hands are cast in light as they rest tenderly on the boy's back,
welcoming his wayward child home.

Before a word of contrition has escaped from the son's lips, and
while his motives for return remain famously unclear (is he truly
repentant? or just desperate?), while the son was yet a great way off,
the father, at great cost to his own reputation, runs to embrace his
child.[5] Jesus's story contains what writer Tobias Wolff called "surely

the most beautiful words ever written or said:"[6] "But when he was yet a great way off, his father saw him, and had compassion, and ran, and fell on his neck, and kissed him" (Luke 15:20 KJV).

But in Jesus's story it is not only the prodigal child whom the father welcomes home. Though it is most often called the parable of the prodigal son, Jesus himself gives the story a different title: "There was a man who had two sons" (Luke 15:11), and the story is about both. Both sons are lost, but for entirely different reasons.[7]

The prodigal son breaks the rules while the elder brother keeps them all ("I never disobeyed your command," Luke 15:29), but both are running from the Father to get control of their lives. The two sons represent the two different audiences listening to Jesus's story: the moral failures gathering around Jesus ("the tax collectors and sinners" of Luke 15:1) and the morally upstanding ("the Pharisees and the scribes" of Luke 15:2), whose very virtue keeps them from seeing how much they too need the grace of God. "So [Jesus] told *them* [both audiences] this parable" (Luke 15:3) about two different ways of running from God. No matter your story, you can find yourself in this story.

At the end of Jesus's parable, the father goes out to meet his older son as well, and that son complains, "Look, these many years I have served you ... yet you never gave me a young goat, that I might celebrate with my friends" (Luke 15:29). His very complaint makes it clear that in his own dutiful, obedient way, the older son has also been avoiding his father all of his life.

And yet the Father goes out to each son—down another road, after another son. We are all embraced as we are, not as we should be. And everything we have to say about following God begins and ends in that embrace. It's all of grace.

GRACE: FULL VOLUME

In the Garden of Eden, *this* was what the serpent called into question—the goodness of God (Gen. 3:4–6). And that question remains today underneath every temptation we face: Do you believe the Lord intends good for you? If only we could see how much God desires our good, then we would never choose against God's will for our lives.

Therefore, the remedy to our deepest wound and the antidote to Satan's most venomous lie is a sure and certain confidence in the goodness of God toward us. Only those who believe in his grace will have the power to obey him.

Because we are relentless in trying to justify our lives, because we will use anything, even our virtue, to keep God at a distance, we can't hear this song of grace too loudly or too often. We always need to hear it at full volume. All the way up. Undiluted. In all of its shocking candor. Grace abounds.

I'm thankful for those writers who, against the fear that such talk of God's lavish grace will lead to a life of license, dare to keep turning up the volume on grace—all the way to full blast. Amazing grace. This is the song that breaks into our hearts and changes everything. Grace changes everything. Believe the gospel of grace. Come and rest.

AND YET ...

And yet, after a while, having heard this song of grace over and over, and after singing it myself again and again, when I looked at my own life I began to feel a growing distress. By this time I had become a pastor, and though I preached about this grace, the distance in my own life between the grace I proclaimed and the life I was living—that gap was not shrinking. Grace covered me, but why wasn't it changing me?

Increasingly, I felt like a fraud. Yes, grace covers that too. But "just believe the gospel" was beginning to sound like a threadbare refrain.

Not to mention, when I read the Bible itself, I felt the need to turn down the volume on passages such as, "Without holiness no one will see the Lord" (Heb. 12:14 NIV).

Nor did I know what to make of the Old Testament prophets. What would Isaiah have to say about my worship (Isa. 1:11–20)? Was I making the very same mistake that Amos and Ezekiel had warned against, the mistake of presuming upon God's grace (Amos 3:2; Ezek. 16:49)? As a pastor, was I doing the same thing Jeremiah castigated the false teachers for: "They have healed the wound of my people lightly, saying, 'Peace, peace,' when there is no peace" (Jer. 6:14)? In an effort to emphasize grace, was I "healing the wound of people lightly" and so hindering the deeper healing that was needed?

Most disturbingly, I felt the need to turn down the volume on Jesus himself. It's one thing to say, "No *ifs*, *ands*, or *buts*." But here was Jesus saying, "*If* you love me, you will keep my commandments" (John 14:15), and, "You are my friends *if* you do what I command you" (15:14). Preachers of grace (as I hope to be) tell us it's not what we do that makes us right with God—it's what Jesus has done. At the same time, Jesus himself says to us, "Not everyone who says to me, 'Lord, Lord,' will enter the kingdom of heaven, but the one who *does* the will of my Father" (Matt. 7:21). And then Jesus tells these frightening stories that make it sound as if we will be held accountable for what we have done with the talents he's given us (Matt. 25:14–30) and for the least among us (vv. 31–46).

I had a way of explaining (explaining away?) such passages, but I felt as though I were editing Jesus. That didn't seem right.

I couldn't get away from the fact that when I read certain voices in the Bible, I felt I was missing something vital. Moreover, I had become skeptical about the possibility of experiencing real transformation.

The lever of "just believe the gospel more" wasn't working. I couldn't make the grace I preached about drip down from my head into my heart. I knew the benefits of the gospel, but did I know the Benefactor? I knew the arithmetic of grace, but I wondered if I knew the Author of it.

OBEY JESUS ... MORE

As I was agonizing over these questions, I was introduced to two other writers who turned up the volume of a very different tune.

Dietrich Bonhoeffer's *The Cost of Discipleship* and Dallas Willard's *The Divine Conspiracy* are both commentaries of sorts on Jesus's most famous sermon, the Sermon on the Mount. Though written decades and continents apart, these two books join with one voice to convey a markedly different emphasis as to what is really ailing our spiritual lives today.

For Bonhoeffer, writing in the 1930s, the great illness of the church is not our lack of familiarity with grace but rather our over-familiarity with it. He writes:

> Cheap grace is the deadly enemy of our Church. Cheap grace means ... the preaching of forgiveness without requiring repentance ... grace without discipleship, grace without the cross ... Those who try to use grace as a dispensation from following Christ are simply deceiving themselves ... We confess that,

> although our Church is orthodox as far as her doc-
> trine of grace is concerned, we are no longer sure that
> we are members of a church which follows its Lord.[8]

That hit home because that's exactly what I had been doing—using grace as an excuse not to follow Jesus. I wasn't doing it consciously, but I was so adamant to emphasize grace that I had begun to use it to diminish the call to discipleship. I found in Bonhoeffer an answer as to why I felt uneasy: "The only man who has a right to say that he is justified by grace alone is the man who has left all to follow Christ."[9] This was a very different message from Manning's "[Grace] works without asking anything from us."[10]

As a Lutheran pastor, working in the tradition of the preacher of grace par-excellence Martin Luther, Bonhoeffer had asked, "What happened to all those warnings of Luther's against preaching the gospel in such a manner as to make men rest secure in their ungodly living?"[11] That question cut me because I feared my preaching was having precisely this unintended consequence. In an effort to relieve overly tender consciences that still felt condemned (because they didn't fully trust in the finished work of Christ), was I making the too comfortable rest secure in their apathy when what they most needed was to be jolted awake just as Bonhoeffer had jolted me?

Against the refrain that what we need to be most wary of are moralizing tendencies in our churches that ask people to "do more" or "try harder," Bonhoeffer perceived a more insidious danger. He said, shockingly, "The word of cheap grace has been the ruin of more Christians than any commandment of works."[12] This was a very different tune than the one I'd been singing or hearing.

In calling the church back to discipleship, Bonhoeffer found a successor in philosopher and author Dallas Willard. Willard calls discipleship "The Great Omission" in the church today. He denounces American evangelicalism in particular for using grace to excuse discipleship and thereby eviscerating the gospel of its living content, the important call of "learning from [Jesus] how to live my life in the Kingdom of God now."[13]

Willard accuses the church of truncating the gospel, turning it into what he calls "a gospel of sin management."[14] He claims that we have reduced life with God to a "bar-code faith,"[15] wherein simply by our verbal confession, we exchange our sins for Christ's righteousness and thereby acquire our ticket for heaven when this life is over. For Willard, such a gross distortion allows us to miss Jesus entirely. "It is now understood to be part of the good news," he laments, "that one does not have to be a life student of Jesus in order to be a Christian."[16]

DEMAND: FULL VOLUME

Here was a markedly different diagnosis for what is most ailing the church today and, consequently, such a different prescription for health. Willard and Bonhoeffer both turn up the volume of the song "Follow Jesus." Obey your Lord, because the cost of not following him is in every sense greater than the cost of discipleship that Jesus demands.

And because we are prone to excuse ourselves with the consolations of grace, and because we are awash in a sea of consumerism that leads us to define the gospel mainly in terms of the practical benefits it brings us, and because we can be given to sloth[17]—we need to hear these voices that turn the call to follow Christ all the way up to full volume. Undiluted. The only way to know God is to follow him.[18] Only those who obey will have the power to believe.

This too is a song that breaks into our hearts and changes everything. Obey Jesus. Come and die.

AND YET ...

And yet, this message, "Want it more, be more sold out, run harder," left me more exhausted than ever and stripped me of the very assurance grace had given me in the first place.

These writers were some of my heroes and men of deep personal piety. But for my part, I lacked a category to hold these voices together: the gospel of extravagant grace that requires nothing from us and the gospel of radical discipleship that demands everything of us.

Which is it: come and rest *or* come and die?

GRACE OR DEMAND?

We suspect this is a false choice. We know it doesn't have to be either/or. We know both of these messages are thoroughly biblical and sorely needed (Matt. 11:28–30; Luke 9:23). And we can see how either message by itself can be dangerous. The call to be *radical* can make you exhausted, but the call to be *ordinary* can make you apathetic.[19]

No one wants to pit these songs against each other, but how do we hold them together? *Balance* may not be the best word because it might suggest a 50/50 split; what we need is 100 percent of both. How can we hear both of these songs without compromising either? How can we sing both of these melodies full volume, in harmony, so that the resulting song is not a cacophony of competing strains, but a rich symphony?

This became my overriding question, both as a pastor and as a follower of Jesus. I knew both knobs needed to be turned all the way up, but I wasn't sure how to do that. I suspected it had something to do with the Holy Spirit, but I wasn't sure how he fit in.

GRACE AND DEMAND

Several years into my ministry, I read something else Bonhoeffer had written. Though I had read these words before, this time they jumped off the page at me:

> "Only those who believe obey" ... and "only those who obey believe" ... If the first half of the proposition stands alone, the believer is exposed to the danger of cheap grace, which is another word for damnation. If the second half stands alone, the believer is exposed to the danger of salvation through works, which is also another word for damnation.... It is all-important that the pastor should be ready with both sides of the proposition: "Only those who obey *can* believe, and only those who believe *can* obey."[20]

Both must be said. Yet many of us lack a framework to hold them together. How do we walk along the apex of the roof without falling off on either side—into "the danger of cheap grace" or "the danger of salvation through works"? Put another way, how do we close the gap between the life the Bible talks about and the lives we know?

UNION WITH CHRIST IS THE SONG WE NEED TO HEAR

Extravagant grace and radical discipleship meet in the person of Jesus himself. After all, wasn't this the man who welcomed prostitutes yet who told his own disciples that to entertain a lustful look was to have "already committed adultery" (Matt. 5:28)? Wasn't this the man who dined with tax collectors yet told his own, "If your right hand causes you to sin, cut it off" (Matt. 5:30)? Undiluted grace and uncompromising obedience meet in the person of Jesus. He is always full of both.

And while it is wonderful news that we can now be found right with God outside of ourselves, it is even more wonderful that he himself is not outside of us, but "deigns to make himself one with us."[21] As we have emphasized, becoming a Christian means more than believing Christ did certain things for you long ago. It means that Christ joins his life to yours in such an intimate and comprehensive way that the prevailing metaphor for this union in the Bible is marriage (Eph. 5:32). It's a metaphor, but it's not *only* a metaphor because the Holy Spirit, the bond of this connection, is not metaphorical. The Holy Spirit is real, which means if you are "in Christ," Christ has truly made himself one with you.

And because of your union with Christ, these songs of "Extravagant Grace" and "Radical Discipleship" can no more be separated in your life than Christ himself can be torn in two.[22] These two melodies meet in harmony in him in whom they have always met.

CHRIST IS THE SOLE SOURCE

The problem with either "just believe the gospel … more" or "just obey your Lord … more" is that alone, they leave us focusing on *ourselves* as the real agent of change. There's something *we* need to do, even if that something is *do nothing but believe*. Either song, by itself, places *us* at the center.

But union with Christ displaces us from the center of our own lives. It tells us we can discover who God created us to be only through living in vital union with his Son. It tells us the work of Christ *for us* cannot be separated from the person of Christ *in us*. Otherwise, we run the risk of loving his benefits more than we love the Benefactor.[23]

Union with Christ says that the one who made heaven and earth dwells within you. He not only holds the lever of change, but he also promises that when you abide in him, through faith *and* obedience, his living water will flow out of your life. He is the fount—and from him flows every blessing.

THE DOUBLE GRACE

The power and grace are all from him, and now we have the privilege of abiding in him (see chapters 11–13 on abiding in Christ). By living in union with him, we receive what John Calvin calls "a double grace." By double grace, he means (to use the Bible's own words) that both justification *and* sanctification flow out of our union with Christ (1 Cor. 1:30). To illustrate this double grace, Calvin uses a picture from nature—the light and heat of the sun:

> Christ, our righteousness, is the sun. Justification,
> its light; sanctification, its heat. The sun is at once
> the sole source of both such that its light and
> heat are inseparable. At the same time, only light

illuminates and only heat warms, not the reverse. Both are always present, without the one becoming the other.[24]

From the one sun come light and heat. Each is distinct, and yet life is not possible without both. But both are made possible only by their source, "the sun of righteousness" (Mal. 4:2). So when we are united to *this* Jesus, we have full access to his amazing grace that covers us and we have full access to his power that enables us to obey his commands.

THE TRAGEDY OF TOLSTOY

Let me give you some concrete examples of how union with Christ helps you in your daily walk with God. We began this chapter with Leo Tolstoy, best known as the author of *War and Peace* and *Anna Karenina*. Perhaps not as well known is that later in life he became a follower of Christ:

> I have lived in the world fifty-five years, and after fourteen or fifteen years of my childhood, for thirty-five years of my life I was … a nihilist in the sense of one who believed in nothing. Five years ago I came to believe in the doctrine of Christ, and my whole life underwent a sudden transformation.[25]

Jesus's Sermon on the Mount particularly moved Tolstoy. Yet, by any measure, Tolstoy couldn't live out the demands of Christ. As his wife complained:

There is so little genuine warmth about him; his kindness does not come from his heart, but merely from his principles. His biographies will tell of how he helped the laborers to carry buckets of water, but no one will ever know that he never gave his wife a rest and never—in all these thirty-two years—gave his child a drink of water or spent five minutes by his bedside to give me a chance to rest a little from all my labors.[26]

Tolstoy himself was deeply troubled over his inability to live up to the Sermon on the Mount. He wrote in a letter to a friend:

It is true that I have not fulfilled one thousandth part of them, and I am ashamed of this, but I have failed to fulfill them not because I did not wish to, but because I was unable to.[27]

Tolstoy took the demands of Jesus seriously. When he read the Sermon on the Mount, he didn't blithely say, "I love the Sermon on the Mount" (like some might say today) as if it were just some impossibly beautiful ideal. Tolstoy took Jesus at his word—"Love your enemy," "Pray for those who persecute you," "Do not repay evil for evil"—he heard these with the seriousness they deserve and faced the gap in his own life with ruthless honesty. He didn't use the grace of Christ as an excuse not to follow him.

And yet, what is tragic is that Tolstoy didn't know how to hold the demands of Jesus alongside the grace of Jesus in a way that enhanced both without canceling either. He was honest about the gap, but instead of motivating him to "press on," this gap crushed and defeated him. He died alone in a train station, an unhappy man.

The point of Tolstoy's story is not "don't seek Christ's kingdom with all your heart or you too will be devastated." For Jesus says in that very sermon, "Seek first the kingdom of God and his righteousness" (Matt. 6:33). The question is: How can we do that in a way that leads to life instead of in a way that leads to exhaustion and cynicism?

Union with Christ! It enables you to face the gap with clear-eyed honesty but also with unfettered hope. You can hear the high call of Christ not as a bar to live up to but as an ennobling reality to live into. This was the very image the apostle Paul drew on when he said, "Not that I have already obtained all this, or have already arrived at my goal, but I press on to take hold of that for which Christ Jesus took hold of me" (Phil. 3:12 NIV).

You see? The gap doesn't defeat Paul. But it doesn't lead him to passivity either. It inspires him to pursue Christ, who has already taken hold of him. You have been given life by the Author of life; now press on to live more and more into this abundant life. Every life is better with Christ at its center, but that means Christ must become, more and more, the animating center of all you do and say—that's union with Christ.

THE DOUBLE GRACE APPLIED

Here's a more current example of how union with Christ helps us live the life Christ calls us into. By most any standard, the statistics on pornography use are alarming, and increasingly, even secular scientists are coming to acknowledge its widespread and destructive effects.[28] How can union with Christ help in this battle that so many are facing?

You can see how either song alone is insufficient to rescue us. "Just believe the gospel … more" can leave you with the suspicion that you don't believe the gospel enough, or even at all. Maybe you truly do believe or want to believe that Jesus is better, but you wonder if the healing and transformation Jesus talks about is even possible, at least for you. That song alone can leave you cynical and stuck.

On the other hand, the "Just obey Jesus … more" song can lead you to the terrifying possibility that perhaps you are one of the people to whom Jesus will say, "I never knew you."

I must not be a Christian if I keep doing this, if I keep falling into this rut. That song alone can leave you ashamed and exhausted.

The same principle applies with any addiction or sin pattern, from pornography to alcohol to pills to work. We become enslaved whenever we seek to salve our pain and heal ourselves with anything other than Christ. We become addicts to sin.[29]

You may not renounce God, but it's clear that God is not your real god. He's not the one you reach for when your heart is troubled. Something else is. And this *something else* is stealing your life from you. Even more maddening, it's with your permission!

That's why Tolstoy's personal story is so heartbreakingly poignant. He came face to face with his own inability to change himself. He couldn't do it. We can't do it. How does union with Christ break the cycle? At the root! When anxious and distressing feelings arise, you can know you are not alone.

You are in Christ: When you feel defeated and ensnared, like you are never going to get over this particular sin, habit, or hang-up;

when your enemy accuses you, and your heart tells you to retreat in shame, you can rehearse and remember, "I am in Christ. I am one for whom he died." The work of Christ sets you free from sin's penalty. So rather than turning away from God, you can turn toward Christ precisely when you might be tempted to hide from him. You can boldly approach his throne with confidence because you remember you are completely covered by Christ's righteousness. Only those who believe can obey.

Christ is in you: You are not left with your own resources. The obedient, powerful, merciful Jesus dwells within you. Christ in you is greater than anything that threatens you (1 John 4:4). The person of Christ sets you free from sin's power. When it feels as though you are drowning in a sea of trouble, you don't have to medicate your feelings or reach for solutions that might temporarily relieve but ultimately destroy you.[30] You can choose instead to draw on Christ's strength, and you will find that you are strengthened. You can take one step, even in the dark. You can make one new choice. You can hold on for one more minute. Only those who obey can believe.

And this is where (as we said in the introduction) our imaginations are so necessary. Our union with Christ is real, but invisible. We must use "the eyes of [our] hearts" (Eph. 1:18) to look not at what is seen, but what is unseen (2 Cor. 4:18). When temptation comes, you can say, "That's not who I am anymore. I'm in Christ and Christ is in me. Christ, help me to be the person I am in you—by grace." You can cling to him and find that he is a complete savior—he frees you from sin's penalty and power—that is the double grace! And life is not possible without both.

THE SONG OF SONGS

Union with Christ is the song we need to recover and hear today as the heart of the gospel. The song of grace without union with Christ becomes impersonal, a cold calculus that can leave you cynical. The song of discipleship without union with Christ becomes joyless duty, a never-ending hill that can leave you exhausted.

To the imposters, who are a million different people from one day to the next, to the frustrated idealists who can't change their mold—that's right, you can't. But when the life of God comes into your life, he can, and he promises that he will (Rev. 21:5).

Union with Christ holds together what so many of us are struggling to hold together. It allows us to sing of a grace that asks nothing of us to love us—*amazing grace*—but at the same time, demands everything from us—*my soul, my life, my all.*

Part II

UNION WITH CHRIST: WHERE DID IT COME FROM? WHERE DID IT GO?

People from vastly different backgrounds gather at our church in Los Angeles—some have never before set foot in a church, others have been in churches for years, and some even have professional theological training. Yet a common denominator is that few, if any, have heard much about union with Christ. Our understanding of this central reality of salvation is vague and shadowy, such that union with Christ can easily get relegated to an optional aspect of living the Christian life.

This next section of the book aims to show you I'm not inventing anything here. Though union with Christ may be unfamiliar to us, it is nothing new. I have claimed (and quoted others claiming) that union with Christ is central to the Bible's story and central to the way Christians have historically understood salvation. The next three chapters will support those claims.

In chapter 4, we'll see how union with Christ is stitched throughout the Bible. In chapter 5, we'll trace the idea through a brief tour of church history. In chapter 6, we'll suggest some reasons why we don't hear much about union with Christ today.

I'm a somewhat suspicious reader myself, always interested in where ideas have come from and how they've changed over time. If you are like me, then you're probably already asking the questions that these next chapters set out to answer.

However, if you're not so much interested in history or theology, or if you are just anxious to learn *how* union with Christ will change your life (part 3 of this book) or even more specifically, *how do I put this into practice?* (part 4), then don't feel bogged down by these background chapters. I think this section is important, supplies a necessary foundation, and will be rewarding. But if you are already convinced that union with Christ is pivotal and needs to be embraced afresh, you might want to skim these chapters and come back to them at the end.

Chapter 4

UNION WITH CHRIST IN THE BIBLE

If union with Christ sounds intriguing to you, but also only vaguely familiar or somewhat new, I hope you're also asking, "That sounds fascinating, even beautiful, but is it in the Bible?" Not only is union with Christ *in* the Bible, but I believe it's also the best lens with which to read the *whole* Bible.

WHAT IS THE WHOLE BIBLE ABOUT?

What is the Bible's central message and unifying theme? Spread among sixty-six books and spanning more than a thousand years, how do all the disparate pieces, distinct voices, and various literary genres fit together into one coherent whole? Reading straight through the Bible can be confusing, even discouraging. Many a resolution to read the Bible cover to cover has gotten bogged down and eventually abandoned in the quagmire of Leviticus.

Sandra Richter, in *The Epic of Eden*, describes what she calls the "dysfunctional closet syndrome," in which she compares the Bible, particularly the Old Testament, to a closet jam-packed with all kinds of stuff—clothes, shoes, books, games—but so disorganized you don't know where to put things or how to find things when you need them. So we shut the door and tell ourselves that we'll sort it all out someday. Sound familiar?[1]

I've found that to be a helpful metaphor for how many people approach the Bible. You may pluck out an item here and there (such as a proverb, or a psalm, or a story like David and Goliath), but most of us are just not sure where everything fits.

Richter suggests a better way. She says that we can best honor the biblical writers by appreciating the *one* story they were trying to tell. "We forget," she writes, "that this book was cast upon the waters of history with one very specific, completely essential and desperately needed objective—to tell the epic tale of God's ongoing quest to ransom his creation."[2] The Bible is the truest and best of redemption stories.

It opens with two people and all creation in perfect harmony with God. They walk and talk with God in intimate communion, and "it was very good" (Gen. 1:31). But quickly things go very bad, as our first parents choose to disobey God and lean on their own understanding. But rather than leave Adam and Eve to their shame, God mercifully seeks them out. God's first words to them after their betrayal are not "What have you done?" but "Where are you?" (Gen. 3:9).

Where are you? That may be the best three-word summary of the Bible in the Bible. The whole rest of the book is the unfolding narrative of God's relentless pursuit to restore humanity, now banished from God's presence by the presence of our sin, to God's original intent—unbroken, unhindered communion with him and with one another and with all creation.

If you want to understand how all the pieces fit—the purity laws of Leviticus, the tabernacle instructions in Exodus, the founding of Israel, the establishment of the monarchy and its subsequent failures, the exile to Babylon and the return to rebuild Jerusalem and the temple, the wisdom literature and the prophets—these can all be subsumed under the overarching story of God's initiative to restore what was lost in Eden.[3]

To demonstrate this, Richter documents the parallels between the opening of Genesis and the closing of Revelation to show that these parallels are by no means incidental. The New Jerusalem is all that Eden was meant to be and more—a fruit-filled paradise, animated by a cosmic river, graced by the Tree of Life. This city will need no temple to house God, for God himself will dwell there (Rev. 21:22), except now not with one couple but with a multitude no one can number from every nation (5:9).[4]

So, what is the Bible all about? The Bible is the grand story of God restoring our communion with him. Everything between the opening of Genesis and the end of Revelation is part of God's plan for how that restoration will take place. God's purposes have never changed. His original intent is his final intent: that the people of God might dwell in the place of God, enjoying the presence of God—this is the arc of the whole biblical story, from Genesis to Revelation.

THE VICTORY OF GOD

As with every great story, an enemy must be overcome. And the Bible tells the true story of God's slow but inexorable victory over every enemy that has threatened his people and driven them from his presence (from Egypt, Babylon, and Rome to sin, death, and the devil).

How has this great victory of God been achieved? The great King has come. Jesus is the one Moses and all the prophets were writing about and pointing toward. He is the seed of Abraham God promised, the son of David the prophets foretold. Jesus is the climax of the covenants, the one in whom all the Old Testament feasts find their meaning and the one in whom "all the promises of God find their Yes." Jesus is the one who holds the whole story of the Bible together.[5]

And every part of Jesus's life has significance for us and for our salvation. Jesus not only fulfilled all the righteous requirements the law prescribed, but he also "redeemed us from the curse of the law." That is, he bore the consequences of our sin "by becoming a curse for us." The Good Shepherd became the "Lamb of God, who takes away the sin of the world." The cross of Christ is the victory of God.[6]

Christ's death and resurrection are the climax of the gospel story. They are "of first importance" and must always be a central part of the church's proclamation. But don't mistake the *climax* of the story for what the whole story is *about*. Look at the word *atonement*. The word means to make payment or reparation, and it calls to mind the high price Jesus paid for us with his "precious blood."[7] But spell it out: At-One-Ment. This is the heart of our good news—that because of Jesus we can now be "at one" with God. "For Christ also suffered once for sins, the righteous for the unrighteous, that he might *bring us to God*" (1 Pet. 3:18).

This startling revelation of God's love—that he did not spare his own Son but gave him up for us all—this moment in the fullness of time is itself a *means* to an even more glorious end: communion with God. All the works of God's redemption, even creation itself, are but means to this end. Communion with God—this is what the whole Bible is about!

COMMUNION WITH GOD

Union with Christ is the doorway to communion with God. Christ, in uniting his life to ours, gives us access to the presence of God the Father (Eph. 2:18). And every other gift God gives us pales in comparison to this gift of God himself.

What will make heaven, heaven is the presence of God. And one day we will see him "face to face" (1 Cor. 13:12) and dwell with him and enjoy him in a way far greater than Adam and Eve ever could in the first garden.[8] Not only does our union with Christ open the door to this gift when this life is over; but it begins now—"We are God's children *now*" (1 John 3:2). "Our citizenship *is* in heaven" (Phil. 3:20).

God has made a way for humanity to be joined to him by becoming one with us. What was lost in Eden has now been more than restored. And that's how the whole story ends: "And I heard a loud voice from the throne saying, 'Behold, the dwelling place of God is with man. He will dwell with them, and they will be his people, and God himself will be with them as their God'" (Rev. 21:3).[9]

Union with Christ is how the Bible's great unifying theme—communion with God—has come to pass. Don't you see? *Union with Christ—not only is it in the Bible, but it's what the Bible is all about!*

MORE THAN AN ORGANIZED CLOSET

This is about so much more than having your closet straightened out, or knowing how to read the Bible better. The reward is not even that the arc of the story now makes sense. The real reward of embracing our union with Christ is that you can now find your place in the story.

You are not at the center of this narrative—Jesus is. It's his party. He is the guest of honor. But because of him, you are invited. You are invited into the grandest party and the greatest community there could ever be: the life of God. You have been given access! Not eventually. Not one day. Now.

This access is like no other we have ever experienced. Whether you voted for the current president or not, none of us would expect him or her to take our phone call. We wouldn't think, *Well, I voted for him. Surely I now have access to him.* You might believe that he cares about the concerns of citizens in general, but no one expects the president of the nation to care about your particular concerns, nor to get involved personally.

A lot of us approach God like the president: we assume he's much too important and busy to care about little old me. But union with Christ tells you that you are united to the one who always has access and who lives to give you access to the executive office of the universe. This isn't just about how to read the Bible; this is about living with a whole new frame of confidence. You are united to the enthroned king above all kings, "the ruler of kings on earth" (Rev. 1:5).

Could anything, then, be more important to our lives than a robust, living understanding of our union with Christ? The effects of this union ripple out and give shape to our most basic questions about identity, meaning, and purpose. But before we examine these ripple effects in part 3, let's zoom in now to look at the importance of union with Christ to the New Testament writers in particular. If it's the thread that unifies the whole Bible, then you'd expect to find it stitched through the New Testament, and that is, in fact, what you find.

UNION WITH CHRIST IN THE APOSTLE PAUL

It's easiest to spot this theme in the apostle Paul, but it is by no means unique to him.

The reality of union with Christ is expressed by Paul in a phrase so commonplace, so conspicuous in his letters that its significance can easily be overlooked, and often has been. It's captured in the little two-word phrase "in Christ."

We might be accustomed to reading past "in Christ" as just part of a greeting: "To all the saints in Christ Jesus" (Phil. 1:1). But for Paul, being "in Christ" changes everything about you. "If anyone is in Christ, he is a new creation" (2 Cor. 5:17). It is the linchpin on which everything hangs. It would be difficult to overstate the importance of this little phrase for Paul.

New Testament scholar Constantine Campbell claims that union with Christ is, if not the center, at least the key to understanding Paul's writings.[10] A key provides something that is necessary to make sense of the whole. Campbell does an exhaustive study of every use of the phrase "in Christ" in Paul's letters and draws this conclusion:

> Union with Christ is the "webbing" that holds it all together. Union with Christ is connected to every-thing else ... Every Pauline theme and pastoral concern ultimately coheres with the whole through their common bond—union with Christ.[11]

Paul uses the phrase "in Christ" (or "in him" or other closely related phrases) over 160 times in the letters attributed to him.[12]

Once you start looking for it, you'll see it everywhere. For example, Paul uses the phrase "in Christ" *eleven times* in the single Greek sentence that corresponds to Ephesians 1:3–14. He begins the sentence by writing, "Blessed be the God and Father of our Lord Jesus Christ, who has blessed us *in Christ* with every spiritual blessing" (v. 3). Every spiritual blessing that God gives us, he has given us "in Christ." Christ is the fountain, and our union with him is the fountainhead from which all blessings flow. *Come thou fount of every blessing!*

To capture what this new reality entails, Paul employs a variety of metaphors. We are united to Christ like parts of a body (1 Cor. 12), like living parts of God's temple (1 Cor. 3), like a husband and wife in the bond of marital union (Eph. 5). Or, our union with Christ is like new clothes that we put on (Eph. 4).

Let's pause on one of these metaphors for a moment. Paul says you are united to Christ like the parts of a body are related to its head. Could any relationship be more essential? You can get away from your parents or spouse; you can lose your limbs and still live (as some martyrs have experienced). You can even become disconnected from your head at the end of your life (as other martyrs have tragically demonstrated). But as our life in Christ is eternal, we can never be separated from him, our head. Nothing "in all creation, will be able to separate us from the love of God in Christ" (Rom. 8:39).

This means your relationship to Christ is closer, more central, more defining, and more important than any other relationship you have or ever could have—closer than your relationship with your parents, your spouse, your children, even your own body! Indeed, it is "closer than any other union which man can possibly imagine."[13]

It can be tempting to read past "in Christ" as simply a biblical-sounding phrase. But once you grasp the significance of this phrase for Paul, you'll never read past it again, and you'll begin to see it on almost every page of his letters.

UNION WITH CHRIST IN THE GOSPELS

Where did Paul get such a radical idea—that those who believe in Christ are actually united to him? From Jesus himself, who appeared to Paul on the road to Damascus and said, "Why are you persecuting me?" (Acts 9:4). It shook Paul to the core to realize that by persecuting Jesus's followers, he was persecuting Jesus himself. They are vitally connected.

"In Christ" is Paul's two-word summary for something Jesus talked about many times, but most conspicuously in the gospel of John and most memorably in John 15:

> I am the true vine, and my Father is the vine-dresser.... Abide in me, and I in you. As the branch cannot bear fruit by itself, unless it abides in the vine, neither can you, unless you abide in me. I am the vine; you are the branches. Whoever abides in me and I in him, he it is that bears much fruit, for apart from me you can do nothing. (vv. 1, 4–5)

To believe in Christ is a personal, dynamic, living reality in the gospel of John. Truth is not an abstract idea we ascribe to; truth is a living person we are connected to (John 14:6). That's why John again and again (and again in 1 John and 2 John) talks about *abiding*. *Abide* is John's word to describe our union with Christ.

To know Christ is to be connected to him, personally, vitally, and organically, like branches to a vine. And a life of abiding in Christ—living out of our union with him—is the abundant life (John 10:10). This explains why John says we can find life only in Christ (John 1:4) and that if we are not connected to Christ, we will wither (15:6).

It seems clear enough that union with Christ is essential to Paul and John. But you can see it assumed in the other gospels as well. While Matthew, Mark, and Luke don't use the language of *abiding* or *in Christ*, they do repeatedly talk about the *kingdom of God* (or *kingdom of heaven*), and those realities are inseparably related.

Because the language of *kingdom* is foreign to us, we may not know what to make of it. But life in the kingdom is the main theme of Matthew, Mark, and Luke (Luke 4:43).[14] The kingdom life is the life Jesus himself embodied and inaugurated (Matt. 3:2). So Jesus could say, while standing in the midst of an astonished crowd, "the kingdom of God is in the midst of you" (Luke 17:21), because *he* was standing in their midst. He could say, "The kingdom of God has come near" (Mark 1:15 NIV), because *he* had come near.

Our union with Christ, Jesus's abiding presence in us, is what makes life in the kingdom of God possible for us today, here and now. The union with Christ that John and Paul describe is *how* the life in the kingdom that Matthew, Mark, and Luke talk about comes to pass. It's because the living seed has been planted in us (to reference a parable found in Matt. 13; Mark 4; Luke 8) that this new kingdom life can bear fruit through us (John 15:5).

Take the Sermon on the Mount, for example. The life Jesus describes in the Sermon on the Mount is impossible on our own. This is kingdom life, and it's only possible if you are united to the

King, which is why, reading the sermon closely, it's not addressed to all humanity. He addresses this sermon to his disciples. "His disciples came to him … and [he] taught them" (Matt. 5:1–2). The Sermon on the Mount describes the new kingdom life Jesus now makes possible for those who are connected to him. Union with Christ is the gateway to this new life.

UNION WITH CHRIST IN THE REST OF THE NEW TESTAMENT

The introductions of Peter's letters show that Peter also regards union with Christ as foundational to the gospel (1 Pet. 1:3–4; 2 Pet. 1:4). He goes on to say that followers of Christ are "like living stones … being built up as a spiritual house" (1 Pet. 2:5); we are integrally built together and God dwells within us through his Spirit. This is Peter's way of capturing our union with Christ. We can stand firm in God's grace and have peace in our suffering only because, as Peter concludes his letter, we are "in Christ" (1 Pet. 5:14).

Union with Christ is a key theme in other New Testament letters as well. We'll look at the letter of James in a moment and at Hebrews in chapter 10. And we've already seen how the theme of communion with God made possible by union with Christ is the pinnacle of Revelation.

So you see, union with Christ is central to the New Testament writers, central to Jesus, who says, "Apart from me you can do nothing" (John 15:5), and central to understanding the Bible as a whole. Union with Christ is what makes salvation a powerful, living reality for us. As one writer sums it up, "Until we are united to Christ, what he has achieved for us helps us no more than an electricity mains supply that passes our house but is not connected to it."[15]

WHAT'S AT STAKE?

The two most common complaints I hear about reading the Bible are "I just don't get anything out of it" and "I don't understand it." Union with Christ addresses both of these concerns.

First, realizing that Christ is in you changes the expectations you bring to reading the text in front of you. No longer are they just words on a page. The Bible is "living and active" because the living Christ is actively speaking through these words.

The same Spirit who *inspired* the words of Scripture long ago now lives in you and speaks through these same words and *illuminates* them as you read today. The one spoken of on the pages is the same one who speaks through them. So you can come to the Bible expecting to hear from and commune with the one who stands at the center of it: Christ. Union with Christ is how the Bible becomes a burning bush out of which God speaks.[16]

Second, as we saw in the previous chapter, union with Christ allows us to hear all the different voices of the Bible—the voices of grace *and* the voices of demand—in ways that complement one another, instead of clashing with one another.

For example, you may read about God's unconditional love that is not dependent on what you do in Ephesians 2:8–9. But then you read Jesus saying, "You are my friends *if* you do what I command you" (John 15:14). "If"? What's that doing in there?

You may hear that grace means there is nothing you can do to make God love you more or less, that God loves you because he loves you because he loves you (Deut. 7:7–8)—not because of the works you do, but because of what Jesus has done (Rom. 4:5). But then Jesus himself tells us, "Not everyone who says to me, 'Lord, Lord,' will enter the kingdom of heaven, but the one who *does* the will of my Father" (Matt. 7:21).

Any conscientious reader of the Bible at some point asks, "How do I reconcile these voices?" Are they incompatible? Is the Bible inconsistent? Does the Bible teach an extravagant grace that asks nothing of us, or radical discipleship that demands everything from us? Which is it?

We know that's a false choice. But practically, we often don't know how to hold these voices together.[17] And so we may tend to focus on one message and skim over the other, or as we saw in the last chapter, we may turn down the volume on one voice as we turn up the volume on another. (We might read the letter of James through the lens of Galatians, for example.) Or, back to where this chapter started, we give up trying to sort it out and push it all back into the closet. And close the door.

The church is in desperate need of a way to express the grace of the gospel *and* the demand of the gospel in a way that enhances both without canceling either. If you have ever asked these questions, union with Christ is your answer.

For example, the letter of James, like the Sermon on the Mount, sets a very high bar for the Christian life. James uses strong language. "You adulterous people! Do you not know that friendship with the world is enmity with God?" (James 4:4). Either we turn down the volume on James ("Now he doesn't mean …") or it becomes a cudgel with which to batter even the most faithful among us. Who can read the letter of James in good conscience and not cry out, "Who then can be saved?"[18]

Only union with Christ allows us to read James not as a crushing burden but as an uplifting possibility. The letter of James *is* a litmus test—are you in Christ? If you are, then James becomes encouraging, even beautiful to you. You *can* persevere under trial (ch. 1), have a living faith (ch. 2), tame your tongue (ch. 3), rest in not knowing what tomorrow will bring (ch. 4), and love the poor (ch. 5), because you are married to Christ. James describes the life that Christ died to enable you to live.

The Bible teaches us that we can be united to Christ, and our union with Christ, in turn, teaches us how to read the Bible. If you are united to Christ, then from him come both grace and demand, which together lead to a life of joy. Listen for the dynamics in Jesus's own words:

> As the Father has loved me, so have I loved you. Abide in my love. [*You hear the grace in this.*] If you keep my commandments, you will abide in my love, just as I have kept my Father's commandments and abide in his love. [*You hear the demand following right after. And then you hear the consequence.*] These things I have spoken to you, that my joy may be in you, and that your joy may be full. (John 15:9–11)

Chapter 5

UNION WITH CHRIST IN THE HISTORIC TRADITION

One day in 1677, a young man named Henry Scougal sat down to write a letter of spiritual comfort to a distressed friend. And though Scougal's life would be tragically cut short a year later at the age of twenty-eight, his letter was copied, passed around, and soon published. You could say it went viral. It's still in print today.

About half a century later, two brothers by the last name of Wesley were given Scougal's letter by their mother, Susanna, who had cherished the letter herself. The brothers, in turn, were so taken by it that they shared it with their friend George, who upon reading it, commented, "I never knew what true religion was till God sent me that excellent treatise." That friend was George Whitefield, who went on to become one of the greatest preachers of the eighteenth century and a catalyst of what would come to be called the Great Awakening. Though he had been in church and a practicing Christian for years, Whitefield traced his own conversion back to reading Scougal's letter.[1]

The letter turns around a question that every age has asked in different ways: What is the heart of true Christianity?

Scougal's answer was that true Christianity consists not in the trappings of religion, not in going to church or in the saying of prayers, not in the making of orthodox affirmations or any external form. Rather, Scougal wrote, true Christianity consists in a "union of the soul with God, a real participation of the divine nature, the very image of God drawn upon the soul, or, in the apostle's phrase, *it is Christ formed within us … a divine life.*"[2]

His letter has come to be called, and the title says it all, *The Life of God in the Soul of Man.*

I remember first reading Scougal's letter and finding his wording both familiar and shocking. This talk of participation in the divine life was not how I heard the gospel described in any church I had yet visited. In fact, some might consider Scougal's language to be downright dangerous, even heretical. It may sound more "new age" than "old school."

But his letter did carry the endorsement of several respected names in the theological tradition of the church. And it was grounded in biblical texts as well. To the questions "What *is* the good news that Christ brings to this world?" and "What lies at the *heart* of the gospel?" Scougal's answer—union with Christ—presented a historical riddle to me.

And the seed of the book you now hold in your hands began with this historical riddle, which provoked me as a young seminary student reading many of the "big names" of church history. Why was it that so many of these writers talked about the gospel in a way most of us don't hear it today? Why has union with Christ disappeared as a controlling category—or even as a common phrase we use—when we talk about the gospel? Whatever happened to union with Christ? That particular question will be the focus of the next chapter.

But for the remainder of this chapter, we will trace, in an extremely abridged fashion,[3] this theme of union with Christ through some of the seminal voices of what historian Hans Boersma has called "The Great Tradition," by which he means "the broad consensus of the church fathers and medieval theologians."[4] We will keep following this thread through the Reformation and up through some surprising voices in the twentieth century.

If union with Christ is truly the "fountainhead of the gospel,"[5] then you would expect to find it emphasized over and over, across the centuries and across theological traditions. And, in fact, that is precisely what you find.

Before we jump in, two caveats are in order. First, to demonstrate that union with Christ has been a dominant theological theme for two millennia would require at least an entire book, and from a master of the tradition—not merely one chapter from me. Perhaps someone else will endeavor to write that book. Here I'll give just a sampling of representative voices and recommend that if you'd like to learn more, the endnotes to this chapter can direct you to further reading.

Second, I am well aware that these theologians differ on significant points, and I don't mean to imply, by quoting them next to each other, that all of their views harmonize (even when it comes to what union with Christ *means*).[6] My goal is to show that one thing they all do agree on is that union with Christ is central and significant.

UNION WITH CHRIST IN THE EARLY CHURCH

Three of the most important voices of the early church were Irenaeus (AD 130–200), Athanasius (296–373), and Augustine (354–430).

Irenaeus, a most important defender of Christianity in its earliest days, emphasizes throughout his writings the significance of Christ's *incarnation* for our life as his followers:

> The Word of God was made man, and he who was the Son of God became the Son of Man, that man, having been taken into the Word, and receiving the adoption, might become the son of God. For by no other means could we have attained to incorruptibility and immortality, unless we had been *united* to incorruptibility and immortality.[7]

The incarnation, Irenaeus says, paved the way and made possible our participation in God's life, such that now we can be united with the incorruptible, immortal life of God.

In the next century, Athanasius was a heroic voice at the first council of Nicaea in 325, crucial for upholding and defending the full divinity of Christ. And Christ's full divinity is necessary for our salvation. "For," Athanasius famously wrote, "[Jesus] became man that we might become divine."[8]

Likewise Augustine, the one name from the early church you probably have heard of, and whose influence is still felt today, speaks of our union with Christ in his seminal work, *The Trinity*:

For surely if the Son of God by nature became son of man by mercy for the sake of the sons of men (that is the meaning of *the Word became flesh and dwelt among us*), how much easier it is to believe that the sons of men by nature can become sons of God by grace and dwell in God; for it is in him alone and thanks to him alone that they can be happy, by sharing in his immortality; it was to persuade us of this that the Son of God came to share in our mortality.[9]

Historian Donald Fairbairn traces the theme of communion with God through the writings of the church fathers in order to demonstrate why the early church did not struggle as much with what we struggle so mightily with today—integrating theology into our daily lives:

They were able to articulate the connection between the doctrines of the faith and the Christian life in a clearer and more persuasive way than we are usually able to do…. The way the early church avoided the problem of divorcing doctrine from Christian life was by understanding all of Christian life in direct connection to God's life…. Doctrine, as they understood it, pointed beyond itself to God, in whose life human beings are called to share.[10]

For the early church fathers, the incarnation and its continuing importance were central to the idea of salvation because knowing

God was not merely a theological exercise but an invitation to commune with God. Theology meant understanding your life as enfolded within God's own life.

To show that this understanding was innate to the faith of the early believers, and not just theologians, we can read the story of Felicitas, a second-century martyr. Charles Williams (one of the Inklings, a literary discussion group comprised of C. S. Lewis and J. R. R. Tolkien, among others) writes in his book on the history of the Holy Spirit in the church:

> Her name was Felicitas; she was a Carthaginian; she lay in prison; there she bore a child. In her pain she screamed. The jailers asked her how, if she shrieked at *that*, she expected to endure death by the beasts. She said: "Now *I* suffer what *I* suffer; then another will be in me who will suffer for me, as I shall suffer for him."[11]

This sense of *another in me*, says Williams, "in a sentence defined the Faith."[12] And so from the pens of the theologians to the cries of the martyrs, we can see that union with the indwelling Christ was the sum and substance of the gospel in the early church.

To capture this immeasurable gift of our communion with God, the church fathers used two remarkable Greek words: *theosis* and *perichoresis*.

The Greek word *theosis* is often translated into English as "deification," and for that reason it is often misunderstood and thus avoided. We fear, particularly in the Western church, any implication that human beings in some sense become gods themselves or get absorbed into God's life. Yet *theosis* was the church fathers' way of talking about what the apostle Peter describes, "He has granted to us his precious and very great promises, so that through them you may become partakers of the divine nature" (2 Pet. 1:4). These theologians were careful to stress that *theosis* did not mean human beings become divine in the same way that God is divine (eternal, infinite, omnipotent, all knowing, etc.). They staunchly maintained a Creator/creature distinction. Yet they were comfortable, in ways we rarely are today, talking about our participation in God's own triune life.[13]

If you spell out the other Greek word, *peri-choresis*, you can hear in English what the word conveys: *peri* (from which we get words such as *perimeter*) and *choresis* (from which we get our word *choreography*)—a dancing circle. The word describes the interrelationship of the persons of the Trinity. That in everything God the Trinity is and does, each of the three persons relates to and engages with each of the other persons. Like an eternal dance, the "choreography" of the Divine Being is singular in its diversity and diverse in its unity. And for the church fathers, one beautiful way of understanding our salvation is our being invited into this dance.

If this sounds foreign to our ears today, Jesus himself promised much the same thing in John: "In that day you will know that I am in my Father, and you in me, and I in you.... If anyone loves me, he will keep my word, and my Father will love him, and we will come to him and make our home with him" (John 14:20, 23).

In emphasizing our participation in God's life, Irenaeus, Athanasius, and Augustine were simply building off the rich biblical foundation we sketched in the previous chapter. It's important to remember as we run through these theologians that our confidence is not in their words but in the Scriptures they were faithfully trying to exposit.

UNION WITH CHRIST IN THE MIDDLE AGES

For the Middle Ages, we'll jump in by way of a great work of art from the time period: Dante's *The Divine Comedy*. This epic poem about a soul's journey to the face of God is widely recognized as a masterpiece of world literature. Dante's pilgrim has three guides along his journey: First, the Roman poet Virgil, who represents classical wisdom and knowledge. Then, Beatrice, the love of Dante's life. His final guide is someone whom, as I read the poem for the first time, I had never heard of—Bernard of Clairvaux, a twelfth-century monk whose great theme was communion with God through our union with Christ.

Dante's admiration is the main reason I would choose Bernard of Clairvaux from among the many voices we could choose in the Middle Ages (Anselm, Bonaventure, Thomas Aquinas, etc.). Bernard is a towering figure of medieval theology, and he holds a distinguished place in the history of Christian spirituality as someone of whom all sides (theologically) speak favorably. In the Catholic Church, Bernard is known as "the mellifluous doctor," a reference to the brilliance of his theological mind and the beauty of his speech. But he was also a seminal influence on the Protestant Reformers, with Luther and Calvin both quoting him extensively and with admiration.[14]

If there is a controlling theme in Bernard's works, it is love, specifically the soul's journey through the love of God to union with God. So taken was Bernard with this theme that he chose the Song of Songs, the biblical poem celebrating the passionate love of a young married couple, as his lifelong theological project (unfinished) to represent the intimate union between Christ and his bride, the church.

Unfortunately for us, he barely made it through the first chapter of the Song of Songs (on which he wrote eighty-six [!] sermons). But isn't it remarkable that Bernard thought he could interpret the whole Bible through a love poem celebrating marriage? That for him, Romans and Galatians should be seen through the lens of the Song of Songs? That he saw the intimate love of God and communion with him as the lens for understanding all of the Christian life?

Bernard was clear that our union with Christ is not a marriage of equals but is nevertheless a real spiritual marriage to be experienced in this life, sealed by the kiss of the Holy Spirit.[15] In one of his sermons, Bernard writes:

> Oh happy kiss, and wonder of amazing self-humbling which is not a mere meeting of lips, but the union of God with man. The touch of lips signifies the bringing together of souls. But this conjoining of natures unites the human with the divine and makes peace between earth and heaven.... "For he himself is our peace, who made the two one" (Eph. 2:14).[16]

UNION WITH CHRIST IN THE PROTESTANT REFORMATION

Martin Luther (1483–1546) also relied on the New Testament imagery of marriage to affirm the reality of the believer's union with Christ, stating:

> Faith … unites the soul with Christ as a bride is
> united with her bridegroom. By this mystery, as
> the Apostle teaches, Christ and the soul become
> one flesh (Eph. 5:31–32). And if they are one flesh
> and there is between them a true marriage … it
> follows that everything they have they hold in
> common, the good as well as the evil. Accordingly
> the believing soul can boast of and glory in what-
> ever Christ has as though it were its own, and
> whatever the soul has Christ claims as his own.[17]

Luther is famous for his formula *simul iustus et pecator* ("simultaneously righteous and sinner"), but while we remember the formula,
we may forget that he grounds it here in union with Christ! The
mystery of the marriage union between Christ and the soul is what
allows sinful people to truly possess Christ's righteousness and allows
Christ to take upon himself our sin, death, and condemnation.[18]

Reading the Protestant Reformer John Calvin (1509–1564)
firsthand surprised me. While many of his terms were familiar (e.g.,
justification and atonement), the way he talked about salvation as a
whole was quite foreign to me.[19] For instance, Calvin writes, "This is
a wonderful plan of justification that, covered by the righteousness of
Christ … they should be accounted righteous outside themselves."[20]
This was a familiar idea, but I was unprepared for how he clarifies
what he means by "outside themselves":

> Therefore, that joining together of Head and mem-
> bers, that indwelling of Christ in our hearts—in

short, that mystical union—are accorded by us the highest degree of importance, so that Christ, having been made ours, makes us sharers with him in the gifts with which he has been endowed. We do not, therefore, contemplate him outside ourselves from afar in order that his righteousness may be imputed to us but because we put on Christ and are engrafted into his body—in short, because He deigns to make us one with him.[21]

Here I was, about to become a pastor in that same Reformed tradition, and yet I was amazed to hear one of our theological heroes write about salvation in terms that I had rarely heard from evangelicals, much less Calvinists. I was also not prepared for how much Calvin would write about union with Christ and the Holy Spirit. Here he is again:

We must understand that as long as Christ remains outside of us, and we are separated from him, all that he has suffered and done for the salvation of the human race remains useless and of no value to us. Therefore, to share in what he has received from the Father, he had to become ours and to dwell within us ... for, as I have said, all that he possesses is nothing to us until we grow into one body with him ... To sum up, the Holy Spirit is the bond by which Christ effectually unites us to himself.[22]

For Calvin, union with Christ is not—cannot be—an optional aspect of our salvation. The person of Christ is our salvation. Every benefit of the gospel comes to us through and only through our union with him. For Calvin, the mystery of our spiritual connection to the living, incarnate, crucified, resurrected, and ascended Lord is what it means to be "saved."[23]

Calvin and Luther were both adamant to uphold the idea that righteousness from outside of us is imputed to us (not *infused* within us) and that we are saved completely by the righteousness of Christ alone, through faith. But in our effort to uphold this most important idea of the Reformation—justification by faith alone—is it fair to ask if we've lost hold of what was also important: a robust understanding and enjoyment of our union with Christ? When I read one of Calvin's most famous historical students, B. B. Warfield (1851–1921), who wrote of Calvin, "above everything else, he deserves, therefore, the great name of *the theologian of the Holy Spirit*,"[24] I was stunned and left wondering, *What?* and *What happened?*

PURITANS

The Puritans of the sixteenth and seventeenth centuries continued the Reformation reliance on union with Christ as central to salvation and the Christian life. Writer J. I. Packer summarizes, "The thought of communion with God takes us to the very heart of Puritan theology and religion."[25] And scholar Tudor Jones agrees that for the Puritans, union with Christ "is not to be understood as the achievement of a few heroic souls but a divine gift received by all true Christians." As a movement concerned with earnest personal experience of God, biblical orthodoxy, and simplicity of worship, the Puritan emphasis on union with Christ for individual piety should make sense to us by this point in our historical tour.[26]

In a page or two we will hear from John Owen, one of the most famous Puritans. But for now, here's Puritan preacher Thomas Goodwin: "Being in Christ, and united to him, is the fundamental constitution of a Christian."[27]

NINETEENTH AND TWENTIETH CENTURIES

After the Puritans, as I've suggested earlier in this book, this thread of union with Christ as the central reality of salvation fades into the background and is, for the most part, lost to laypersons. William Evans, in his history of union with Christ, says it loses its central and defining role at this point and becomes relegated to simply an optional aspect of Christian life and experience.[28] Among theologians and academics, the thread continues, albeit faintly.

At the risk of oversimplifying, let's skip ahead a few centuries to an important voice of nineteenth-century American Protestantism, B. B. Warfield. He is perhaps best known today as a defender of the inspiration and authority of the Bible, but he also wrote and preached on union with Christ. Here, in his sermon "Communion with Christ," he speaks of it:

> The appeal is clearly to the Christian's union with Christ and its abiding effects. He is a new creation; with a new life in him; and should live in the power of this new and deathless life … The pregnancy of the implication is extreme, but it is all involved in

the one fact that if we died with Christ, if we are
His and share His death on Calvary, we shall live
with Him; live with Him in a redeemed life here,
cast in another mould from the old life of the flesh,
and live with Him hereafter for ever. This great
appeal to their union and communion with Christ
lays the basis for all that follows. It puts the reader
on the plane … of "in Christ Jesus."[29]

And to show that the significance and centrality of union
with Christ has not been completely forgotten, I'll add three other
significant twentieth-century voices. John Murray, longtime professor of systematic theology at Westminster Theological Seminary,
concludes:

Nothing is more central or basic than union and
communion with Christ. Union with Christ is
really the central truth of the whole doctrine of
salvation not only in its application but also in its
once-for-all accomplishment in the finished work
of Christ.[30]

Theologian Sinclair Ferguson adds:

The dominant motif and architechtonic principle
of the order of salvation should therefore be union
with Christ in the Spirit. This lies at the heart of
evangelical theology.[31]

Lastly, theologian and professor Robert Reymond, in his career-defining work, summarizes the idea:

> Union with Christ is the fountainhead from which
> flows the Christian's every spiritual blessing—repen-
> tance and faith, pardon, justification, adoption,
> sanctification, perseverance, and glorification.[32]

FOUR MORE VOICES: JOHN OWEN, JONATHAN EDWARDS, KARL BARTH, AND C. S. LEWIS

In closing, I thought we'd look at these four names unlikely to be found together. John Owen (1616–1683) is arguably the greatest English theologian; Jonathan Edwards (1703–1758) is arguably the greatest American theologian; Karl Barth (1886–1968) is arguably the most important theologian of the twentieth century; and C. S. Lewis (1898–1963) is *in*arguably the most popular theological writer of the last hundred years. Regardless if we are aware of it, these four voices have had a decisive influence on Christian history and thought. So rather than treat them in their respective historical periods, I thought I'd pull them out so we could see, as distinct as their voices are, how integral union with Christ is to each.

I'll admit John Owen can be difficult for modern readers to read. But it is not without reason that the word "Communion" is inscribed on his gravestone. Owen calls union with Christ "the greatest, most honorable, and glorious of all graces that we are made partakers of."[33]

Sinclair Ferguson, in his book *The Trinitarian Devotion of John Owen*, demonstrates that communion with God and union with

Christ through the Holy Spirit is the great unifying theme of Owen's works. For Owen, nothing is more practical to the Christian life than understanding this vital union and understanding that it is not abstract, but real and personal. Ferguson concludes:

> Owen's great burden and emphasis in helping us to understand what it means to be a Christian is to say: Through the work of the Spirit, the heavenly Father gives you to Jesus and gives Jesus to you. You have Him. Everything you can ever lack is found in Him; all you will ever need is given to you in Him ... For the Father has "blessed us in Christ with every spiritual blessing in the heavenly places."[34]

Could anything be more helpful to your daily living and devotion to God than to realize this—that the Father sees you and all you do through the lens of your union and fellowship with Christ?[35]

At the center of Jonathan Edwards's theology is the idea that God's own glory is the end for which God created the world and all things. Edwards says, "The beams of glory come from God, and are something of God, and are refunded back again to their original. So that the whole is of God, and in God and to God; and God is the beginning, middle and end in this affair."[36] Edwards biographer George Marsden says, "That last sentence encapsulated the central premise of [Edwards's] entire thought ... Perfect goodness, beauty and love radiate from God and draw creatures to ever increasingly share in the Godhead's joy and delight."[37]

That's a remarkable statement from one of Edwards's best readers. But it distills why, for Edwards, God's glory and human happiness are not two differentiated things. True human happiness cannot be found or experienced apart from God's glory. "Therefore God's glory and human flourishing are one and the same."[38]

It is a beautiful dance: our highest joy is found in God's glory, and God is most glorified in us when we find our highest joy in him. And it is at the cross of Christ that we see God's glory most clearly because the cross is our best picture of who God is: God providing from within his own life the gift of bringing us back into his life.[39] For Edwards, this is the gospel—not any benefit that Christ brings, but that, above all, Christ brings us into communion with God. "The ultimate end of creation, then, is union in love between God and loving creatures."[40] So it should not be surprising that Edwards did not hesitate to speak of our "participation in the life of God."[41] It's in this participation, this communion with God, that God's glory and our highest joy fuel each other. And so Edwards concludes, "By virtue of the believer's union with Christ, he doth really possess all things."[42]

Next we turn to Karl Barth, who is a controversial name in some quarters and unknown in others, but is still considered by many to be the most influential theologian of the twentieth century. Barth considered union with Christ to be "the principle controlling Christian existence ... Whatever else may distinguish [the Christian life], it is to be understood primarily and decisively from this standpoint."[43] It may be fairly said of Barth's theology as a whole, "Not since the apostle Paul has one phrase [in Christ] so dominated a theologian's work."[44] And you can see this emphasis on the abiding importance of our union with Christ carried on, albeit in different ways, in the works of two theologians who were influenced by Barth, T. F. Torrance[45] and Dietrich Bonhoeffer.[46]

Lastly for us, there is C. S. Lewis, sounding very much like the church fathers, whom he read widely, and with whom our historical-theological tour began. If, when you began to read this book, union with Christ sounded vaguely familiar to you, there's a good chance it is through the influence of Lewis, who writes this of our union with Christ:

> The whole dance, or drama, or pattern of this three-Personal life is to be played out in each one of us: or (putting it the other way round) each one of us has got to enter that pattern, take his place in that dance. There is no other way to the happiness for which we were made ... Once a man is united to God, how could he not live forever? ... But how is he to be united to God? How is it possible for us to be taken into the three-Personal life? ... Now the whole offer which Christianity makes is this: that we can, if we let God have His way, come to share in the life of Christ. ... The whole purpose of becoming a Christian is simply nothing else.[47]

CONCLUSION

I've left out so many important voices for whom union with Christ was a crucial theme (Maximus the Confessor, Thomas Aquinas, Bonaventure, Julian of Norwich, Martin Bucer, Richard Baxter, John Bunyan, Thomas Boston, John Williamson Nevin, Charles

Hodge—just to name a few), and I haven't even touched on the Eastern church fathers or the Orthodox branch of the church, in which the idea of *theosis* has remained prominent.[48]

But at the risk of getting lost in this crowd of theologians, I felt it was important to show beyond doubt that this theme of union with Christ, besides being biblically central, is also historically critical—that many of the formative voices of church history saw union with Christ as integral to understanding why the gospel is good news. I hope this chapter has convinced you how necessary it is for us to recover this forgotten jewel.

Before we conclude this chapter, I should note that union with Christ is making a comeback. There has been an explosion of interest in both theological circles[49] and academic circles.[50] My hope as a pastor, and my goal with this book, is to return union with Christ to the central place it held for much of Christian history—not as the province of scholars, but as a living reality, central to the life of all believers. This is what we are missing today, and nothing is more personally helpful, theologically significant, or pastorally needed than a recovery of union with Christ.

To answer our opening question: The heart of the good news is our union with Christ and our communion with God. It is the arc of the entire biblical narrative and the core truth of the whole Bible's teaching concerning salvation. From the early church, through the centuries, and even now, theologians have agreed that the entirety of our relationship with God is captured in our union with Christ.

The question that follows then is this: Why would so many of us have a hard time recounting the practical and devotional significance of union with Christ? If John Murray is right that nothing is more central or basic, then why is union with Christ neither central nor basic in our understanding of what it means to be a Christian?

Whatever happened to union with Christ?

Chapter 6

WHATEVER HAPPENED TO UNION WITH CHRIST?

Scientists tell us that something called dark energy makes up about 75 percent of the universe. But the fascinating thing is, as one of today's leading scientists admits, "no one knows what it is."[1] So there's something real, but invisible, and central to the world in which we live, something that permeates all we see and know, and not only do we rarely talk about it, but we're not even sure where to start.

If you're wondering, *Why do I need to know about union with Christ? Is it really necessary? I've gotten along fine thus far without understanding it.* Perhaps you feel that union with Christ is like dark energy—invisible, mysterious, impractical, because it's true that you can get through your whole life having never once thought about dark energy. And most of us do.

But we have seen, in the last two chapters, that union with Christ is central to the gospel, biblically and historically. The first and greatest benefit of our salvation is that Christ unites us to himself. For this reason, John Murray says, "Nothing is more central or basic than union and communion with Christ," for it "is the central truth of the whole doctrine of salvation."[2] As with dark energy, it's entirely possible for something to be central, and for us to *know* that it's central, but still not know what it is. Yet unlike dark energy, understanding union with Christ will change the way you live your life each day. It will give you hope and purpose, and it was never meant to be reserved for specialists.

A recent book claims, "Union with Christ may be the most important doctrine you've never heard of."[3] But why is that? Why haven't we heard of it? If nothing is more central or basic to our salvation, then why is union with Christ neither central nor basic for so many of us?

Our neglect of this reality is not necessarily intentional, but neither is it just a blind spot. There are several factors at work in our culture at large that make union with Christ seem less important, less central, even less real.

UNION WITH CHRIST IS HARD TO TALK ABOUT
And We Like Clear Explanations

If, prior to reading this book, hearing "union with Christ" gave you a vague sense of "Yeah, I know what that means, I *think*," that might be because it's difficult to talk about and hard to understand without using pictures.

So pictures are exactly what the Bible gives us. Union with Christ—what is it? It's like marriage (Eph. 5). It's like the relationship of a human body to its head (1 Cor. 12) or stones to a building (1 Pet. 2). Even Jesus uses an extended metaphor of vine and branches to describe our union with him (John 15). The number of metaphors tells us how important this is; the variety tells us how far reaching. But the fact that metaphors must be used at all tells us there is no way to describe or explain union with Christ directly.

I hope to show you that nothing is more practical to living your faith than union with Christ. Yet because it relies on the language of poetry—similes and metaphors—and because it speaks of our participating in heavenly realities while we walk on the ground, it can come across as obscure, or too heavenly minded to be any earthly good. This brings us to a second reason we don't talk about it today.

UNION WITH CHRIST IS AN ENCHANTED REALITY
And We Live in a Disenchanted World

The writer B. F. Westcott said, "If once we realize what these words 'we are in Christ' mean, we shall know that beneath the surface of life lie depths which we cannot fathom, full alike of mystery and hope."[4] Lewis Smedes adds, "It is [a] whole new reality."[5] It's not a reality we can contain in our heads but one that contains us and that underwrites a whole new way of living in an enchanted world. And by *enchanted* I mean what poet Gerard Manley Hopkins refers to when he writes, "The world is charged with the grandeur of God."[6]

This conviction, that the world is charged with God's grandeur, fills the writings of G. K. Chesterton. The subtitle of his classic book *Orthodoxy* says it well: *The Romance of Faith*. For Chesterton, there is a romance to faith, a sacredness in the mix of things that moves against what he calls "the suicide of Modern thought." Written over one hundred years ago, the book is a reaction to the modern notion that only what is empirical or observable can be real and true. In perhaps the most famous chapter of that book, "The Ethics of Elfland," Chesterton writes:

> The only words that ever satisfied me as describing Nature are the terms used in the fairy books, "charm," "spell," "enchantment." ... I left the fairy tales lying on the floor of the nursery, and I have not found any books so sensible since ... it has taken me a long time to find out that the modern world is wrong and my nurse was right ... this world is a wild and startling place.[7]

Our loss of enchantment did not happen overnight. In *A Secular Age*, philosopher Charles Taylor asks, "Why was it virtually impossible not to believe in God in say, 1500 in our Western Society, while in 2000 many of us find this not only easy, but even inescapable?"[8]

Taylor's book charts how and why Western culture has become increasingly disenchanted over the last five hundred years. He coins a number of terms to describe this growing disenchantment. It used to be that people assumed we lived in a world infused with the supernatural, charged with the presence of God and other invisible powers. But today, Taylor says, we live inside "an immanent frame," in which we see the world as completely physical and purely natural, without any supernatural trace or element.[9] Within this "immanent frame," Taylor also speaks of the "buffered self," a self that is insulated and autonomous, "not open and porous and vulnerable to a world of spirits and powers."[10] In our disenchanted world, the buffered self no longer needs to look beyond itself for meaning. It only needs to look within.

Also contributing to this sense of disenchantment, some (by no means all) of our leading scientists have tried to convince us that there is a necessary division between faith and science, that you have to choose between the natural world and supernatural realities.[11] The late Stephen Jay Gould said that purely naturalistic answers to where we came from and why we are here are more than sufficient. "We may yearn for a higher answer," Gould said, "but none exists. This explanation, though superficially troubling, if not terrifying, is ultimately liberating and exhilarating."[12]

But what Gould conceives of as liberating, Chesterton considers soul narrowing. "How much larger your life would be," Chesterton says, "if your self could become smaller in it."[13]

As an odd sort of proof that no amount of scientific or technological advance can eradicate our sense of the supernatural, look at the number of movies and television shows today that contain supernatural or spiritual themes. No sooner does one area of our culture try to convince us nothing exists beyond the visible world than another stream rushes in to fill the void.

It seems that if we take mystery and enchantment out of our intellectual diet, we become starved for it. Could it be that our particular moment's obsession with vampires and zombies is, in fact, an indicator of our hunger for enchantment? And that if we can't find it where it's meant to be found—at the center of reality—we will try and settle for our own created substitutes?

Union with Christ is an enchanted reality. It tells us that the most important things about our lives cannot be seen or touched with our senses. It tells us that there are extraordinary depths running just below the surface of our lives, which is an overarching reason it doesn't enjoy a more robust reception today. So many voices in our secular age have conspired in chorus to convince us we live in a disenchanted world. But over the decrees of "This world is all there is," Shakespeare's retort still stands, "There are more things in heaven and earth, Horatio, than are dreamt of in your philosophy."[14]

UNION WITH CHRIST DISPLACES US FROM THE CENTER OF OUR LIVES
And We Live in a Self-Centered World

To some extent, self-centeredness is innate to being human. Our experience of the world is always filtered through our own perspective, so it's natural that our first frame of reference is "How will this affect me?" However, while in some times and places a culture will collectively urge people to subordinate their personal desires in favor of the family, the group, or the nation, it's fair to say our particular culture feeds and nourishes our self-centeredness, encouraging us to enthrone ourselves as the sovereign of our own lives. Do your own thing.

What was once seen as the deadliest of sins—pride—is now embraced and cherished as essential to human flourishing: embrace yourself, express yourself, promote yourself.

Illustrations of our self-centeredness abound, but here's one of my favorites. In 2006, thousands of American college students filled out a survey. They weren't told what it was, but it was actually the Narcissistic Personality Inventory (NPI), a psychological evaluation that asks for responses to statements such as "I am an extraordinary person," "I am more capable than other people," "Everybody likes to hear my stories," and "If I ruled the world it would be a better place."

The NPI has been given to college students for several decades. By looking at the change in responses over time, a recent study shows a 30 percent increase in narcissism over the last thirty years. Even more striking, in the 1950s, 12 percent of teens agreed with the statement "I am an important person." In the 1980s, just thirty years later, 80 percent of teens agreed with that same statement.[15] By our own reckoning, we live in an increasingly self-centered world.

Perhaps, then, another reason it's difficult, if not impossible, for us to embrace union with Christ is because it displaces us from the center of our own lives, where we naturally love to be. It tells us that the most important part of our identity comes from outside ourselves and that, therefore, our posture needs to be one of dependence and vulnerability, of waiting and trust. To an age that embraces self-promotion as fervently as our own, union with Christ will come across not only as bizarre and strange but even distasteful and offensive.

Here's an everyday example of just how difficult this displacement can be. When a married couple begins to consider the other's needs alongside, if not before, their own, their sense of self is being displaced. Each must learn to replace "I" with "we" as their primary frame of reference in order to form a healthy partnership. But when you are used to doing things your own way, this displacement can be uncomfortable. It can be hard to embrace the fact that it's no longer just you.

Similarly, when Christ unites himself to us, as a bridegroom to a bride, our sense of self must necessarily change. Nothing humbles us, nothing puts us in our place like union with Christ. And because humility is not something we naturally gravitate toward, especially today, it's not surprising that union with Christ has been pushed to the periphery.

UNION WITH CHRIST DEPENDS ON THE HOLY SPIRIT
And the Spirit Remains Anonymous, Unknown, and Underappreciated

We've seen that union with Christ is an enchanted reality that displaces us from the center of our lives and that we live in a disenchanted, self-centered world. But a variety of other factors speak to why union with Christ is ignored not only in the culture at large but even specifically in the church. Perhaps chief among these is that union with Christ depends heavily on the Holy Spirit. The Holy Spirit is "the bond … by which we come to enjoy Christ and all his benefits … by which Christ effectually unites us to himself … the root and seed of heavenly life in us."[16]

If the Spirit is the means by which Jesus unites us to himself, then it is essential for the Spirit to be known and celebrated in order for union with Christ to be appreciated and embraced. It follows that where the Spirit is not cherished, or is unknown, neither will union with Christ be understood or enjoyed.

Perhaps it is fair to say that two errors predominate today when it comes to the Holy Spirit. Some circles, those that tend to speak of the Spirit easily and frequently, often place their emphasis more on the gifts he brings to individuals (extra-ordinary charismatic gifts) than on his primary role—to highlight the person and work of Jesus. "He will glorify me," Jesus says (John 16:14) of the Holy Spirit in what has been called the "ministry of the Spirit in a nutshell."[17]

J. I. Packer compares the Holy Spirit to a floodlight in front of a house. The floodlight exists not to draw attention to itself but to illuminate the house. In the same way, the Holy Spirit's primary work is to shine light on Jesus and glorify God the Father.[18] This is why Dale Bruner calls him "the shy member of the trinity."[19] But when this primary focus is lost, union with Christ will be lost as well.

On the other hand, other circles of the church, in an attempt to protect against what they see as abuses and misuses of the Spirit's work (such as privileging some spiritual gifts over others as a sign of a higher spirituality), often overcorrect by downplaying or even ignoring the importance of the Holy Spirit's ongoing presence and power in the Christian life. Richard Lovelace says that all too often the Christian's relationship to the Holy Spirit is "like that between the husband and wife in a bad marriage. They live under the same roof, and the husband makes constant use of his wife's services, but he fails to communicate with her, recognize her presence and celebrate their relationship with her."[20]

As a result, many of us are not sure of whom we are speaking when we talk about the Holy Spirit. Sinclair Ferguson says:

> The assertion that the Holy Spirit, once forgotten, is now forgotten no longer needs rephrasing. For while his work has been recognized, the Spirit *himself* remains to many Christians an anonymous, faceless aspect of the divine being.[21]

And as long as the Holy Spirit remains unknown or under-appreciated, or where his primary role is obscured, so too will union with Christ be minimized and marginalized. The end result of all this is that both Pentecostals and Presbyterians downplay union with Christ, but for entirely different reasons.[22]

UNION WITH CHRIST IS IRREDUCIBLY MYSTERIOUS
And We Live in a Sound-Bite Culture That Prefers Simplistic Answers

This is related to what we said earlier, but we don't avoid union with Christ merely because it's enchanted. It's also because, since it's enchanted, we can't contain it, control it, or explain it. And this is fantastically hard for a solution-focused, technique-oriented, productivity-minded people like ourselves to accept.

With unprecedented amounts of information at our fingertips—in our pockets, even!—we are able to cull a dizzying array of knowledge within seconds, to collect life hacks for any conceivable task; and therefore, we are less and less accustomed to sitting with questions that require sustained, subtle, and difficult work from us. Is it fair to ask if we have become impatient, even lazy?

As we communicate ideas today, simplicity is "in." We like sound bites that we can possess quickly and digest easily, as opposed to nuance and depth that we must wrestle with at length. So we keep it simple. Give me your two-minute pitch or TED talk in under twenty. Say what you need to say in 140 characters. Better yet, just post a photo.

Even within the church, we seem to have developed an allergy to mystery. We prefer bullet points or fill in the blanks to parables that leave us scratching our heads. We prefer a theology we can articulate neatly to mysteries that will stretch and engulf us.

Historian Hans Boersma says that up until the fifteenth century, people viewed the world as a "mystery," by which he means people believed that the world contained realities beyond what could be seen, touched, measured, or even understood. In his book *Heavenly Participation*, Boersma says that recovering a sense of mystery is "the most urgent task facing the church today." And yet, he laments,

> To speak of creaturely participation in heavenly realities ("heavenly participation") cannot but come across as outlandish to an age whose horizons have narrowed to such an extent that bodily goods, cultural endeavors, and political achievements have become matters of ultimate concern.[23]

This loss of mystery reveals itself in our pragmatically driven churches. See our tendency to want every sermon to "make it practical," to give us action steps or things to do. See our prayer lives, too often narrowed to to-do lists for God. See the rise of church shopping, church hopping, worship wars, and other evidences of the language of commerce and ownership invading our spiritual lives.

To be sure, we should strive to proclaim the gospel clearly (Col. 4:4). But sometimes our desire for clarity ends up narrowing our view of the gospel, even to the point of placing us at the center of it. But we are not the center of the gospel because we are not the center of the universe. When we make the gospel primarily about us, we make it small.

Union with Christ says that Christ is not simply at the center of our lives; he is at the center of all creation and holds all things together, visible and invisible (Col. 1:16). He is "before all things" (v. 17), the creator of all things (John 1:3), the sustainer of all things (Heb. 1:3), and the one in whom all history finds its purpose (Eph. 1:10). This is the Christ to whom we are united!

Of course this would be impossible for us to get our heads around. Its very grandness—this is the *definition* of epic—makes it difficult to fathom. Jesus not only compares our union with him to the most intimate union that exists, that of the Trinity (John 17:21). He goes further, saying that because of our union with him, we are invited into this most sacred union, the very triune life of God (John 14:20, 23). This union is spiritual, "in a real way surpassing our power of analysis."[24] It is "breathtakingly extravagant,"[25] even mystical, "mysticism on the highest plane."[26]

Granted, the word *mysticism* has become problematic—if by *mysticism* one means unmediated access into God's presence or that we become absorbed into God or become divine ourselves.[27] But perhaps our justifiable wariness of a new-age spirituality has made us too skeptical of a robust, healthy, Christian one that not only tolerates but also moves toward mystery.

As Augustine urges, "We have heard the fact, let us seek the mystery."[28]

We rarely hear language like this in churches today. But where mystery is explained away rather than embraced, where heavenly participation is clarified ("Now I'm *not* saying …") rather than celebrated, union with Christ will not be widely known or enjoyed. It will remain "the most important doctrine you've never heard of,"[29] and we will be much poorer for it.

WHY WE NEED TO RECOVER UNION WITH CHRIST

Union with Christ is not a fact we can put in our pocket, but rather a key to open a door into a whole new reality. We can't fill in the blank and file it away. This truth will fill us and remake us.

As we've noted, union with Christ has become a hot topic in academic circles today. But the one place it's not a hot topic is the one place it most needs to be—in the seats and pews, the homes and offices, the apartments and cubicles of so-called ordinary Christians.

So as we close this chapter, in light of all the reasons we don't talk about it, here's why we need to: Union with Christ is strong precisely in those places where we in our secular age tend to be weak.[30] It gives us an ability to speak into the void created by our disenchanted, self-centered world, which has only narrowed our vision and caused us to forget who we are.

It opens our eyes to what we have felt to be true since the time we were children. We may think we've outgrown those childish ways, but as G. K. Chesterton said, he had to grow up to discover that the fairy tales he'd loved as a child were in a sense more true than any book he'd read since.

J. R. R. Tolkien wrote *The Lord of the Rings*, one of the most popular books of the twentieth century. Why would people in a primarily secular, scientific age still crave fairy stories—ones in which animals can talk and magical things happen, in which the small and the weak can triumph over the strong and powerful, in which victory can be snatched from the jaws of almost certain defeat by an act of self-sacrificial heroism?

Tolkien suggests that we love these stories because they point to an underlying invisible reality, "a fleeting glimpse of Joy, Joy beyond the walls of the world" that we feel in our bones must be true, in spite of all the evidence to the contrary. We love these stories, he claims, because they are hints and echoes of the one true story we were made to hear: the gospel, the most magical story of all.[31]

Once upon a time, the King of the universe disguised himself as a baby. He grew up and did wonderful, beautiful things: fed thousands of people from one small lunchbox, calmed a storm by speaking to it, made sick and broken people well, and brought the dead back to life. Then, in an act of heroic self-sacrifice, he let himself be killed. He died a gruesome death on a cross.

But what looked like tragedy and certain defeat turned into joy and victory a few days later when he came back to life. Jesus broke open "the pitiless walls of the world,"[32] and he makes new life possible for all of us. Tolkien says:

> The peculiar quality of the "joy" in successful
> Fantasy can thus be explained as a sudden glimpse
> of the underlying reality or truth … The Gospels
> contain a fairy-story, or a story of a larger kind
> which embraces all the essence of fairy-stories.…
> This story begins and ends in joy.… There is no
> tale ever told that men would rather find was

true, and none which so many sceptical men have accepted as true on its own merits.[33]

This same conviction pervaded the writings of Tolkien's friend C. S. Lewis. For Lewis, literature was a window to a world more real. He puts it famously:

> For if we take the imagery of Scripture seriously ... then we may surmise that both the ancient myths and the modern poetry, so false as history, may be very near the truth as prophecy. At present we are on the outside of the world, the wrong side of the door. We discern the freshness and purity of morning, but they do not make us fresh and pure. We cannot mingle with the splendours we see. But all the leaves of the New Testament are rustling with the rumor that it will not always be so. Some day, God willing, we shall get *in*.[34]

Union with Christ doesn't narrow your world. It opens the door to a world larger and more exciting, more mysterious and more dangerous, than you ever imagined. But in order to live in it, your imagination must be captured by a new story so that you too can keep pressing onward and upward toward life in this new world, even today as you walk with both feet on the ground.

Part III

UNION WITH CHRIST: WHAT PROBLEMS DOES IT SOLVE?

Remember that trunk we found in the attic in the introduction of this book? It was filled with papers that proved you had indeed been abducted as a baby. You'd long suspected something was amiss with these people who called themselves your parents. And now your suspicions have been confirmed.

Your real parents, according to these papers, are extraordinary people—brilliant and talented—and their DNA is in you. It dawns on you that this new knowledge will change everything about your life, but you can't stay in the attic forever. It's time to walk down the stairs. As you descend back into your everyday life, you'll notice that it feels like you are seeing the world through new eyes.

Now that we know what union with Christ is and why we need it, where it came from and where it went, in this next part we will

come down from the attic and start to see how it will change your
life. Union with Christ is a whole new mindset. It offers surprising
answers to our oldest questions:

> Identity—Who am I?
> Destiny—Where am I headed?
> Purpose—What should I be doing?
> Hope—What can I hope for along the way?

You now have this wonderful new knowledge about who you are
and where you came from, but as you walk back into your old life,
you wonder what all this will mean. From this point on, nothing will
be as it once was.

Chapter 7

A NEW IDENTITY: WHO AM I?

Once upon a time there was an old man who wished so dearly to have a son that he carved a boy out of wood. That night when the man fell asleep, a fairy entered the workshop and brought the puppet to life.

The fairy tells the puppet that if he proves himself to be "brave, truthful, and unselfish," he can become a real boy.

The puppet must overcome many obstacles in his quest to become real. On his way to his first day of school, he meets Honest John the Fox and Gideon the Cat, who play upon his vanity and entice him to star in a traveling puppet show. But this moment in the spotlight results in his being locked in a cage. He mourns the consequences of his bad choices, and he vows to the fairy that he will do better. She sets him free, but he's immediately lured away from his good intentions by the prospect of a place called Pleasure Island.

On Pleasure Island, the puppet meets a boy named Lampwick, and together with the other boys on the island, they begin having the time of their lives, with no rules or authority to inhibit them. They don't realize that the island harbors a terrible curse: the boys who go there become donkeys. That is, by exercising their autonomy, they literally make jackasses of themselves and become slaves. Lampwick turns into a donkey. And when the puppet sprouts ears and a tail, he realizes he's made another grave mistake and decides it's time to return home.

He manages to escape the island and runs home, only to discover that the old man, Geppetto, has ventured out to rescue his wayward wooden son and been swallowed by a giant whale, Monstro. Determined to rescue his father, the puppet jumps into the sea, and Monstro swallows him up as well. The puppet devises a plan to make the big fish sneeze them out—which works, but the whale is furious and smashes their raft. The puppet swims, dragging Geppetto into a cave, but Monstro smashes the cave as well. They flounder in the sea until finally washing up on the shore.

When Geppetto awakes, he sees his son lying facedown in a pool of water, and he mourns bitterly. But the good fairy arrives and decides that the puppet has proved himself to be brave, truthful, and unselfish, and so Pinocchio is brought to life as a real boy.

THE STORIES WE LOVE

Pinocchio, based on Carlo Collodi's 1883 novel, is one of Disney's most celebrated films (and one of only a handful of movies to have a perfect rating on Rotten Tomatoes). But have you ever noticed how many of the stories we love center on the search for identity? *Beauty and the Beast, Cinderella, The Frog Prince* … all stories of a new identity granted or a true identity recovered.

And it's not just fairy tales. Ralph Ellison, author of the classic novel *Invisible Man*, was once asked, "Would you say that the search for identity is primarily an American theme?" He answered, "It is *the* American theme."[1]

Think of the classic stories of American literature; from Huckleberry Finn on the river to Jay Gatsby on his dock, from Luke Skywalker not knowing who he really is to Princess Elsa feeling terrified that people will discover what she's really like—these are all stories about identity.

Perhaps the theme of identity dominates our stories because the search for identity dominates our lives. Like Pinocchio, we long to make ourselves real. Like Jay Gatsby, who "didn't want you to think I was just some nobody,"[2] we will do whatever we can to prove that we're somebody. Or, as Rocky put it in that most American of films, "All I wanna do is go the distance … [so I'll know I'm not] just another bum from the neighborhood."[3]

The main idea of this chapter is simple but revolutionary. Union with Christ gives you a completely new self-understanding found *outside* of yourself in Christ. Union with Christ gives you a new identity. In fact, that's one way to define the Christian faith: faith is finding your identity in Christ.[4]

Against the prevailing mindset of our day—you are what you make of yourself—union with Christ tells you that you can discover your real self only in relation to the One who made you. You are not, you *cannot* be, self-made. Union with Christ tells you that you can only understand who you are in communion with God and others. And that is a wildly countercultural claim.

A NEW MINDSET

When Paul says, "If then you have been raised with Christ, seek the things that are above," he's not asking us to live with our head in the clouds. He's talking about our mindset, which is why he goes on to say, "*Set your minds* on things that are above" (Col. 3:1–2). This new mindset gives us a new way of understanding who we are, which is the *next* thing he says: "For you have died, and your life is hidden with Christ in God" (v. 3). Christ is now your life, and that is the *next* thing he says: "Christ who is your life" (v. 4).

Why is this good news—that you must look outside yourself to find yourself? How is that even possible? How can *my* life be *defined* by someone else and still be my own? That sounds life denying rather than life giving. It sounds like I'd have to give up … myself.

Paul is saying union with Christ not only gives you a new identity; it gives you a new mindset, a new grid through which to filter everything that happens to you. For it's not so much what happens to you that defines you, as how you *interpret* what happens to you.[5] Your mindset is the lens through which you see the world and yourself. Your identity, therefore, is formed by your mindset. And you can change your mindset, says Stanford social scientist Carol Dweck.[6] But again, why would you want to?

For you to want the new mindset Christ offers and the new identity it confers, you have to see it in sharp contrast, even collision, with the mindset you've previously been living under. You have to see it as a more attractive, more compelling option.

CHOOSE YOUR OWN IDENTITY

The other day my three-year-old daughter walked past me, singing, "Don't let them in, don't let them see, be the good girl you always have to be." But it was under her breath, like in a horror film. As she turned to the chorus, her voice grew louder and more assured:

> It's time to see what I can do
> To test the limits and break through!
> No right, no wrong, no rules for me,
> I'm free! Let it go! Let it go![7]

Princess Elsa from the film *Frozen* has captured the modern secular Western mindset perfectly. Autonomy. Authenticity. Individuality. Freedom. If the dominant mindset we are living under today could be summed up, it would coalesce around these themes. David Brooks labels it "the Big Me."[8] Philosopher Charles Taylor calls it "the culture of authenticity."[9] Alternately named the iWorld,[10] Expressive Individualism,[11] or the Age of the Selfie, this mindset assumes we each have a true, authentic self hidden within us and the path to human flourishing involves discovering and expressing that true self. We must be free from any external authority or expectations that might constrain who we really are. Because, as Kanye West recently put it, "I'm nothing, if I can't be me."[12]

When I was a little kid, we had these Choose Your Own Adventure books. They were popular because they allowed you, as a reader, to make choices about the direction of the story you were reading. They put you in control of the narrative. Today we have an entire cultural narrative of Choose Your Own Identity, which also suggests that you are in control of your own story. You are free to choose.

Professor Barry Schwartz, in his popular TED talk "The Paradox of Choice," calls this prizing of individual freedom and choice "the official dogma" of all Western industrial societies. "The official dogma runs like this," he says. "If we are interested in maximizing the welfare of our citizens, the way to do that is to maximize individual freedom," because freedom is considered to be good and valuable in and of itself, even essential to being human.[13]

These assumptions are woven through the fabric of our society, from our advertising, "Be a rebel, make your own rules" (says J. C. Penney—even *J. C. Penney!*), to our legal discourse, "The heart of liberty," our Supreme Court has declared, "is the right to define one's own concept of existence, of meaning, of the universe, and of the mystery of human life."[14]

Perhaps the clearest picture of the mindset of our day is our love affair with Apple. It's no coincidence that the *bitten* apple has become the iconic symbol of modern Western culture, because it represents what's most valued among us: autonomy and independence. After all, they don't call it a wePhone.

PROBLEMS WITH "THE OFFICIAL DOGMA"

What's wrong with Choose Your Own Identity? Undoubtedly it has some enormous benefits. It empowers the individual to pursue her dreams. "We're gonna make our dreams come true … Doin' it our way," sang *Laverne and Shirley*. It offers the hope of unprecedented social mobility. "We're movin' on up," sang *The Jeffersons*. And it places a welcome accent on equality and justice for all. "Everyone is special in their own way … we're all in this together," sang *High School Musical*. These are our cherished ideals.

But Choose Your Own Identity falls short of delivering on its promises. It fails to satisfy. I'll list five besetting problems with this mindset and then show you how union with Christ offers a more compelling alternative for understanding who you are.

First, Choose Your Own Identity's accent on unlimited freedom often leads to paralysis. Take your career. No one wants to go back to the days of "My daddy was a farmer, so I must be a farmer." But when you can do *anything*, and it's up to you to choose, then that long list of possibilities, coupled with the significance of your choice, can be paralyzing. The weight of the possible is heavy indeed.

Second, and closely related to the first, this mindset leads to greater anxiety. In *The Weariness of the Self*, Dr. Alain Ehrenberg explores why depression has become the most diagnosed mental disorder in the world. It's empirically true that the incidence of anxiety and depression is higher today than it has ever been. After studying the history of depression, Ehrenberg concludes that the phenomenon is on the rise today because of increased feelings of "inadequacy," arising from a social context in which "success is attributed to, and expected of, the autonomous individual."[15]

Suppose you are one of the rare individuals who actually *does* know what you want to do with your life. Great! Now all you have to do is go do it. And do it well. And keep it up. That's an unrelenting pressure that no amount of success can relieve because the question is always, "Now, what will you do next?" And if you don't make it or can't make it? If it's all up to you, and you fail, then who do you have left to blame? Age of anxiety, indeed.

Third, having more choices actually makes us more discontent. Barry Schwartz explains why the idea that more choice equals more happiness is "completely wrong." He describes his recent experience shopping for a pair of blue jeans. So many choices: button fly or zipper fly? Relaxed, easy, or slim fit? Stonewashed or acid-washed? "I walked out of the store—truth!—with the best fitting jeans I'd ever had. I did better.… But—I felt worse. Why?"

He concludes that increased choices have led to increased expectations of how good a good choice *should* be (with so many choices, surely one of them is almost perfect), which leads to increased *dissatisfaction* with whatever choice you end up making. "Expectations have gone through the roof,"[16] and with them our rising discontentment.

Take dating and marriage. With such high expectations going in, it's hard not to slip into thinking, "if only" you'd made a different choice, then you'd be happier. And you might be. But when you pit the imagined possibilities of what you *don't* have against the real limitations of what you *do*, it inevitably leads to dissatisfaction with whomever you choose. Or, it might make you reluctant to choose at all—commitment phobic. So, Schwartz concludes, even though we have it better than we ever have, we're less content than we've ever been.

Fourth, the freedom-enthroning narrative of Choose Your Own Identity ends up robbing us of the very freedom it promises. Never has a culture talked about freedom more but experienced it less. You'll recall that Ralph Ellison said the search for identity is *the* American theme. But he continued, "The nature of our society is such that we are prevented from knowing who we are."[17]

Take the film *Frozen* again for a moment (yes, I've seen it a few times). The irony of Princess Elsa's chart-topping song "Let It Go" is that she is singing about her choice to exercise her power to be free, while (please notice) she is locking herself inside an ice prison of her own making! She sings, "I'm free!" while ensuring that she won't be.

From *Frozen* to *Pinocchio*, autonomy can't break the curse. It only ends up imprisoning you in the labyrinth of your constantly shifting desires. And so the poet W. H. Auden wrote:

> Each in the cell of himself
> Is almost convinced of his freedom.[18]

Fifth, this mindset affects how we view God. Choose Your Own Identity leads us to treat God as "a convenient, yet distant deity."[19] We may co-opt God into our plans, but we don't want him making plans for us. In our quest to discover our true selves, it's hard *not* to see God simply as an authority figure who will constrain us and impede our freedom. In our disenchanted, pragmatically driven world, we may try to keep God "on call" for when we're in trouble or need help. God becomes a stagehand to the play we are writing and starring in. And we try on new identities like so many costumes as the play moves from one scene to the next.

I've gone into such detail on the prevailing Western mindset because our mindset is like a pair of glasses through which we see ourselves and everything else. While we're looking through them, we may not realize that they are there, or that we have a choice. We simply take our view for granted. We assume that what we are seeing is "just the way it is."

But the official dogma of Choose Your Own Identity doesn't have to be the way it is. In the words of one student exhausted by the furious pursuit of proving herself, "I had no idea there was another way to be ... that I don't have to go through life like I always have."

A WEARY WORLD REJOICES: UNION WITH CHRIST

Rejoice! There is another way to be. You don't have to go through life as you always have. The Christian mindset is so foreign it can seem unreal, like a fairy tale. But union with Christ is real because the Holy Spirit is real. You truly are united to Christ by the Spirit of God.

Scholar Todd Billings points out that union with Christ is strong precisely where our modern secular Western mindset tends to be weak.[20] Let's look back for a moment at the weaknesses we just sketched and see how being united to Jesus, and the new mindset he provides, can give us what we're looking for.

First, to our paralysis. Union with Christ gives us permission to rest. We don't have to be burdened by the weight of the possible. We do have so many choices. But union with Christ says there is one choice more important than any other choice you will make: *Thy* will be done or *my* will be done? As long as your will is set on following Christ, you can rest in the choices you make. You don't have to be frozen in fear because your life is no longer in your own hands. You can surrender your plans to Christ, who has joined his life to yours.

Second, to our anxiety, to that old way of trying to justify our existence by our own work. Union with Christ tells us "You have died" to that way of living. To the angst that comes from thinking you're not allowed to fail, or to the feelings of inadequacy that come from believing you have. To those human questions, *Am I significant? Have I done enough? Am I accepted?* the answer is "Your life is now hidden with Christ in God" (Col. 3:3 NIV).

This is the precious biblical truth of justification (Gal. 2:16). You no longer have to justify your life. You don't have to worry, like Jay

Gatsby, about others thinking you're a nobody. You don't have to go the distance, like Rocky, to prove you're not a bum. Christ marries himself to you, and in a wonderful exchange, you give him all your sins and he gives you all of his righteousness.[21]

In Christ, you are significant—he makes you so. In Christ, you are secure—he gathers you to himself and keeps you safe (Isa. 40:11). In Christ, you are accepted. But that acceptance no longer has to be earned or maintained; it is granted by grace and guaranteed in Christ. This doesn't mean you stop working, but it does mean you now work in a totally new way. You no longer work *for* approval; you work *from* approval.

American Idol was one of the most popular television shows of all time, and for the contestants, one of the most nerve jangling. A single missed note could cost you the competition, but winning could change the course of your life. At the end of each season, when the competition was over and the winner had been crowned, she took up the microphone and sang one more time. But she was no longer singing to win; she was singing because she had won. It was no longer a contest. She had nothing more to prove or earn. Instead, the chosen and honored performer could sing with all her heart, delighting in her gifts for the benefit of others. That's the freedom from anxiety the gospel gives. You have already been chosen and crowned in Christ, so now you can do what you do with all your energy, delighting in whatever gifts God has given you for the benefit of serving others.[22]

Third, to our discontentment and dissatisfaction, one united to Christ can say, "I have learned in whatever situation I am to be content.... In any and every circumstance, I have learned the secret of facing plenty and hunger, abundance and need" (Phil. 4:11–12). What is this secret Paul learned (and please note even Paul had to *learn* it)? The secret is that his life is now empowered by the presence of Christ, which is why he immediately follows these words with "I can do all things through [Christ] who strengthens me" (v. 13). Union with Christ is the antidote to our discontentment. You shall not want if the Lord is your shepherd.

Fourth, to our longing to be free. Barry Schwartz concludes his TED talk on the paradox of choice with the image of a fish in a fishbowl, and he asks: How free is that fish? Yes, of course the fish is confined, but to shatter the fishbowl, to remove all constraints, would not improve the fish's situation. In fact, it would destroy him. Schwartz says, "The absence of some metaphorical fishbowl is a recipe for misery, and, I suspect, for disaster." And then ends flatly, "Thank you very much."[23]

Schwartz's unanswered question is ours as well: Which boundaries will set us free? Union with Christ tells you that Jesus is the center and circumference of authentic human existence. Jesus is the *center*—we can't understand ourselves without understanding who he is and what he has done for us. And Jesus is the *circumference*—he sets the boundaries of what it means to be human. Your real identity, your real self, is waiting to be found in him.[24]

Ralph Ellison writes, "When I discover who I am, I'll be free."[25] Union with Christ says you were made to be a part of God's family and that only by finding your place here will you be free. When you become a Christian, God sends the Spirit of his Son into your heart who cries out, "Abba! Father!" (Gal. 4:6). This is the great biblical truth of adoption, that in Christ, you have been adopted into God's family. Living in any family constrains your freedom, but living in this family is what you were made for. This Spirit of adoption, the Bible says, sets you free (Rom. 8:15) because you've finally found the boundaries that fit you. You have found your place. You are home.

J. I. Packer comments, "Our understanding of Christianity cannot be better than our grasp of adoption.... Adoption is the highest privilege that the gospel offers."[26] But by now you can see that this most precious gift of adoption flows out of what is even more basic and most precious, union with Christ. If you are united to him, "you will be free indeed" (John 8:36).

Fifth, to a God who is convenient, yet distant. Union with Christ says God is closer and more intimate than we ever imagined. He's not a stagehand in the play you are writing and starring in. You are no longer the star of the show. It's not about you. He displaces you from the center of your life. But this new role means you get to be part of something bigger than your own autobiography. You are invited into God's story, the biggest and best story of them all.

If you are in Christ, your life and your story become enfolded by another story, Another's story. You don't have to discover or craft, create or achieve, invent or reinvent your own identity. Your identity is found not deep within yourself but *outside* of yourself. Your self-understanding becomes inseparable from who God says you are in Christ. Who are you? Your identity is no longer a construct of your own preferences and choices, accomplishments or affiliations. You no longer stand alone. You no longer get the credit or the blame, the applause or the jeers. The German martyr Dietrich Bonhoeffer sums it up in his poem "Who Am I?"

Who am I? They mock me, these lonely questions
of mine.
Whoever I am, Thou knowest, O God, I am thine![27]

TWO TESTS AND ONE EXERCISE

I'm tempted to stop here on this high note, but something else needs to
be said. Perhaps like me, you've seen a "Who I Am in Christ" list of the
wonderful things the Bible says are true about my life in Christ. The list
can vary in length, from ten to one hundred points long; for example:

I am loved (1 John 4:10)
I am free (Gal. 5:1)
I am a child of God (John 1:12)
I am a new creation (2 Cor. 5:17)

Why do we have trouble getting these truths to stick? How can
this not feel like mental gymnastics, like trying to convince yourself
of something too good to be true? How do we "set our minds," and
keep setting our minds, on Christ?

The Bible uses marriage and adoption to describe how your
union with Christ changes your identity. Both of these metaphors
include a legal aspect and a relational one. On the day either relationship is legalized, you begin to possess the full rights and privileges of
a spouse, or a child. But it will take time, even years, for you to fully
inhabit your new identity.

Think about what brings about this change, however. Does a
new wife keep a copy of her marriage license on her bedside and take
it up and read it over every morning and evening? *It's true, it's true,*

I'm legally married. Wow. No, what turns a legal truth into a living one is living in that new relationship. It's a product of living out of your new identity. How do we know we are doing that? How do we know we are growing in our new identity in union with Christ? Here are two tests and one exercise.

Test 1: Radically Threatening

The first test by which you can determine whether the radical nature of union with Christ is sinking in is to ask this: Are you threatened by it? Before you can rest in the comfort of your new identity in Christ, you have to sense how frightening it can be. Union with Christ gives us a new identity, but to accept it requires leaving behind the life we have always known.

Before Orphan Annie could allow herself to be adopted by Daddy Warbucks, she had to first give up hope of her parents coming back for her. In order for us to embrace the joy of "Christ … is your life" (Col. 3:4), we must face the terrifying vulnerability of our true condition—without him we can do nothing.

Jesus will not be an accessory to your identity. Jesus must become the center, which means anything that had been in the center must be displaced. *You* must be displaced, and this is threatening. Victor Hugo, in his masterpiece *Les Misérables*, describes his main character, Jean Valjean, receiving an act of extreme grace as "the hardest assault, and the most formidable attack which he had yet sustained." Hugo continues:

> [Valjean felt] his hardness of heart would be com-
> plete, if he resisted this kindness; that if he yielded,
> he must renounce that hatred with which the acts

> of other men had for so many years filled his soul,
> and in which he found satisfaction; that, this time,
> he must conquer or be conquered.[28]

To embrace our union with Christ may feel like a most formidable attack because it will entail leaving behind the life we've known. If this offer sounds threatening to you, Hugo would assure you that's a good sign the new reality is sinking in.

Test 2: Radically Comforting

Why would you ever choose something so traumatic? Because otherwise you'll never be able to escape from what journalist Malcolm Muggeridge calls "the tiny dark dungeon of the ego."[29] Only another, coming in from outside of our lives, can set us free from our obsessive self-concern.

This is the second test to see if union with Christ is replacing our former, self-made identity: Are you comforted by it? Are you experiencing the freedom and confidence union with Christ brings? Like the Mickey Mouse costume my friend used to wear at Disneyland, this is a new identity we must choose to put on each day. "Put on the new self" (Eph. 4:24). But when we do, and as we go through life as one who is hidden in Christ, then those lists of "Who I Am in Christ" will cease to be abstract truths *outside* of us. These are not simply words on a page—these are realities rooted in our union with Christ.

> I am forgiven.
> I am loved.
> I am redeemed.

I am a new creation.

I am a new self.

Like Pinocchio, we too must decide which voices we will listen to if we want to become who we were made to be. We too must overcome the enslaving curse of thinking that freedom means autonomy and the ability to do whatever we want. Unlike Pinocchio, the gospel tells us we can't save ourselves by being brave and truthful, nor can our consciences set us free.[30] But also like Pinocchio, the gospel tells us a new life is made possible by a Father who has loved us into being.

"You are not your own" means you are no longer on your own. What could be more comforting than that?

An Exercise: Reframe the Conversation

You can exercise your new identity as one who is united to Christ by reframing the conversation inside your head. The constant voice that narrates your life, that begins speaking to your soul when you wake up each morning, naturally talks in terms of "I"—*What do I want to do? What does this mean for me? ... I think I need to ... I ... I ... I ...*

But you can practice the truth that Christ has married his life to yours by including him as your constant conversation partner. *What should we do? What are you trying to teach me?*

Instead of a running conversation with yourself, which only reinforces the broken idea that I ... I ... I am at the center of reality, choose instead to converse with Christ about what you see, what you hear and read, about what is happening and what you're afraid of.

It's more robust than What Would Jesus Do? because that question keeps Jesus external to you. Instead, reframe the conversation as a way to live in your union with Christ. Just as physical exercise can reshape your body, so this spiritual exercise, over time, can reshape your self-understanding. The more you do it, the more it will become second nature. And you will discover that Jesus truly is the "friend who sticks closer than a brother" (Prov. 18:24).

There was a story on the radio program *This American Life* in which an interviewee was contrasting her experience as a black woman growing up in America with now living as a foreigner in Paris. She said, "I was always an outsider. And I feel most inside right now where I'm most outside. That's what freedom is about though. It's not about nothing left to lose. It's about nothing left to be. You don't have to be anything."[31]

That's the freedom of the gospel you have through your union with Christ: there is nothing left to be, because you are already his.

Union with Christ grounds us in a way no other mindset ever could. If you choose to find your identity in Christ, you will lose nothing of what makes life beautiful and free. You will move from searching for an identity to being found in Christ (Phil. 3:9).

Chapter 8

A NEW HORIZON:
WHERE AM I HEADED?

Jean Vanier was a French philosophy professor who became dis-
illusioned after witnessing man's inhumanity to man in two World
Wars and seeing so many people suffer. In particular, Vanier was
burdened by the situation of the mentally disabled in Paris. How
could they be locked away in such dehumanizing conditions? Were
they not human?

Vanier had an idea to start what he called L'Arche—a community where people with and without intellectual disabilities could live
alongside one another, working together, playing together, praying
together, serving side by side and learning from one another. These
L'Arche communities spread throughout the world, and it was to one
in Toronto called Daybreak that Henri Nouwen came in 1986.

Nouwen had reached the pinnacle of professional success. He'd
taught at Harvard, Notre Dame, and Yale Universities, but he felt
he was losing his soul in the process. So at the height of his career,
he gave it all up and went to Daybreak. And light indeed began

to break for Nouwen there, among his neighbors with disabilities. Living alongside them, he came to learn from them what it meant to be truly human.

You see, Nouwen had fallen into the trap that many of us fall into—of thinking that joy and fulfillment will come through climbing the ladder in our respective fields, through expert competency, financial independence, or the acclaim of our peers. And yet Nouwen learned at Daybreak something he probably could never have learned at Harvard. The teacher became the student, and his teachers were the ones he thought he'd come to help.

He learned from these men and women with disabilities, those for whom need was a constant and who were always dependent on others. While living with those who *had to* receive, he began to learn *how to* receive. He finally found the fulfillment he craved when he came to the end of placing any confidence in himself. Only then could he begin to rest in God's love and care. That's what his brothers and sisters with disabilities taught Henri Nouwen—that in receiving, in letting ourselves be loved and loving in return, only then are we becoming *human*. This posture of humility and vulnerability is not the horizon we naturally set for ourselves.

WHAT'S YOUR HORIZON?

Novelist Walker Percy says, "I have learned that the most important difference between people is between those for whom life is a quest and those for whom it is not."[1] And Percy's novels are filled with questers, or to use one of Percy's favorite words, "wayfarers." He writes, "Such a view of man as wayfarer is, I submit, nothing else than a recipe for the best novel-writing from Dante to Dostoevsky."[2]

Maybe it's a recipe for the best stories because these are questions we all face. At transition points—*where am I going?* In times of boredom—*what am I doing with my life?* At times of suffering—*what is all this for?* When these questions arise, if you don't have a compelling horizon, you feel aimless and adrift.

Maybe that's why we love those underdog sports movies, such as *Hoosiers*, *Rudy*, and *Rocky*. What do they all have in common? They all have a horizon that propels the characters through hardship and exhaustion toward a worthy end. Any sacrifice is worth it if they can reach that goal. As Nietzsche said, "If you have your *why* for your life, you can get by with almost any *how*."[3]

UNION WITH CHRIST GIVES YOU A NEW DESTINY

As with any trip, you have to know where you're going before you can chart out how to get there. One of the oldest metaphors for life with God is that of a journey through a treacherous wilderness to a promised land. We'll use this image of life as a quest to frame our next three chapters.

Where are you headed? This chapter aims to set that horizon and show you that union with Christ gives you a most surprising and glorious destination.

Contrary to what the prevailing Western mindset tells you, you don't have to make your own destiny. Your destiny is not left for you to carve out or create for yourself, which is only a recipe for depression when you've failed, pride when you've succeeded, or exhaustion when you see all that's left to do.

Nor is your destiny assigned to you by blind fate, something toward which you move inescapably, like poor Oedipus. But neither is your destiny simply to get a great job or get married or have a family—as good as those things might be. Your destiny is much grander than that. And neither is your destiny just a vague sense of going to heaven someday and being reunited with all those you have loved and lost. Sweet as that prospect might be, perhaps it explains why the promise of heaven can come across as quite boring to children—what does one *do* all day?

When you become a Christian, Christ unites his life to yours. "You are not your own" (1 Cor. 6:19); you gain a new identity. And along with your new self-understanding, union with Christ also tells you that you have a destiny that's glorious and specific to you, one that gives new shape and purpose to each day. You have a horizon that can propel you through hardship and exhaustion. Any sacrifice will be worth it. But to get where you want to go, you may, like Henri Nouwen, have to go by a way you never expected.

WHERE YOU CAME FROM

In order to know where you're going, you have to know where you came from and what you were made for.

> Then God said, "Let us make man in our image, after our likeness."… So God created man in his own image, in the image of God he created him; male and female he created them. (Gen. 1:26–27)

The biblical scholar Walter Brueggemann says, "There is one way in which God is imaged in the world and only one: human-ness!"[4] God created us in his image and pronounced over us and all creation, "Very good" (Gen. 1:31).

But what does it mean to say that we are created "in the image of God"? You may know that for much of history, scholars have talked about the "image of God" mainly in metaphysical terms—that is, we image God in our ability to reason, to create, to exercise authority, or in our conscience, or in our desire for community. And certainly a case can be made for each of these.[5]

In his groundbreaking book, *The Liberating Image*, Richard Middleton shows that the term "image of god" was a familiar one in ancient Egypt and Mesopotamia. But the phrase had a specific meaning: the king was the "image of God" and no one else. The king was thought to be god's representative on earth. So if you wanted to honor god, or the gods, you had better honor the king, the "image of god."[6]

Moreover, if a king reigned over larger regions than he could visit regularly, he would erect statues, *images* of himself, to represent his rule and reign to his subjects who could not see him in person. So in the ancient world, when a person heard the phrase "image of god," that's what came to mind—*the king and his statues spread throughout his empire.*[7]

Do you see, then, how amazing, even revolutionary, the Bible sounded to those who heard it in this context? To those for whom the king, and only the king, was the "image of god," to hear Genesis 1:27 say of *all* men, *and women*, "In the image of God he created him; male and female he created *them*" must have been astounding. They would hear the Bible saying that every one of you is created to be royalty, walking images of the true God, all over the earth. You. Me.[8]

Also in those ancient cultures, the king was often considered to be the sole mediator between the god(s) and the people. He had access. He was the priest. So the early readers would hear Genesis 1 saying not only are you royalty, you are royalty *and* you are a priest.

You were created to represent God and have access to God. You are a *royal priest*. We don't often put those words together today (royalty and priesthood), but this sheds light on this strange phrase we read throughout the Bible, from Exodus, "You shall be to me a kingdom of priests" (19:6), on into the New Testament, "You are … a royal priesthood" (1 Pet. 2:9).[9]

The first images of God, Adam and Eve, were created to live in perfect communion with God, as royalty under God, with access to God. Today it must still be acknowledged as one of the most daring acts of theological imagination to believe that every human being is created in the image of God. As C. S. Lewis puts it, "There are no ordinary people. You have never talked to a mere mortal."[10]

Perhaps this is why we yearn to be significant, for someone who matters to say to us, "You are so special." This isn't mere sentimentality. It reaches down into the roots of what we were made for. And yet, is this how we see ourselves or one another? As royalty?

WHAT'S OUR PROBLEM?

Carl Rogers, the father of client-centered therapy, concluded after decades of observing thousands of clients, "The central core difficulty in people, as I have come to know them, is that in the great majority of cases they despise themselves, and regard themselves as worthless and unlovable."[11]

Even if Rogers overstates the case, we can agree something is amiss. George Saunders, a contemporary writer, recently gave a commencement speech that went viral. He asked the graduates of

Syracuse University what he called "the million dollar question ... What's our problem?" Saunders said,

> Here's what I think. Each of us is born with a series of built-in confusions that are probably somehow Darwinian. These are: (1) we're central to the universe (that is, our personal story is the main and most interesting story, the *only* story, really); (2) we're separate from the universe (there's *us* and then, out there, all that other junk—dogs and swing-sets, and the State of Nebraska and low-hanging clouds and, you know, other people), and (3) we're permanent (death is real, o.k., sure—for you, but not for me).

Saunders continued,

> We don't really believe these things intellectually ... we know better—but we believe them viscerally, and live by them, and they cause us to prioritize our own needs over the needs of others, even though what we really want, in our hearts, is to be less selfish, more aware of what's actually happening in the present moment, more open, and more loving.[12]

This diagnosis of human nature—built-in confusions that lead us to think that we are central to the universe—is actually no different from what the Bible says. Saunders was saying the same thing the Bible says: something is wrong with us. And we know it.

A MARRED MASTERPIECE

The only sculpture Michelangelo ever signed was the *Pietà*, his statue of Mary holding her crucified son. Installed in St. Peter's Basilica in Rome in 1500, the *Pietà* remained there, mostly undisturbed, until 1972, when a vandal broke past security and smashed it repeatedly with a hammer. The attack shattered Mary's left arm and also resulted in severe damage to her nose, veil, and left eye. This treasure of Renaissance art became a marred masterpiece. Over the next year, a team of experts gathered up the shards and slivers of damaged marble and painstakingly pieced them back together.[13]

As with the *Pietà*, an enemy has entered into our world and savagely attacked human beings, leaving us damaged and defaced. The image of God in us has not been completely lost or erased, but it has been marred and disfigured. Our enemy is not only outside of us. There is also an enemy within that threatens to undo us. George Saunders calls it "built-in confusions ... somehow Darwinian." The Bible refers to it by a simpler name: "sin."

Sin is an unpopular word today, associated with rule breaking and forbidden pleasure. In Los Angeles where I live, one of the reasons Christianity is unattractive to many is because it's seen as life denying and pessimistic, judgmental and hypocritical.

I suppose that was my impression as well, and why I wanted nothing to do with Christianity as a young adult. Then I encountered another masterpiece of medieval art, *The Divine Comedy*, by the Italian poet Dante. His poem is a classic of world literature. Deep into the story, a couplet caught my eye:

> Love is the seed in you of every virtue
> And of all acts deserving punishment.[14]

It may not seem like much printed on this page, but those lines changed my life. Everything we do, Dante is saying, the good things or the bad things, every virtue or vice, we do for love. We are lovers. We are creatures of desire. It's simply a question of where that desire is directed. Dante was the one who showed me that sin was not the breaking of rules so much as my misdirected love. My desire was not the problem, but I desired the wrong things. For Dante, sin is loving the wrong things, or to be more precise, loving the right things in the wrong way.[15]

Now here is a definition of sin that is old yet thoroughly modern (and thoroughly biblical). Jesus says he is "the true vine" (John 15:1), implying that there are other vines from which we will strive to take life and sustenance. Sin is abiding in something other than Jesus to give us significance and joy. In terms of our last chapter, sin is constructing an identity around anything other than God. Sin is that which defaces the image of God in us and keeps us from flourishing.

This explains Jesus's curious statement "Apart from me you can do nothing" (John 15:5). It's curious because it seems as though we can do a lot of things apart from Jesus, and that most of the time we do. But Jesus is saying that apart from him we can do everything but live.

The Christian doctrine of sin proves to be a remarkable resource in helping us understand ourselves, but it's intelligible only against the background of a profound Christian optimism about the created potential of humanity. The caricatures of Christianity paint it as pessimistic and life denying. But in fact, Christianity is the true humanism. We are royal masterpieces, yet we are marred. The glorious image of God in us needs to be restored, and it is worth the effort of restoration.

THE PERFECT IMAGE OF GOD

How will this restoration take place? If the image is marred in all of us, how can we know what the image should look like? "No one has ever seen God," John admits, but Jesus "has made him known" (John 1:18). Jesus is "the image of the invisible God" (Col. 1:15).

Jesus not only shows us who God is; he shows us who we, as human beings, are meant to be. Jesus is the perfect image of God, not defaced by sin. Philosopher Peter Kreeft writes, "We are half-men, he is perfect man. We are inhuman humans, he is perfect humanity. We are alienated from ourselves, he is perfectly himself … He is more us than we are."[16] Colossians 1:15 also tells us that in Jesus Christ the nature of humanity, as our Creator intended it, has been fully revealed.

This explains why Blaise Pascal once said, "Not only do we only know God through Jesus Christ, but we only know ourselves through Jesus Christ."[17] Or as Karl Barth wrote, Jesus is "the real man."[18] What does a real man look like? Look at Jesus. What is a human being supposed to be? Look at Jesus's life.

Jesus, the dependent, obedient, compassionate Jesus, the humble king, the royal servant. While he walked on this earth, Jesus loved God with all his heart and mind and soul. He always preferred his Father's will above his own, and he loved others to the point of laying down his life for them. The Son of Man shows us what it means to be fully human.

Oh, great, you might be thinking. *Just be like Jesus! I can't do that! Not helpful.* Seeing the distance between who we are and who God made us to be can make us discouraged. It's an impossible horizon. And it would be ... were it not for our union with Christ!

To restore to us our created dignity, God became one of us. He became a man to restore what the first man lost. As the "last Adam," he came to recover what the first Adam had squandered (1 Cor. 15:45). Jesus came to show us what it means to be human. He came to pay our debt. He came to *atone* for us, that we might be *at one* with him. In Christ, God has united his life to ours and made it possible for our lives to be made new (Col. 3:10).

Just as the *Pietà* had to be restored by master artists, who painstakingly pieced together the broken shards of the existing statue and at great expense and effort restored the ruined master-piece, so God, the original master artist, used the material of his existing creation and at great expense and effort set out to pains-takingly restore his ruined masterpiece.

This means Jesus is not some impossible horizon in the dis-tance, far removed from the realm of possibility or your everyday life. He is very near. This is the nearness that union with Christ brings: you are in Christ and Christ is in you. Adam and Eve, in their shame, tried to cover themselves with fig leaves (Gen. 3:7). You, though, are covered completely by Christ. Christ fully covers us in all of our shame.

Christ now sets you free to be your true self: the self you are by grace, not the self you are by nature.[19] The tarnished image of God in you has been fully redeemed (bought back out of bondage) and is now being fully restored. And one day, it will be finished.

YOUR DESTINY—THE IMAGE OF GOD RESTORED IN YOU

In this chapter, we've looked back in order to look forward, but all to arrive at a most practical point: "Where am I headed?" You no longer have to rack your brain or wait for an answer to fall from heaven. You never need to feel aimless again.

Jesus came from heaven in order that the image of God might be restored in you.

And because of Jesus, we now know what that image looks like. He rescued you in order that you might become fully human. This idea is captured in a single verse: "For those whom he foreknew he also predestined to be conformed to the image of his Son" (Rom. 8:29). Why are you here? To become like Jesus. Why are you here? To become a human being. That's your new horizon.

WHAT THIS DOESN'T MEAN

Conformed to the image of Jesus doesn't mean that our self is annihilated. Years ago, a young woman in the church I was serving said, "I feel like I'm a glass of water. That I'm supposed to be poured out, so Jesus can fill me up. But sometimes I wonder, what part of me will be left?" In an effort to say what is true—"I must become less so that he might become greater"—sometimes we suggest something false, that our individuality is given up when we give ourselves over to Christ.

But our self is not obliterated by our union with Christ; our self is fully realized. God the Creator clearly delights in our unique particularity. From sunsets to snowflakes, he makes endless variations of beautiful things for the sheer joy of it. He never repeats himself and never runs out of ideas. He is the master artist, an infinite creator, not a factory. We can see from looking around us in the world that his goal is not uniformity.

And he created each one of us, distinctly. "We are [God's] workmanship," the Bible says (Eph. 2:10). The word used there is *poiema*, where we get the English word *poem*. You are God's poem, his work of art. There's no one else he made quite like you. So when he becomes one with you, he still preserves and delights in your unique particularity. As he restores his image in you, as you become more like his Son, you are becoming more and more yourself—more and more the *you* God dreamed up when he first dreamed you up.

"We are God's *poiema*, created in Christ Jesus," the verse continues, "for good works, which God prepared beforehand that we should walk in them." Not only does God call you toward the glorious horizon of being conformed to the image of his Son, but he also has in mind specific manifestations that this image will take in you. Isn't that encouraging? That you can reflect his image to the world in ways that no one else can? He not only made you as you, but he also planned good things for you to do.

This is the destiny God sets for each one of us—to more and more discover who you truly are as you more and more give yourself over to him. This is identity (you are created uniquely by God) and destiny (to have the image of God restored in you) and what to do along the way (walk in the good works he prepared beforehand) all in one.

Could anything stand in sharper contrast to our current accent on expressive individualism? This is a radically different vision of what makes for a fully human life! The joy and fulfillment we are looking for can never be found by expressing ourselves, but only by giving ourselves over to God. Only if we seek what we were made for—to know God and to love him above all else—will joy and fulfillment follow. But if we seek to please ourselves, we will find neither.

In following Christ, we don't become something less than ourselves. Nor do we become something more than human. We become more and more human, more and most ourselves.

WHAT THIS DOES MEAN

Where is your life headed? Now you have an answer. Jesus is your horizon. And because he deigns to make us one with himself, this horizon is not only beautiful but also accessible. Jesus already went the distance, and now he takes hold of you to bring you there.

One day, you will see him face to face, and that face will have a form you recognize. But you will not only see him. On that day, "when he appears we shall be like him, because we shall see him as he is" (1 John 3:2). This glorious destiny is where you are headed.

Until that day, we are to "put on the new self, which is being renewed in knowledge after the image of its creator" (Col. 3:10). What does this verse mean by "renewed in knowledge"? One writer says it is our "'progressive ability to recognize God's will and command' and to live in accordance with it."[20] As we walk in this new self, we become human.

Not only is the image of God in us being renewed in knowledge, but our entire self is being transformed. This is how the New Testament dares to speak: "We ... are being transformed into the same image from one degree of glory to another" (2 Cor. 3:18). The glory that belongs to Christ, the brilliant blazing image of God, is becoming more and more our own.

You might think, *It sure doesn't feel like it!* And though we'd be sheepish ever to claim it for ourselves, Jesus prays for us that we would know we share in his glory (John 17:22). Without becoming gods, yet we are becoming more and more like the God-man, Jesus. In Christ, you are becoming more and more like God's vision of you, for you.

We often say, "I'm only human," in reference to our mistakes and foibles, as a recognition of our limitations. But who ever dreamed that being a human could mean something so glorious? That even as careful a theologian as John Calvin could say, "The purpose of the gospel [is] to make us sooner or later like God; indeed it is, so to speak, a kind of deification"?[21]

What a destiny! Like our fully human brother Jesus, we as humans will share in God's glory. We will be raised bodily, but we dwell in heavenly glory in God's presence (1 Cor. 15:40). Our destiny is not only to see him but also to be like him. And this glorious end is not only beautiful beyond description; it is assured. What God has begun in us, he will complete (Phil. 1:6).

NOW WHAT?

> But something is wrong. [Modern man] has settled everything except what it is to live as an individual. He still has to get through an ordinary Wednesday afternoon.... What does this man do with the rest of the day? the rest of his life?[22]

Walker Percy reminds us that this glorious destiny must take a very mundane shape. What am I supposed to do today? That will be the focus of the next chapter, but in closing this one, let's reflect on a few of the implications of the new destiny that your union with Christ gives you.

BOASTING IN YOUR WEAKNESSES

When you know that your destiny is to have the image of God uniquely restored in you, and you hear Jesus say, "Apart from me you can do nothing" (John 15:5), it ceases to sound like a threat and becomes instead a doorway to "I can do all things through [Christ] who strengthens me" (Phil. 4:13).

By nature, we resist vulnerability. We hate to see our weaknesses exposed, much less to boast in them. Rather, they are more often occasions for us to think, *I'm unfit to be a Christian if I did that.* But one of the great discoveries of the Christian life is coming to see our failings as occasions to praise Christ for his complete sufficiency. Welsh preacher Martyn Lloyd-Jones puts it, "We must never look at any sin in our past life in any way except that which leads us to praise God and magnify his grace in Christ Jesus."[23]

Instead of feeling shame, you can come to boast in all the things that remind you of how far you fall short. "The pain of having arrived at the utter end of any confidence in myself had brought me into the heaven of God's love and care," says writer Leanne Payne.[24] You can boast in your weaknesses because you see them move you further along toward your goal of being dependent on God. You don't just learn *from* them; you learn *by* them.

REJOICING IN YOUR SUFFERING

Everything that happens to us, good and bad, and everything we strive for, can now be interpreted through this new prism—the image of God being restored in you.

"We rejoice in our sufferings," the apostle Paul says (Rom. 5:3). Not that suffering is joyful or good in itself, but you now have a context and a horizon that makes any hardship endurable, even redeemable. Every ounce of suffering becomes a stepping-stone as God's workmanship is being perfected in you. To quote C. S. Lewis once more:

> [We are] a Divine work of art, something that God is making, and therefore something with which He will not be satisfied until it has a certain character.... Over a sketch made idly to amuse a child, an artist may not take much trouble.... But over the great picture of his life ... he will take endless trouble—and would, doubtless, thereby *give* endless trouble to the picture if it [could feel].... It is natural for us to wish that God had designed for us a less glorious and less arduous destiny; but then we are wishing not for more love but for less.[25]

The restoration work may be painful, but Christ, the master artist, is taking endless trouble to restore God's image in you. "In all this you greatly rejoice, though now for a little while you may have had to suffer grief in all kinds of trials" (1 Pet. 1:6 NIV).

REASSESSING YOUR WINS

How do you measure success? How do you know when you "win"? With this new horizon, Paul doesn't just say that his past accomplishments are as *nothing* compared to "the surpassing worth of knowing Christ Jesus" (Phil. 3:8). He says more than this: "Whatever were gains to me I now consider loss" (v. 7 NIV). It wasn't just that those former wins don't compare; it's that he considers them losses because they distracted him and kept him away from his true glory and highest good: knowing Christ.

When being conformed to Christ is your horizon, every accomplishment, every promotion, every trophy becomes a potential hurdle, something that might lead you away from that which is better—knowing Christ and being conformed to his image.

Your win is to become a human being, to become more like Jesus: dependent and obedient, humble and compassionate. Above all, your win is becoming someone who loves.

For this is what characterizes Jesus above all, what he prized above all things (Matt. 22:37–38). Because love was central in the life of Christ, love is at the heart of the image of God. Your win is learning how to love. And your greatest losses are your failures to love.

This means we will become people who prize relationships. For relationships, even and especially difficult relationships, are the school in which we learn to deny ourselves and love others.

Leo Tolstoy once defined boredom as "the desire for desires." With this new horizon, how could we ever again be bored or aimless? To have as our goal that Christ be formed in us (Gal. 4:19) makes ordinary life exciting, even on a Wednesday afternoon. Every day has purpose because this purpose stands over every day.

If we find ourselves wishing for a less glorious, less arduous destiny, if we find ourselves wondering, *Is any sacrifice worth it?* we can hear Christ whispering to us, "I have told you this so that my joy may be in you and that your joy may be complete" (John 15:11 NIV). Press on.

Chapter 9

A NEW PURPOSE: WHAT AM I HERE FOR?

Writer Søren Kierkegaard sums up our last chapter by saying, "Now, with God's help, I shall become myself."[1] Your life is a quest to discover, and more and more to live into, the person God originally made you to be; for the image of God to be restored in you; for Christ to take form in the contours of your life. That is your horizon. It is a beautiful thought.

But what does this look like each day? As with any quest, the real adventure is found in the journey itself, the step-by-step walking. Knowing your destination is not enough. Sooner or later, you have to start moving. As Walker Percy says of the pilgrim, "He still has to get through an ordinary Wednesday afternoon…. What does this man do with the rest of the day? The rest of his life?"[2]

What should I be doing? Here's how the apostle Peter answers that question:

> Therefore, preparing your minds for action, and
> being sober-minded, set your hope fully on the

grace that will be brought to you at the revelation of
Jesus Christ. As obedient children, do not be conformed to the passions of your former ignorance,
but as he who called you is holy, you also be holy
in all your conduct, since it is written, "You shall be
holy, for I am holy." (1 Pet. 1:13–16)

Notice how Peter sets the horizon—the revelation of Jesus
Christ and the grace of "When he appears you shall be like him."
But he also lays out the path for walking toward it: be holy in all
your conduct. That's what we should be doing, pursuing holiness as
a way of life each day.

And all God's people said … "Yuck."

THE BIG BROCCOLI IN THE SKY

I don't like broccoli. Even though I now live in Los Angeles where
you're *supposed* to like healthy food, I still associate it with my
mom saying, "Eat your broccoli! It's good for you." It's something
unpleasant but good for me, something I don't enjoy but know I
should. Grit your teeth and take it.

Holiness is like broccoli for many of us. We know we're supposed to want it, but we don't, not really. And we might even think
the good news is that we no longer need to pursue it.

Psalms talks about "the beauty of holiness" (29:2 KJV), but beauty
is not what comes to mind when we hear "holiness" today. Holiness
sounds stifling, boring, even off putting.

I remember years ago trying to encourage a couple who were
going through a difficult time. They faced one setback after another

with no relief in sight. They felt as though God had abandoned them. With less sensitivity than was needed, I turned to one of the oldest reasons why God allows trials in our lives. "When God seems absent," I said, "he can be doing his most important work in us. As a loving Father, he's training us as his children to trust him." And I quoted the book of Hebrews: "He disciplines us for our good, that we may share his holiness" (Heb. 12:10).

I'll never forget their response because it was so refreshingly honest: "Holiness? Who wants that?"

Exactly. Who wants that?

GOD WANTS HOLINESS FOR YOU

In the Bible, holiness is not an optional extra reserved for the cloistered few or only those most advanced. It is God's expectation for all of his people at all times and places.

When the Lord brought Israel out of Egypt, he made clear the purpose underlying their redemption:

> You yourselves have seen what I did to the Egyptians, and how I bore you on eagles' wings and brought you to myself. Now therefore, if you will indeed obey my voice … you shall be my treasured possession …; and you shall be to me a kingdom of priests and a holy nation. (Exod. 19:4–6)

He didn't save them because they were morally superior; he made that clear (Deut. 9:5). But now that he had rescued them and called them to himself, God commanded his people to be different: "Be holy, for I am holy" (Lev. 11:44). And we've just seen that this command is repeated verbatim in the New Testament, in 1 Peter.

To be holy means to be set apart for God's purposes, which is why in the Old Testament inanimate objects, such as bells or pots, are sometimes referred to as "holy" (Zech. 14:20–21)—not because the pots or bells were morally pure, but because they were wholly consecrated to God's use. Set apart for God.

When used in reference to human beings, holiness means to be set apart to reflect God's character in all of our ways—his goodness and love, his kindness and compassion, his concern for justice and the poor.

Far from being optional, holiness is expected, even necessary for our salvation. "Without holiness no one will see the Lord," the book of Hebrews warns (12:14 NIV). This is not a reference to the holiness of Christ being credited to us from outside of us by faith (which Hebrews does talk about elsewhere). This verse is talking about our personal holiness and what the biblical writers with one voice assume: if God's life has indeed come into our lives, then our lives will necessarily reflect the light of God's life. Martin Luther and John Calvin, who both emphasized the necessity of "faith alone" for salvation, also both made it clear that faith never exists "alone" in the life of a believer. "We are saved by faith alone, but saving faith is never alone."[3]

A true and living faith rooted in Christ will always bear the fruit of Christ's Spirit. So, to that common question "God, what is your will for me?" the Bible answers, "This is God's will: that you become holy" (1 Thess. 4:3 NET).

GOD REDEEMED YOU FOR HOLINESS

Holiness is the great end underlying everything God has done for us in Christ. Look at Ephesians 1:4: "He chose us in him before the foundation of the world, that we should be *holy* and blameless before him." If you are a follower of Christ, God has saved you for a purpose, for you to live a holy life.

This is the reason Christ gave himself up for his bride, the church, "that he might sanctify her, having cleansed her … so that he might present the church to himself in splendor, without spot or wrinkle or any such thing, that she might be holy and without blemish" (Eph. 5:26–27). And this is the reason J. I. Packer says, "Holiness is the goal of our redemption."[4] God wants you to pursue this strenuously, like a determined athlete. "Run in such a way as to get the prize" (1 Cor. 9:24 NIV).[5]

THREE REASONS WHY WE MAY NOT PRIZE HOLINESS

And yet it seems obvious that we don't prize or pursue holiness. If we're honest, we probably feel like that couple: "Holiness? Who wants that?" We don't want holiness for at least three reasons.

It's Undesirable

Even the word *holiness* has become tarnished, both inside and outside the church. It suggests something negative, restrictive, prudish, uncool, and undesirable.

When I was a little kid, my sister and I used to watch *Little House on the Prairie*. The character we loved to hate was Mrs. Oleson—arrogant, exacting, overly proper, and legalistic, and that's the image I had of holiness. Hypocrisy. Hardness. Very unattractive.

Many of us today hold that same image, so much so that the word *holy* is almost always used pejoratively, as in "holier than thou" or "holy roller." The call to be holy is often viewed as a big *no* to anything pleasurable or fun. It may retain the sense of being set apart, but not in a good way.

It's Unnecessary

A second reason holiness is not prized among us is that we might think the good news of the gospel is that we no longer need to pursue it. "Holiness? Isn't that what Jesus died to give us?"

Yes. The grace of God alone makes humanity right with God. But sometimes, our efforts to stress what is unique and compelling about Christianity (grace!) can lead to a conclusion that is dangerously false—that what we do and how we live don't matter to God, so daily obedience and a life of holiness are unnecessary.

In a recent interview, actress Keira Knightley said, "If only I wasn't an atheist, I could get away with anything. You'd just ask for forgiveness and then you'd be forgiven."[6] And that's how the gospel is sometimes misrepresented—as a blank check—which might explain why there are so many people who believe in God but so few who love godliness. In rightly emphasizing what God has saved us *from*, too often we lose sight of what God has saved us *for*.

It's Unattainable

A final reason we may not prize holiness today is that it seems too hard, too demanding. We cannot see ourselves being able to attain it. To attempt to be holy seems like a recipe for discouragement and inevitable failure.

It's easy to become cynical (*It's not possible*), or resigned (*If it is possible, it's not for me*), or defeated (*I tried that, but I just can't*). A friend put it to me memorably a few years back:

> I see where I am. And I see, way in the distance, where I'm supposed to be. The person God wants me to be. But the distance between these two points seems hopelessly long with steep mountains and impassable rivers between. I'll never get there. So why even try?

HOLINESS IS BEAUTIFUL AND GOOD

My children have a CD they listen to in the car sometimes, a series of questions and answers covering the basics of the Christian faith set to music. One of the songs goes like this:

> What were Adam and Eve like when God made
>   them?
> God made them holy and happy.[7]

In the Bible, those two words go together. Holiness is not a *no* to happiness but a resounding *yes*. But how can we become convinced that the call to be holy is a call to be happy, a call to fullness and joy? How can we learn that holiness is not just desirable but also beautiful?

Jonathan Edwards says that God's holiness is the *most* beautiful thing about him:

As the beauty of the divine nature primarily
consists in God's holiness, so does the beauty of
all divine things. Herein consists the beauty of
the saints, that they are *saints*, or holy ones: it is
the moral image of God in them, which is their
beauty; and that is their holiness.[8]

Edwards is saying, in his seventeenth-century way, that
holiness is the most beautiful thing about God and his people.
Holiness is not only good, but it is also attractive. It draws us in.

We saw in our last chapter that there is only one person who
always reflected God's character in all of his ways: Jesus. And we
saw that holiness, rightly understood, looks like Jesus. He lived
the most holy, most beautiful, most human, most free life anyone
ever lived. Who wouldn't want that?

That's what it means for us to live a holy life—to see the
beauty of Jesus and follow after him.

You'll never want holiness until you are convinced that it's
not meant to be a burden. Rather, in light of our last chapter, this
is what God has created you to be and has now re-created you
to become. Your destiny is for the image of God to be restored
in you. That's beautiful. And the path toward that destiny is to
follow Jesus today and each tomorrow. "His commands are not
burdensome" (1 John 5:3 NIV). But how can this be true? How
can holiness become not simply an ideal belonging to Jesus but a
reality belonging to us?

Once again, union with Christ is the answer to our riddle.

UNION WITH CHRIST IS THE ANCHOR OF HOLINESS

So many of our fears and suspicions surrounding holiness concern our lack of it.

Union with Christ tells you that you are in Christ. And the Bible insists that in Christ, our sanctification (the Bible's word for becoming holy) is finished. Paul says, "You are in Christ Jesus, who became to us ... righteousness and sanctification" (1 Cor. 1:30). Christ is your holiness, your sanctification, already, full and complete. In Christ, "you were washed, you were sanctified, you were justified" (6:11). In this sense, holiness is not something we achieve; it is something we receive by faith in total. Already "we have been sanctified through the offering of the body of Jesus Christ once for all" (Heb. 10:10).

Theologian John Murray calls this "definitive sanctification." He adds, "It is a fact too frequently overlooked that in the New Testament the most characteristic terms that refer to sanctification are used, not of a process, but of a once-for-all definitive act."[9] The Bible talks about our holiness being complete and finished because Christ has joined his life to ours. Hebrews says, "We have *this* as a sure and steadfast anchor of the soul" (6:19). What is "*this*"? It is God's promise that in Christ we are holy and acceptable in his sight; that we are safe and secure, anchored in Christ; and that nothing can snatch us from his hands (John 10:28).

Think about what an anchor does. It protects us from the wind and the waves; that is, it guards us from those things that make us doubt God's care for us. These "waves" can be outward circumstances (*If God loves me, why is this happening?*) or inward doubts and dispositions (*If I really loved God, why would I be doing this? Or feeling this way?*). If our hope is anchored in our own experience or efforts, we will never be settled.

When it comes to a life of holiness, our anchor is being united to Christ and the holiness Christ has already achieved for us. Just as an anchor gives a ship confidence that it will not float away or be overturned, so our union with Christ gives us confidence that our holiness does not fall with our failures or rise with our successes. It's not up to you to keep it up. Remember, union with Christ means that when God looks at you, he sees your life hidden in Christ's perfect life and perfect obedience. It is finished. Thank God! You are safe. You are secure. You are anchored. You are completely holy in Christ.

UNION WITH CHRIST IS THE ENGINE OF HOLINESS

But union with Christ is not only the anchor; it is also the engine of our holiness. The gift of holiness in Christ doesn't make the pursuit of it unnecessary. We are to be holy as God is holy (Lev. 11:44). That's a command. We are to "grow in ... grace and knowledge" (2 Pet. 3:18); we are to "grow up in every way into him" (Eph. 4:15). We are to be "transformed by the renewal of [our] mind" (Rom. 12:2).

In the Bible, holiness is both what we already are and what we are called to become. It may sound strange, yet this is how God has always interacted with his people. He set Israel apart as his people and then called them to be holy. He repeatedly reminded them that his choice of them was not in any way based on their moral fitness (Deut. 9). Rather, God said to them, "I've set you apart; now live like it. I've made you holy; now be holy. I've redeemed you and set you free; now go live as free people, not as slaves. It's done. Now do it." We are declared holy that we might become so.

How is union with Christ our engine, propelling us forward? J. C. Ryle puts it this way: "Jesus is a complete Saviour. He does not merely take away the guilt of a believer's sin, he does more—he breaks its power."[10] Or, as we sing with the old hymn "Rock of Ages":

> Be of sin the double cure,
> Cleanse me from its guilt and pow'r.[11]

Jesus cleanses us from both the penalty and the power of our sins—he is the double cure. He not only declares us holy, but he also empowers us to be holy. Union with Christ means Christ is in you. The presence and power of Jesus now dwells within you by his Spirit. That's why he's called the *Holy* Spirit, because he is none other than the presence and power of the obedient Christ himself. And just as Christ lived a completely holy life and was able to overcome every temptation, so now, because he is within you, he gives you a new disposition to live for him.

One of the underdog sports movies I mentioned in the previous chapter was *Rudy*, based on the true story of a young man who loved Notre Dame football and wanted nothing more than to play for the team. He was a walk-on, undersized, too small, too slow—but he practiced harder and worked harder than anyone else on the team. At one point in the film, the coach says, "I wish God would put your heart in some of my players' bodies." And that's exactly what God has done for us. He's taken the heart of Christ and placed it in all his players. Do you see what power we have?

WHY WE NEED AN ANCHOR AND AN ENGINE

"You are in Christ" gives you assurance. "Christ is in you" gives you power. Together they help us move out in confidence.

If we base our objective standing before God on our subjective day-to-day performance, we have a recipe for spiritual depression. One writer puts it, "Many acknowledge that we are justified by the righteousness of Christ, but seem to think, at least they act as if, they must be sanctified by a holiness they themselves have acquired."[12] This has been called "the key error of the Christian life,"[13] grounding our confidence before God and others on the sinking sand of our shifting performance. On the days you "do well," you feel great: started the day early in prayer, helped a stranger at the supermarket, even found a clever and smooth way to introduce the gospel into a conversation with your neighbor. Check. Check. Check. You're flying high. You're a great Christian!

But just a day later, you woke up late. You were short with a coworker, and you blasted the horn at someone on the road, who turned out to be the neighbor you just yesterday talked to about Jesus. You come crashing down and wonder, *What's wrong with me? What kind of Christian am I?* Up. Down.

But this is how so many of us are living, and it can only result in our feeling defeated (*I'll never get there*) or cynical (*No one gets there*) or resigned (*Why even try?*).

Unless you grasp and live out of your union with Christ, the call to holiness will be oppressive, unbearable, and impossible. No matter how earnest or committed you may be, you'll keep falling in the same ditches, over and over. You'll remain defeated by the same demons, be they alcohol or envy or greed or unkindness.

The Greek poet Pindar coined a phrase that captures how these two images, anchor and engine, can work together. He said, "Become what you are."[14] In calling us to be holy, God isn't asking us to make up something lacking in us. We don't obey from a deficit. We obey out of fullness. And that makes all the difference, as we'll see in a moment.

There are three places in the New Testament that capture this dynamic beautifully.

Most succinctly is John, who says, "Everyone who thus hopes in him purifies himself as he is pure" (1 John 3:3). The more you know you have it, the more you'll want it.

Paul makes the same point in Philippians: "Not that I have already obtained all this, or have already arrived at my goal, but I press on to take hold of that for which Christ Jesus took hold of me" (3:12 NIV). Christ Jesus had already taken hold of Paul to do for him what Paul could never do for himself, be holy. But in celebrating that he has been given this gift, Paul is clear to say, "Not that I have already obtained all this." He presses on, like a champion runner, toward holiness, toward Christ! Further up and further in! But he doesn't press on under the cloud of needing to measure up. He's full. He's covered.

Here's one last example. "To the church of God that is in Corinth, to those sanctified in Christ Jesus, called to be saints" (1 Cor. 1:2). You see? Already "sanctified" and yet "called to be saints." In fact, throughout the New Testament, the word *saint* captures the mystery of holiness we've been discussing.

Today we use *saint* to refer to extraordinary examples of exemplary character, like Mother Teresa, or unsung heroes of uncommon

self-sacrifice. "She's a saint," we say. But the biblical writers, address-
ing groups of people with debilitating and persistent sin, call their
readers "saints" (Eph. 1:1), even though the contents of these letters
make clear their lives are far from saintly. It's an undeserved but
ennobling compliment! Saint! Become what you are.

IS HOLINESS UP TO GOD OR UP TO US?

Yes. And union with Christ shows you why this is a false dichotomy.
Only God can change us, and God is faithful. "He who began a good
work in you will bring it to completion" (Phil. 1:6). Becoming holy
(sanctification) is by faith alone. Christ is the root and only source
of our holiness.

At the same time, the biblical writers do not shy away from talking
about our exertion. Jesus says, "Strive to enter through the narrow
door" (Luke 13:24). "Make every effort," Peter adds (2 Pet. 1:5).

Jerry Bridges provides a summary:

> No one can attain any degree of holiness without
> God working in his life, but just as surely no one
> will attain it without effort on his own part. God
> has made it possible for us to walk in holiness. But
> He has given to us the responsibility of doing the
> walking.[15]

When we fail, or when we are afraid, we have an anchor—we
are in Christ. When we are tired, or when the road looks too long,
we have an engine—Christ is in us. This doesn't mean, of course,
that there is not ongoing, even debilitating, sin in our lives. The

battle rages on. But the final outcome is certain. And so is the strength to endure.

UNION WITH CHRIST MAKES HOLINESS BEAUTIFUL AND ACCESSIBLE

Christ has made holiness a reality for you (you are in Christ) and a possibility for you (Christ is in you). Before we turn to some everyday examples of what this looks like, one final word needs to be stressed.

I recently taught my son Jack how to ride a bicycle. He was terrified. At first he kept turning around to make sure that I was right there beside him. But you can't move forward if you are always anxiously checking behind you. When Jack was able to hear my voice, "I've got you. I've *got* you," and he could trust that I was right there, then he was able to move forward in confidence. *Dad's got me!*

One of the reasons why holiness is so scary or unattractive for us is that we see it as a bar we can never reach or yet another thing we've failed to do. We do fail. We fall. And when we do, we fear that God is disappointed in us, that he is scowling. So we want to pull away from him and hide.

How can you remember *Dad's got me?* What reminds you that he is right there with you? That his affection for you does not change when you "fall off your bike"—if anything, it grows warmer as he rushes to you in compassion?

Well, why did I want Jack to learn how to ride his bike? Not only so he can one day deliver newspapers and start paying rent, but also so he can know the joy of feeling the wind in his hair and so we can ride our bikes together. His little legs can't keep up with me when we walk or run, but on wheels my son and I can experience more life together and enjoy each other's company. We can ride to the ocean.

God wants us to grow in holiness, not as some sort of test or punishment, not even just as preparation for the future, but because he wants us to *enjoy* life with him more. The more we grow in holiness, the more we can enjoy his presence. He wants us not simply to press on but to soar. He wants holiness for us, for our joy. *Now my child can ride with me.*

When you fall, God rushes to you in love and cares for you. But because he loves you, he doesn't want you to keep falling.

Once we understand holiness in light of our union with Christ, it becomes beautiful to us. We see that God is making us beautiful because he is making us like him and he is committed to us over the course of the whole journey. *I've got you. You'll get there! Just pedal!*

Who wants holiness? God wants it for you, for your good. His commands make you *wise*: "Keep them and do them, for that will be your wisdom and your understanding" (Deut. 4:6). His commands make you *free*: "And I will walk at liberty: for I seek thy precepts" (Ps. 119:45 KJV). His commands are always for our *good*: "And the LORD commanded us to do all these statutes … for our good always" (Deut. 6:24). And his commands lead us to *life*: "You make known to me the path of life" (Ps. 16:11).

Do you see? These commands are not burdens; they are the path to life. They are the means God has provided us to abide in his love, which is why Jesus says in John 15:10, "If you keep my commandments, you will abide in my love."

PICTURES OF UNION WITH CHRIST IN THE PURSUIT OF HOLINESS

You are on a quest, and as with any epic quest, there will be dragons. It's not without reason that, in the Bible, the life of faith is often called a fight or a battle. This is the central drama of your life, to "fight the good fight of the faith" (1 Tim. 6:12).

Let's conclude this chapter by looking at how union with Christ helps us in our daily battle with sin.

Take an area that is a struggle for many of us—honoring God's gift of our sexuality. As God created us for intimate union with himself and others, our yearning for intimacy is intense. So it's no surprise that this desire is so easily exploited or distorted.

And yet, watch what Paul draws on to help the Corinthians fight sexual temptation. "Do you not know that your bodies are members of Christ?" (1 Cor. 6:15). He reminds them of their union with Christ. "You are one with Christ," he's saying, "so then how can you unite yourself to another in a way that you know dishonors him?" (see vv. 15–17). He reminds them of their identity in Christ and *then* calls them to holiness. "That's not who you are," he's saying in effect, "and that's not how you need to live any longer."[16]

As opposed to simply saying, "Don't do that," when you battle temptation, instead call to mind your union with Christ. Use the presence of Christ to stand firm against anything that threatens you.

UNION WITH CHRIST WON'T LET YOU REST IN YOUR SIN

There are no happy disobedient Christians. If you are content in running from God's will for you, you have reason to doubt that

Christ's life is in you. For how could the Holy One rest within you as long as you are resting in sin? This is the reason David compares the presence of unconfessed sin to a debilitating bodily weakness: "For when I kept silent, my bones wasted away … For day and night your hand was heavy upon me; my strength was dried up as by the heat of summer" (Ps. 32:3–4). Thank God, he won't let you wander away in peace. He will give you what writer Romano Guardini calls "a holy disquiet."[17]

This is a great benefit of being in community with other believers—when we are deaf or numb or drifting away, we need others to call us back to our beautiful destiny. *Keep pushing! Press on! It's worth it!* We can call each other back to our union with Christ, our anchor and engine.

UNION WITH CHRIST WON'T LET YOU DESPAIR WHEN YOU FAIL

As we grow in Christ and pursue holiness, we will fail. We will not live up to our best intentions. "I do not understand my own actions," Paul says. "For I do not do what I want, but I do the very thing I hate" (Rom. 7:15). How can we fall without despairing? How do we break the cycle of sin and self-loathing?

Samuel Rutherford's letters are classics of devotional literature. He wrote the following in a letter to encourage a friend:

> You doubt … whether you be in Christ or not? …
> I answer … you owe charity to all men, but most
> of all to loving and lovely Jesus, and some also to
> yourself, especially your renewed self; because your

new self is not yours, but [Christ's], even the work
of his own Spirit: therefore, to slander His work is
to wrong himself.[18]

Rutherford is saying that our main obstacle to growing in holiness is that we are not living out of our union with Christ. Where does the strength come from to move out in joy and peace? It begins with the assurance that God is for you—that's your anchor! And the knowledge that God is in you—that's your engine! And the confidence that God is with you and not disappointed in you—that's the hand on your back. These can only come from laying hold of your union with Christ.

Only as we grasp hold of our union with Christ will we be able to fall and not despair, to get up again and not feel ashamed, to keep striving and see God change us "from one degree of glory to another" (2 Cor. 3:18).

What should you be doing? "He chose us in [Christ] before the foundation of the world, that we should be holy" (Eph. 1:4). You can place this as the purpose over each new day: pursue holiness, not as a bar to live up to, but as an ennobling compliment to live into. Become a human being today.

Chapter 10

A NEW HOPE: WHAT CAN I HOPE FOR?

We are more connected today, across the world and in an instant, than humanity has ever been before. But how is our ever-present technology shaping us? In her book *Alone Together: Why We Expect More from Technology and Less from Each Other*, MIT professor Sherry Turkle observes:

> We are changed as technology offers us substitutes for connecting with each other face-to-face.... As we instant-message, e-mail, text, and Twitter, technology redraws the boundaries between intimacy and solitude.... Teenagers would rather text than talk. Adults, too.... We build a following on Facebook ... [but] wonder to what degree our followers are friends. We recreate ourselves as online personae ... Yet, suddenly, in the half-light of virtual community, we may feel utterly alone.[1]

While magnified by our technology, loneliness is not a recent affliction, nor is it reserved for the isolated few or the sensitive spirits among us. Writer Thomas Wolfe explains:

> The whole conviction of my life now rests upon the belief that the sense of loneliness, far from being a rare and curious phenomenon, peculiar to myself and to a few other solitary people, is the central and inevitable fact of human existence.[2]

Our fear of being alone is so deep and primal it's hard to speak of directly. As we have been looking at life as a quest, we have seen that our union with Christ gives us a new identity, found outside of ourselves. With this new identity, we gain a new destiny, a new horizon—the image of God being restored in us, and a new path toward that horizon: pursuing holiness. But the road is long and the journey is hard. We will need to know that on this way, we are not alone. Every quester needs a companion: Frodo had Sam, Butch had Sundance, even Luke Skywalker had R2-D2.

Union with Christ tells us we are not alone. One of Jesus's names is Immanuel, "God with us" (Matt. 1:23). Jesus is God's promise to us that we are not alone on our journey. We have a loyal friend beside us each step of the way.

To show how union with Christ gives us hope for the journey we will look at two questions: (1) Where is Jesus now? and (2) What is he doing?

WHERE IS JESUS NOW?

If Jesus is "God with us," you might reasonably ask, "Where is he?" Had you asked the New Testament writers this question, they would have answered with one voice: "In heaven, seated at the right hand of God" (see Matt. 26:64; Mark 16:19; Luke 22:69; Acts 7:56; Eph. 1:20).

How much time have you spent thinking about the fact that Christ "ascended into heaven" (John 3:13)? The ascension of Jesus is not often seen to be a critical part of our faith today.[3] Of all the aspects of Christ's life, perhaps no aspect has been more neglected than this: "He ascended into heaven and is seated at the right hand of God the Father Almighty."[4] "At God's right hand"—what does that even mean?

You may have never thought about this, but Christ's resurrection and ascension means Jesus's physical body is alive somewhere at this very moment. Because he is God, Jesus is spiritually present everywhere (Matt. 28:20). But because he is man, Jesus is physically present right now in heaven (1 Pet. 3:22). His risen body is in heaven at the right hand of God. How does that make any difference in my life, practically? Why does the ascension matter?

What Is Heaven?

When the New Testament writers spoke of Jesus ascending into heaven, they did not mean that if you traveled long enough—up, up, up—you'd arrive at heaven. The sky represented for them what it has for every known culture: that which is above and beyond us, that which transcends our understanding and experience. "Ascending" to heaven meant Jesus was returning from whence he came, which was precisely what Jesus said, "I am ascending to my Father" (John 20:17).

That's what makes heaven, heaven—the immediate perceptible presence of God. Yes, God is everywhere (Ps. 139:7–12), but heaven is a different dimension of God's creation, totally pervaded by God's glory (Acts 7:55).[5] Heaven is the place where God's will is always done: "Thy will be done in earth, as it is in heaven" (Matt. 6:10 KJV).

N. T. Wright calls heaven "the CEO's office" from whence Jesus is ruling the world.[6] J. I. Packer compares heaven to the control center of a bustling train station. Standing on the platform, one can't see all the different tracks, let alone make sense of all the coming and going, which train should go where and why and when. Only from the control station, where a Grand Conductor can see all the trains and all the schedules and all the tracks, does each part make sense.[7] We are not privy to that perspective, but Jesus is—as he is in heaven "at God's right hand" (Acts 7:56).

At God's Right Hand

Throughout the Bible, the right hand is a symbol of power and authority (Ps. 110:1). Jesus is now enthroned in the seat of authority, which is why he says, right before he ascends, "All authority in heaven and on earth has been given to me" (Matt. 28:18). He follows that up with, "I am with you always" (v. 20). Then he disappears from their sight. And right here, we are face to face with one of the central difficulties of faith.

We are told God is with us. But we can't see him, touch him, or talk to him in the way we are accustomed to doing these things, so Jesus can seem removed from our earthly experience. "The ascension represents our greatest struggle of faith," writes Philip Yancey, "more than the problem of pain and suffering. Would it not have been better if the ascension had never happened?"[8]

In our confusion, we can be prone to dismiss this heavenly theology and turn our focus toward things more down to earth, more visible, things we think will help us with our daily concerns. But the burden of this chapter will be to show you how the presence of Jesus in heaven now dramatically affects how we see our lives in the world today.

One of the driving convictions of this book is that nothing is more needed to lift us out of ourselves than to know we are connected to the heavenly Christ. If Jesus is in heaven, *what is he doing there?*

WHAT JESUS IS DOING AND WHY IT MATTERS
Jesus Is Seated

What is Jesus doing at the right hand of God? Did you notice? He is seated. "If then you have been raised with Christ, seek the things that are above, where Christ is, seated at the right hand of God" (Col. 3:1).

It's a visual picture of Jesus's words "It is finished" (John 19:30). He's sitting down because the work he came to do is done. The work of atoning for our sins is complete (Heb. 10:10). The record of our debt has been canceled (Col. 2:14).

Atonement is a bestselling novel by Ian McEwan. Set in the years leading up to World War II, it's the story of a thirteen-year-old aspiring writer named Briony from an upper-class English family.

The plot revolves around her witnessing a vivid romantic encounter between her sister, Cecilia, and a family servant-become-friend, Robbie Turner. Later that same day, she sees a crime, a rape. But her imagination mixes these events together with tragic consequences, including the imprisonment of Robbie, an innocent man.

Fast-forward five years, and we find Briony wracked with guilt, knowing she's made a terrible mistake but unsure how to undo what's transpired. She becomes a nurse and cares for wounded soldiers, seeking penance for her past mistakes. But Cecilia won't even speak to her, and Robbie has now gone off to war.

In the movie based on McEwan's novel, something entirely unexpected happens next. The story jumps forward fifty-nine years, and Briony, now old and dying, is a famous writer publishing her twenty-first and final novel, which is the story of her choices as a child and their tragic aftermath. But in the movie's version, the redemption that eluded her in real life, the atonement, is now written into the story. The film ends with "happily ever after."

Critics had mixed feelings about the film because those who'd read the novel knew that McEwan himself chose to end things differently. This is on the novel's last page:

> The problem these fifty-nine years has been this: how can a novelist achieve atonement when, with her absolute power of deciding outcomes, she is also God? There is no one, no entity or higher form that she can appeal to, or be reconciled with, or that can forgive her. There is nothing outside her. In her imagination she has set the limits and the terms. No atonement for God, or novelists, even if they are atheists. It was always an impossible task, and that was precisely the point. The attempt was all.[9]

McEwan leaves us where he left Briony, with the grim realization that without something beyond us, outside ourselves, there can be no atonement. Such a message might not have been palatable for a mass movie audience because it goes against our cherished assumption that we can atone for our lives by the choices we make. But McEwan, a professed atheist, is more honest. No God, no atonement. We may yearn for it, but that's all we can do. As he says, "The attempt was all."

That Jesus is seated means he has completely atoned, "once for all," for your life. He has "put away sin by the sacrifice of himself" (Heb. 9:26). You can't undo your past, but Jesus being seated means you don't have to be defined by it.

That Jesus is seated means you don't have to fear the future either, even the worst that could happen to you. Neither "things present nor things to come" can separate you from God's love in Christ (Rom. 8:38–39).

That Jesus is seated means you don't have to be afraid anymore. "Your life is hidden with Christ in God" (Col. 3:3). You are safe. So when you feel anxious about your life, the road ahead of you on this journey, "seek the things that are above, where Christ is, seated at the right hand of God" (v. 1). And you will have peace. It's not over, but it is finished.

Jesus Is Enthroned

Imagine if you'd been there, on that dusty road listening to the street preacher in the midst of the mighty Roman Empire, where everyone knew who the king was—Caesar. Caesar is Lord. And yet here is a man saying God raised Jesus up and "exalted [him] at the right hand of God," and in so doing, "made him both Lord and Christ" (Acts 2:33, 36).

Jesus may have been crowned on the cross, but it is with his ascension, his exaltation to the right hand of God, that he is enthroned. A certain man, of a certain height and weight, now sits on the throne over the whole cosmos.[10]

If you spiritualize the ascension (or ignore it), then Jesus is no longer a threat to the rulers of this world. But the New Testament writers say that he is not only ascended; he is now enthroned as "the ruler of kings on earth" (Rev. 1:5).

It may not look like Christ is ruling the universe. Today it might look like just a crack of light under a door. But the New Testament writers were confident because they knew the light had dawned (Rom. 13:12) and that one day the door will open, and that light, the Sun of Glory, will flood the whole room.

The gravity of Christ being King is often lost on those of us who have no earthly king. But in the Roman Empire, the tiny church not only survived, but flourished, even amid terrible persecution. They were willing to die because they knew who the real king was. And they believed he was worth dying for. King David's men once said to David, "You are worth ten thousand of us" (2 Sam. 18:3), and we can now say that to our King and make our lives wholly expendable to him and his cause.

When you know that Christ is the seated and enthroned King, you too will be willing to surrender all your plans and ambitions into his hands. Perhaps, with the persecuted church, you can even rejoice when you are counted worthy to suffer dishonor for the name (Acts 5:41) because we know who the real King is, and he is worthy.

Jesus Is Our High Priest, Forever

If the language of Jesus as enthroned king sounds somewhat foreign to us, then the language of Jesus as our "high priest" sounds utterly alien.

In order to embrace the significance of this ancient term, we must appreciate the rich symbolism of the high priest in the Old Testament. That's the imagery from which the New Testament writers are drawing when they call Christ our "high priest forever" (Heb. 6:20).[11]

In the Old Testament, the central act of Jewish worship took place on the Day of Atonement when an offering was made by one man, the high priest. The ceremony is described in detail in Leviticus 16. The high priest stood before all the people as their representative, bone of their bone and flesh of their flesh. He stood between God and the people. He was the mediator.

Before he entered the temple, he cleansed himself by washing, so as to be ritually pure on behalf of the people. In fact, all he did, he did on the people's behalf, as symbolized by his special clothing: an elaborate breastplate adorned with twelve jewels representing the twelve tribes of Israel. That is, he bore the names of the people over his heart (Exod. 28:29) as he entered the Holy Place.

He would take an animal, lay his hands on it, and confess his own sins and the sins of the people. Then he would offer a sacrifice as a symbol of the just judgment of God on all the people's sins. Next, the high priest would take the blood and go behind the veil into the Most Holy Place, which represented the presence of God on earth (Lev. 16:2). There he would intercede on behalf of all the people, praying that God would have mercy and forgive them.

Now this is the imagery the New Testament writers are drawing on when they describe Jesus as our true high priest. Jesus, as our high priest, stands in solidarity with us, whom he represents. He too is a mediator, standing between God and humanity. He consecrated himself by his life of perfect obedience and clothed himself especially for this occasion, but not with jewels. He adorned himself in naked human form, bone of our bone and flesh of our flesh. And he came bearing our names on his heart.

He too offered a sacrifice—not the blood of an animal, but his own. Jesus became both sacrificing priest and sacrificial lamb. "Behold, the Lamb of God, who takes away the sin of the world!" The high priest had to appear year after year, but Jesus "once for all … put away sin by the sacrifice of himself." On a certain Friday afternoon, the true Day of Atonement, Jesus made a way behind the veil into God's holy presence.[12]

What wondrous love is this? God satisfied himself by substituting himself. God the Father was willing to give up God the Son (Rom. 8:32); and God the Son was willing to give himself up (John 10:18).[13] Three days later, Jesus rose from the dead and afterward ascended to the most holy place. He entered into God's holy presence, and there intercedes on behalf of all the people (Heb. 4:14; 9:24).

If this language still sounds archaic to you, let me show you how relevant it is to our deepest concerns. Does God really love you no matter what? It's one thing to say, "I believe there is a god." But can you dare to say, "I am the apple of God's eye" (see Ps. 17:8) or, "God delights in me and sings over me" (see Zeph. 3:17)? Where can such confidence come from, given how insecure we often feel?

Jesus as our high priest means that our confidence to approach God does not rest on ourselves. Our confidence is not in our obedience. Our confidence is not in our faith, our understanding, our feelings, or even our sincerity. God's acceptance of you does not depend on the depth of your understanding that acceptance.

Your faith is absolutely necessary, but it is the object of your faith, not the strength of it, that matters most. Your confidence that God *does* love you—that you *are* the apple of his eye and that he *does* sing over you—is grounded outside of you in the one who "sat down." And that means you can't mess it up.

Not only did he stand in your place two thousand years ago; he now stands in your place before God the Father (Acts 7:55). That means God's benevolence toward you is as sure as Christ being fixed at God's right hand. And he will not be moved. "Consequently, he is able to save to the uttermost those who draw near to God through him" (Heb. 7:25). What security! What eternal security.

When we forget this and look instead to our circumstances for the assurance that God is pleased with us, we are so easily swayed. We assume that God must be pleased with us if things are going well or that God must be disappointed in us when bad things happen. But this only shows that we think we approach God on our own merit in the first place. It shows that we do not understand the gospel. We don't know that Jesus is seated, he is enthroned, and he is our high priest!

Jesus Is Our Sympathetic High Priest

Not only is Jesus our high priest; he is our *sympathetic* high priest.

If you were climbing Mount Everest, you would want a guide who had been to the top, who knows the terrain and is aware of the challenges, who has the resources and the know-how to help you.

The Bible says of Jesus, "For we do not have a high priest who is unable to sympathize with our weaknesses, but one who in every respect has been tempted as we are, yet without sin" (Heb. 4:15). Jesus was made like us "in every respect" (2:17). He was tempted in every way. "Although he was a son, he learned obedience through what he suffered" (5:8).

You may have heard this before but privately wondered, *Really? Jesus understands and can sympathize with me? He might want to, but isn't it like asking a billionaire to sympathize with a homeless man? Don't the circumstances he's coming from make such sympathy impossible?*

How could Jesus understand my struggle with sin, given that he never committed any? C. S. Lewis shows us the folly of this assumption:

> No man knows how bad he is till he has tried very hard to be good. A silly idea is current that good people do not know what temptation means. This is an obvious lie. Only those who try to resist temptation know how strong it is. After all, you find out the strength of the German army by fighting against it, not by giving in.... A man who gives in to temptation after five minutes simply does not know what it would have been like an hour later. That is why bad people, in one sense, know very little about badness. They have lived a sheltered life by always giving in. We never find out the strength of the evil impulse inside us until we try to fight it: and Christ, because He was the only man who never yielded to temptation, is also the only man who knows to the full what temptation means—the only complete realist.[14]

We might sometimes imagine that Jesus overcame sin by his "divine super powers" that are unavailable to us, so he can't really know what it's like. But Jesus was empowered for his ministry by the Spirit (Matt. 3:16). When he was tempted in the wilderness, he battled against temptation with God's Word (4:4, 7, 10). In other words, Jesus had the Spirit and the Word, which is to say, he had the very same resources available to you and me—the Spirit and the Word.

Jesus, our guide, is with us and equips us on this uphill journey, and he is able to sympathize with every challenge we face.

We are not alone. He knows our frame because he assumed it. He knows we are dust because he became it. And now dust sits on the throne of the universe. Our savior is not an idea. He is a real person, able to sympathize with real people.

Jesus Lives to Make Intercession for Us

Jesus is not only our sympathetic high priest; he is also our willing advocate. Have you ever heard it said of someone, "He doesn't just love football; he lives for it"? They mean it stirs his heart and motivates him. What does Jesus live for? The Bible says he "lives to make intercession" for those who draw near to God through him (Heb. 7:25).

In Los Angeles, advancement in the entertainment industry often depends on who you know. Networking is so vital, you will sometimes hear someone say, "Feel free to use my name if it will help." We all understand that some names open doors that would otherwise be closed.

Jesus, our advocate, says, "Go ahead and use my name; it will help." But Christ doesn't just open the door. He takes our hand in his, ushers us to the Father's throne, and stands beside us and pleads for us.

Jesus is our *willing* advocate, not like a fatigued defense attorney groaning, "Ugh, got to go to court again for this one," as if he were weary of pleading for us. God knows we are weary of ourselves.

Think about what this means if you are discouraged, like so many of us are, with your prayer life. Jesus, our willing advocate and high priest, gives us confidence in prayer like nothing else—confidence that our prayers are heard and that they are effective.

When, in our failure and bewilderment, we do not know how to pray as we ought or when we forget to pray altogether, Christ takes what is ours. He takes our mumbled, sputtering, unworthy prayers, our sighs and garbled words, and he purifies them and offers them without spot or stammer to his Father.

Even when you struggle to get the words out, and they are only groans (Rom. 8:26), Christ intercedes and translates our sighs into what is needed. What confidence we can have in prayer, in Christ, that we are heard! "Let us then with confidence draw near to the throne of grace, that we may receive mercy and find grace to help in time of need" (Heb. 4:16).[15]

He Has Blazed the Trail for Us

To use another biblical image, Jesus is not only with us on the journey; he is also at the finish line of the race, waiting for us, cheering us on—"You can do it!"—along with all those who have gone before, the great cloud of witnesses (Heb. 12).

The Bible calls Jesus "a forerunner on our behalf" (Heb. 6:20). As the pioneer, he has gone on ahead and made a place for us, as he promises, "If I go and prepare a place for you, I will come again and will take you to myself, that where I am you may be also" (John 14:3).

In the incarnation, God took humanity into his being forever. And when he ascended to heaven, Jesus imported flesh and blood for the first time into those holy precincts. He paved the way for us so that when we arrive later, no one will be shocked that the likes of us were invited to this party.[16]

In heaven, "a hand like this hand shall throw open the gate of new Life to thee ... We shall be greeted by a face ... that has a form we recognize."[17] Union with Christ means we, as humans, have a place in God's life. Forever. This dignifies humanity like nothing else.

Christ's humanity is not "like some seedy motel room he can't wait to vacate,"[18] as though when he became human, he took a step down, but when he ascended, he discarded that old flesh and went back to being only divine. No, when Jesus says he is "the way" (John 14:6), he doesn't just show the path; he blazes it and carries us along it.[19]

God is now not stripped of humanity but—can we dare to say—adorned by it. Consequently, concerns of humanity matter to God because humanity is forever a part of God's own life. That means justice and care for the poor, the orphan, and the widow are always on God's mind because Jesus is always in his presence.

He Is with Us and for Us along the Way

All this talk of our heavenly participation with the ascended Christ may sound high minded, but what could be more down to earth? When the concerns of life are weighing you down, what could give you more hope than to know that God is with you and God is for you?

Jesus is at the finish line, cheering you on. He is also alongside you on the road, filling you with hope ("You'll make it—I'll see to that," see Phil. 1:6); giving you courage ("Do not fear; I am with you," see Matt. 28:20); and giving you energy (Col. 1:29) and strength along the journey (Heb. 12:12).

Some parts of the church have reminded us beautifully that because of Christ we can know that God is *for* us. "If God be for us, who can be against us?" (Rom. 8:31 KJV). A strong emphasis on the finished *work* of Christ is crucial.

Other parts of the church have reminded us beautifully that because of Christ we can know that God is *with* us. And if Christ is with us, why would we ever need to fear? A strong emphasis on the indwelling presence of the *person* of Christ is also crucial.

But what union with Christ holds together—and why it gives us unrivaled hope on the journey—is that it tells us that God is for you *and* with you. He is with you and he is for you. You may not have thought much about Jesus ascending into heaven. But Jesus promises us, "It is to your advantage that I go away" (John 16:7).

You don't have to "white knuckle it," as if it's up to you to hold on to him. We have Christ within us. "Do you not realize this about yourselves, that Jesus Christ is in you?" (2 Cor. 13:5). We can't be reminded enough that though Christ is physically present in heaven, he is spiritually present with all those who are "in him" (1 John 5:20). To belong to Christ means to have his Spirit, and to have his Spirit means having the risen, ascended, reigning Christ within you, wherever you are.

So Jesus is both with us spiritually and in heaven, at the right hand of God. "The spirit truly unites things separated in space."[20] And now we can see how Christ being in us *and* in heaven makes all the difference for our lives on earth.

In one of his poems, Robert Hass describes a couple deeply in love:

> … and one day, running at sunset, the woman
> says to the man,
> *I woke up feeling so sad this morning because I*
> *realized*
> *that you could not, as much as I love you,*
> *dear heart, cure my loneliness.*[21]

Even the best and most intimate human relationship has its limits. No relationship can cure our loneliness but the one we were made for, the one that is more central, more defining, and closer to you than any other relationship you could ever have: your relationship with Christ. Jesus offers you what no other partner could: unwavering and eternal fidelity—no sickness, not even death, will part you.

Your spouse might be willing to die for you, but Jesus already did. Your spouse might want to understand you more deeply, but only the one who knows you better than you know yourself can deliver you from the tyranny of feeling you are not understood. Jesus is better than any earthly friend. He's the friend you've always wanted.

As your enthroned king, he gives you peace, knowing that he is in full control.

As your high priest, he gives you the security that you always stand safe.

As your sympathetic high priest, he gives you comfort that somebody understands.

As your willing advocate, he gives you confidence, even boldness, before God.

As your trailblazer, he gives you assurance that you'll make it.

And along the way, he gives you hope that behind every sickness there will be healing and that every longing for a better world will be repaid. All this because Jesus is in heaven—at the right hand of God.

Part IV

UNION WITH CHRIST
DAY BY DAY

You could think of this book thus far as an aerial tour of union with Christ. We've looked at it from varying elevations, but now it's time to land and walk around. The reality of our heavenly participation needs to take root in our earthly lives.

Because Christ is real, our union with him needs to make a real difference in how we greet our neighbors and do our jobs. In order for the gap we spoke of in chapter 1 to close, union with Christ needs to change how we experience each new day.

It can be all too easy for "your life is hidden with Christ" (Col. 3:3) to become detached from our day-to-day lives, for this heavenly reality to remain theoretical and abstract.

How do we set our minds on our union with Christ each day so that it fuels our faith and propels us forward on our journey? Moreover, how do we *keep* our union with Christ in front of us throughout the day and over the years? How do we move these truths from our heads to our hearts?

How does union with Christ make a difference on a Wednesday afternoon at 4:00 p.m.?

Part 4 is dedicated to these questions.

Chapter 11

THE ART OF ABIDING

A few years ago, our family took a vacation near Lake Michigan. The beachfront had these small two-person sailboats you could rent. *How hard could it be?* I wondered. I put the boat in the water and fiddled with the ropes and sail. Twenty minutes later, the boat and I were still only a few feet from shore, and I hoped anyone watching would assume my red face was just sunburned. At last, the teenager at the rental stand took pity and gave me an impromptu sailing lesson.

It did get me thinking about what makes a sailboat move. Is it the skill of the sailor? Certainly skill makes a difference, as I learned that day. But no matter how knowledgeable or determined the sailor might be, he needs something else, something he has no control over: the wind. If there is no wind, his boat will not move.

At the same time, the wind can be blowing fiercely without your boat moving, or at least not moving in the direction you'd prefer. You can be stuck, your sail haplessly flapping. Or you can be tossed to and fro by the waves. You can even capsize (which I did later that day, in the middle of the bay).

For you to move, and move in the right direction, certain skills need to be learned and put into practice. Moreover, you'll not be able to *enjoy* the experience of sailing until those skills have become so internalized that you're not even thinking about them. You've practiced them so much they've become second nature. Then you're not thinking about sailing—you're sailing!

Though sailing might be unfamiliar to many of us, it's a good metaphor for our life with God. No matter how determined we might be, we can't change our hearts at the deepest level nor move ourselves forward. No amount of knowledge or grit will avail. We are always dependent on a power outside of ourselves. We need the wind. Without the wind, there is no movement. And as Jesus reminds us, "the wind blows where it wishes" (John 3:8).

Yet at the same time, we are not passive observers. We can't control the wind, but we can catch it. And in order to catch the wind, you have to draw the sail. And in order to draw the sail, certain God-given, time-honored skills need to be learned and put into practice. Otherwise, even if the wind is blowing fiercely, you can be stuck or tossed by the waves (Eph. 4:14) or even "suffer shipwreck" (see 1 Tim. 1:19 NIV).

LABOR TO BE BROUGHT NEAR

Right from the start, I need to address a possible objection that might be troubling you. Perhaps you're saying, "I thought our salvation is all of grace and completely dependent on God. But you're making it sound like I have to *do* something."

Sometimes a desire to express what is true about the grace of God—that there's nothing you can do to make God love you more or love you less—leads to the false assumption that there is nothing then left for you to do. Your life with God is all of grace. Period. And God's grace invites, even requires, your participation. "Grace is not opposed to effort, it is opposed to earning."[1] The Bible calls us to rest in Christ (Matt. 11:28) and, at the same time, to "strive to enter that rest" (Heb. 4:11).

An old Oxford preacher captured this tension when he called us to "labour to be brought near."[2] You can hear both sides: "labor" is an active command and gives us something to do; "to be brought near" is a passive stance and sounds like the responsibility is God's. Yes.

We don't often hear the complexity today of "labor to be brought near," but you'll find it assumed historically by the most stalwart defenders of grace. John Calvin said, "Let us therefore labor more to *feel* Christ living in us."[3] John Owen added, "Labor, therefore, to fill your hearts with the cross of Christ."[4] And Jonathan Edwards exhorted, "We should labour to be continually growing in divine love."[5]

For some, this call to "labor" still sounds suspicious. But might this suspicion reveal something telling about us? Perhaps we're expecting the presence of Christ to be with us each morning the same way the dew is on the morning grass: we just wake up, and there it is.

But if we passively wait for an experience of Christ's presence to fall afresh on us each morning and it doesn't, or if we don't *feel* his presence, then we will complain of periods of being "dry." We might be tempted to blame this dryness on someone else—our church, our friends, even on God himself. But perhaps the reason is because we are not laboring to be brought near.[6] Granted, there could be other reasons why we might feel "dry," many of which are completely out of our control. Seasons of burnout and exhaustion will happen and will require resting with God or a new routine of seeking his face. Nevertheless, we must always keep pressing on to know him (Hos. 6:3).

The Bible captures the dynamic of this dual reality in one remarkable sentence in Philippians 2:12–13. The sentence begins, "Work out your own salvation with fear and trembling," which again sounds like we are responsible. But the verse continues, "For it is God who works in you," which sounds like God is responsible and we depend on him.

Exactly.

Not only do the voices of history convey this shared responsibility in our spiritual progress, but Jesus describes it too. His word for this dynamic is "abide," which even in English captures the sense. On the one hand, the word suggests resting and staying, like a child leaning into his mother's embrace. It's a posture of reliance for care and even survival, like branches depend on a vine, which is exactly the context in which Jesus uses the word. "Abide in me … As the branch cannot bear fruit by itself, unless it abides in the vine, neither can you, unless you abide in me" (John 15:4). This is a relationship of utter dependency. As Jesus says, "Apart from me you can do nothing" (v. 5).

On the other hand, abiding is an *action*. Here is something you must choose to do. Jesus *commands* us, "Abide in me." He commands us to rest in him. Like a dog commanded to stay, we must exert ourselves not to become distracted or move away from our Master. And Jesus makes it clear that the amount of fruit that comes out of our lives will be a direct result of how much (John 15:5) or how little

(v. 6) we heed his commandments. In fact, he goes on to say, "If you keep my commandments, you will abide in my love" (v. 10).

That's why the sailing metaphor is instructive. Life with God is not like a motorboat, where we are in control of the power and direction. But neither is it like a raft, where we just sit back and are carried along. It's like sailing. While we can't control the most important thing—the wind that makes us move—that doesn't mean there is nothing left for us to do. We have to draw the sail to catch the wind. We must labor to be brought near.

How do we do that? How do we draw the sail to catch the wind of God's empowering presence so we can move ahead in joy and confidence?

THE QUESTION BEFORE THE QUESTION

Over the last four chapters, the prevailing metaphor we've used to describe your life in union with Christ is a journey. You are on a journey, a quest. You have been given a new identity, a new horizon, a new purpose for each step along the way; and you have a sympathetic and powerful guide who is with you (that's chapters 7–10 in one sentence!).

In the next chapter we will look specifically at some of the ordinary means God has provided for us to draw the sail to catch the wind of the Holy Spirit, to move forward on this journey. But before we get ahead of ourselves and talk about the specific motions of "drawing the sail," we need to address the question that must come first: Do you want to go on *this* journey in the first place?

If you don't intend to get in the boat, even the best sailing lessons will be pointless.

Several years ago, I trained for a marathon over a period of months. I planned to run the race with a friend who lived far away. I would wake up early in the mornings to run—at first three to four miles but gradually more. Some mornings, I dreaded it. Other mornings, I woke up before my alarm in eager anticipation. Almost always, I was glad that I'd done it when the run was over. But what got me out of bed and into my running shoes morning after morning was the horizon, the goal of finishing that 26.2-mile race and knowing that my buddy was counting on me. All the sacrifices would be worth it for that end.

On our journey, this is where we too must start: Do you want to run this race? Do you want communion with God? This is the great end to which all of our lessons and practice are but the means. This is the quest:

> You have said, "Seek my face."
> My heart says to you,
> "Your face, LORD, do I seek." (Ps. 27:8)

Unless God is the end that you desire, unless he is the one you seek, these calls to "draw the sail" will come across as simply boxes to check, duties to perform, or more items to add to your already long to-do list. You may think you're not moving forward with God because you don't want it enough. But perhaps it's because God is not your true God. He is not really the one your heart is after. You may profess faith in God but be attempting to use him as a means to your own ends, obeying him in order to get what your heart is really seeking. Whatever your heart seeks most—that is your real god.

Until you face this question—*Is God the one your heart most seeks?*—then these calls to "labor" will feel, well, laborious.

DO YOU WANT TO?

It's not a one-time decision. The journey of choosing God will be a daily fight, a clash of wills, an inner conflict that will play out over and over, in a thousand little ways. Writer David Brooks says this road to character is "the most important thing," about you: "whether you are willing to engage in this struggle."[7] Do you see this inner confrontation to be the central drama of your life? Are you willing to engage in this daily struggle?

At times you'll be tempted to despair or to give up. You'll grow weary and disheartened. Don't be surprised by that (Ps. 6:6). That is exactly why you need to answer this most important question first—do you want to go on *this* journey?

If you do, remember what this book is all about: Christ is with you. He's your "running buddy," as it were. He leads you, comforts you along the way, and assures you you'll make it all the way home. He's also your horizon. He is not only our guide; he's our prize (1 Cor. 9:24). And one day "we shall see him as he is" (1 John 3:2).

Is Jesus your horizon? Is this your prayer: "I want to know Christ" (Phil. 3:10 NIV)? Or can you at least pray, with St. Teresa of Avila, "Oh God, I don't love you, I don't even want to love you, but I want to want to love you"? If Christ is not what you want, then it won't matter how clear these sailing lessons are.

But if you do want to abide in him, then let's go!

THE BASIC MOVEMENT OF ABIDING: WALKING WITH GOD

One of the most common metaphors for life with God in the Bible is not sailing, but walking (e.g., Eph. 5:15; Col. 2:6). It seems rather simple, even trite, after the grand high call to know Christ. After all, nothing is more pedestrian than walking. Even a toddler can do it; but it makes an instructive point. Life lived in communion with God is not meant to be rare or extraordinary. It's not the reward of some secret knowledge. The Bible doesn't say, "Grasp the secret of the Spirit"; it says, "Keep in step with the Spirit" (Gal. 5:25). Walking. Keep in step.

This turns out to be one of the most challenging aspects of the Christian life—the simple repetitiveness of it. Left, right, left, right. Again and again, over and over. All the way. Every day. Like a long walk uphill.

Christina Rossetti has a poem that opens:

> Does the road wind up-hill all the way?
> Yes, to the very end.[8]

We might prefer to fly. We may wonder if there are any shortcuts. And there are some, but once you find out what they are—humiliation and suffering—you'll probably prefer to walk.

THE STEP OF FAITH

The first step in life with God is always the step of faith. The most famous definition of faith is the Bible's: "Now faith is being sure of what we hope for, being convinced of what we do not see" (Heb. 11:1 NET).

What do we hope for? Isn't it this? We hope that God really is as great and good as he says he is. Or as King David says in Psalm 56:9, "This I know, that God is for me." Being able to say, come what may, *this I know, that God is for me*—this is the life of faith.

How can we have a sure and certain confidence that God is for us given all that we *can* see? T. F. Torrance, the great twentieth-century English theologian, tells of his service as an army chaplain during World War II. In the heat of battle one day, he came across a young soldier at the point of death:

> As I knelt down and bent over him, he said, "Padre, is God really like Jesus?" I assured him that he was— the only God that there is, the God who had come to us in Jesus, shown his face to us, and poured out his love to us as our Saviour. As I prayed and commended him to the Lord Jesus, he passed away.[9]

I appreciate this story because it acknowledges the cruelty of life. Pain and death, injustice, suffering, and war—these exist and they hurt us. They tear at us. And yet, we have alongside us "a man of sorrows, … acquainted with grief" (Isa. 53:3), who meets us in precisely this place of pain to assure us that—in spite of everything—this God is for us.

In our walk with God, faith always comes first because unless you are *sure* that you are safe with God and *certain* that God is not disappointed in you, you will never seek his face. "For whoever would draw near to God must believe that he exists and that he rewards those who seek him" (Heb. 11:6).

Before we labor to be brought near to him, we must first rest in his favor toward us. This is the step of faith. It is both how we begin (Acts 16:31) and how we move forward in our life with God (Gal. 3:1–5). There is nothing more liberating or life giving than knowing that God has pronounced you innocent—legally innocent—now that you are united to Jesus Christ. This is a once-for-all and irrevocable announcement. It's as real and eternal as the Word of God itself. And it's precisely because that platform of acceptance and favor is so stable that you can live in holiness and in the freedom of the Spirit (see chapter 9).

So we always begin in faith. And following just behind faith, as surely as the right foot follows the left, is repentance.

THE STEP OF REPENTANCE

Repentance is not a popular word today, but as we've seen over these chapters, when Christ calls us to himself, he is calling us into the abundant life (see chapters 8–9). Repentance is not simply feeling sorry for what we've done or confessing where we've failed. Nor is it simply resolving to do better. Rather, repentance is turning back to God in all of life. If sin is running *from* God to get control of our lives, then repentance is turning back *to* God and yielding control to him.

In that clash of wills—*Jesus or you?*—repentance is letting God's quiet voice become louder, larger, and stronger in your life. And because we are turning back to the one who has already accepted and forgiven us, repentance is not only marked by weeping and mourning, but it is also marked by relief and joy. We do mourn (Matt. 5:4) because we hate to grieve him who loves us best (Eph. 4:30). But we also rejoice as we realize that the primary one we have offended

(Ps. 51:4) is the very one who has moved toward us and embraced us (Luke 15:20). Here is a sorrow that leads to rejoicing and leaves no regret (2 Cor. 7:10). Turning back to God is turning back to life!

These two steps of faith and repentance are the basic movement of the Christian life. They are not only how we begin life in Christ (Mark 1:15); they are also the mindset, the disposition, with which we live the entire Christian life. This is how you keep in step with God's Spirit: faith and repentance. Believe and obey. These are the left, right, left, right of our walk with God. You never outgrow or get beyond this.

Let me give you a few images as kindling for your imagination.

Like Pedals on a Bicycle

One of my favorite images for the Christian life is a bicycle. A bicycle must have two functioning tires to move forward. The front tire is *grace*. Grace always leads. The back tire is *demand*. Demand always follows grace (Exod. 20:1–3). But both are needed for the Christian life to move forward (see chapter 3). To extend the analogy, belief and repentance are like pedals for this bicycle. You must keep pressing on both. Yes, occasionally the road will head downhill and you can coast, but if you ignore either tire or attempt to push only one of your pedals, you'll get in a ditch. Attend to both tires, and keep pedaling.

Like Breathing

Faith and repentance must also become like breathing to you. You breathe in the promises of God (God is good; God loves me; God is with me). You breathe out the lies of trying to abide in those other vines (God is holding out on me; I know how my life will work best; I can get the life I want through _____ [insert anything other than God]). Christ says, "I am the true vine ... abide in me" (John 15:1, 4). Breathe in; breathe out.[10] No one thinks about breathing, of course. It's autonomic. But it is also repetitive, continuous, and absolutely essential to life. And to breathe faith and repentance, to abide in Christ, you must start by being very conscious of it. Oswald Chambers says this about abiding:

> In the initial stages it is a continual effort until it becomes so much the law of life that you abide in Him unconsciously.[11]

This is the goal—that by a lifestyle of belief and repentance, by breathing in and breathing out, you've rehearsed this so often that you're able to do it "without ceasing" (1 Thess. 5:17).

Like a Pendulum

To use one more illustration, the dynamic of repenting and believing works like a pendulum. The further it goes in one direction; the further it can go in the other. The more you believe the gospel (God is good; he has united himself to me; I am accepted as I am; he is worth it), the more you will repent (my sin runs even deeper than I thought, but I don't want to stay as I am; I want to trust him; I want to live for him who loved me and gave himself for me). The more you obey God, the more you will believe God. And the more you believe God, the more you will want to obey him. Back and forth it goes, swinging higher and higher, like a pendulum.

THE ART OF ABIDING

Picasso once said, "All children are artists." There is a desire to create in the heart of each child that the grown-up world usually squeezes out. In the same way, abiding is an art, and there is a desire to commune with God in the heart of each person that sin squeezes out.

The Bible says we must "become like children" to enter the kingdom of heaven (Matt. 18:3). Like any art, abiding can at first be delighted in without any training, like a small child dabbling with finger paints or bouncing her hands on piano keys. But for this art to be developed and enjoyed so that it continues to give life to you and others, it has to be practiced, long and hard, with the eventual reward that it becomes second nature. Like sailing or learning a new language or learning to play the piano—after you practice it long enough, you arrive at the place where you no longer have to think about the mechanics of it; you get to just do it.

My downstairs neighbor (and good friend) is a world-class, Juilliard-trained pianist. As the music he plays floats up through the floorboards of my living room, I know that he's not thinking about the notes he wants to play. He is free just to sit down and make beautiful music on the piano. But getting to this point of freedom took hundreds of hours of practice; it required patience and time and discipline. And he will never get beyond the need for discipline—as accomplished and skilled as my friend is, he still practices almost every day.

Abiding, as with any art, requires practice and discipline to reach that point of freedom and enjoyment. And like any artist, you'll need to keep on practicing—repeatedly and habitually—or you'll get rusty.

ALWAYS WE BEGIN AGAIN

It's been said the Christian life is like playing with a yo-yo while walking upstairs. There are a lot of ups and downs, but the overall direction is up. What matters most is not how far along we are but what direction we are facing. How do we keep pressing on and moving up? How do we keep going in the right direction?

To start, we need to be aware of an unexpected danger on our journey.

Much has been written about the importance of a morning routine. The first few choices you make each morning have great power to set the direction of the whole rest of your day. Our next chapter will look at some of the specific practices we can choose to set in motion; but for now, let's emphasize that abiding in Christ takes preparation. First Peter says to prepare "your minds for action" (1:13). In other words, the most important thing you do each day may happen before you *do* anything.

Every morning I wake up and find my heart has reverted to its default position: *I need to prove myself today, handle things, make a name for myself.* Part of "preparing my mind for action" is choosing instead to reorient myself toward God and his mercies, which are new every morning; to remember God relates to me by his grace, not by my performance.

That is, I must start each day with my union with Christ. I must breathe in faith—I am in Christ and Christ is in me. God is good, God is in charge, and God loves me. Above all, what will make this day a good day will be abiding in Christ today, listening to his voice, keeping in step with his Spirit, walking in faith and repentance.

But I can't assume the posture of abiding unless I am sober minded (1 Thess. 5:6), knowing that I must labor to be brought near and that this labor begins again each day.

BEWARE OF THE DRIFT

We must labor to keep our union with Christ in front of us day after day or we will drift. To return to the sailboat analogy with which we began this chapter—what does it take for a boat to drift away? Nothing. If it is not anchored or tied down, it will drift away. "Therefore we must pay much closer attention to what we have heard, lest we drift away" (Heb. 2:1). As the hymn says:

> O to grace how great a debtor *daily* I'm
> constrained to be;
> Let that grace now, like a fetter, bind my
> wand'ring heart to thee.
> Prone to wander—Lord, I feel it—prone to leave
> the God I love:
> Here's my heart, O take and seal it, seal it for thy
> courts above.[12]

The unflagging, unfailing grace of God is always blowing. And every day, it is our union with Christ—the reality that we are bound to him—that is our anchor, keeping us from drifting away, and our engine, the wind in our sails that propels us forward. Each day we wake up and we begin again. "Always we begin again."[13] So today, let us "labor to be brought near," confident that our labor is not in vain. Now for some sailing lessons.

Chapter 12

THE MEANS OF ABIDING

Last summer I started to feel chest pains. Then I made a serious mistake. I went to the Mayo Clinic website (don't ever do that). "Tingling in the arms," hmm, yes. "Pressure on the chest," maybe. Pretty soon I was convinced I was dying. Apparently there is a term for this—*cyberchondria*.

I went to the doctor, and he ran a battery of tests—cholesterol screening, EKG, even a cardiac scan. When I went back the next week to get the results, he asked me, "Are you stressed?" Now, I'm a pastor of a growing church and the father of three young children—that can be stressful. But if you're a pastor and your doctor asks you, "Are you stressed?" you're in a bit of a bind. "Me? Stressed? No, I've got peace like a river, Doc." Actually I think I mumbled, "I don't think so."

He said gently, "Well, sometimes your body trumps what your mind is telling you. As far as these tests show us, you are a picture of health. But your body is telling you that you need to rest more, eat better, and exercise."

I looked on the wall at his credentials: "Johns Hopkins MD." I'd been worried for weeks, tested for days, and this was his diagnosis. "You're telling me that I need to rest more, eat better, and exercise?" I asked, repeating him verbatim. "And then I'll feel better?" So, I thanked my doctor and paid him for telling me something I already knew before I'd ever gone to see him.

But if I knew it already, why wasn't I doing these things? Maybe I didn't understand what I thought I knew. Maybe I wasn't convinced that these basic disciplines were essential to my daily health. Maybe I needed to suffer the consequences of ignoring them before I felt compelled to pay attention to them.

TIME TO MAKE THE DONUTS?

When I was a little kid, Dunkin' Donuts had a television commercial featuring a man who wakes up while it's still dark and mutters to his wife, "Time to make the donuts." He shuffles into his uniform and heads, zombielike, to the donut shop. But it was clear he was not excited and would rather keep sleeping. That's how many of us look at the practices of abiding in Christ. *Time to make the donuts …* but we'd really prefer to hit the snooze button.

Over the years, I have heard (and now given) many sermons on the importance of prayer and Bible reading, but I've noticed these seem to pass in one ear and out the other. We know we ought to (*Yes, yes, I know—rest more, eat better, and exercise*), but most of us find it difficult to sustain the daily habit.

In the last chapter, we looked generally at the journey of life with God: the posture of abiding and the basic movements (believe and repent, repent and believe). The specific means, or practices, of abiding in Christ that we're about to look at are like the bread and water for our journey. They keep us going; they feed and nourish us.

If you've ever been on a long hike, then you know that if you wait until you feel thirsty to drink water, you are in trouble. You'll already be on the verge of dehydration and possible exhaustion. In the same way, if you pray only when you feel a desperate need, you're probably suffering from a sort of soul dehydration and possible spiritual exhaustion. And yet, if you don't put these means of abiding in their place—as nourishment—they can become merely boxes to check, duties to perform, one more thing to do on an already-long list.

As we said in the last chapter, life with God is like sailing. You can't move yourself. You are completely dependent on a power outside of you. You need the wind, and the wind blows where it will. You can't control it. But you can catch it. And to catch the wind, you must draw the sail. To draw the sail, certain skills must be learned and put into practice. But these skills will benefit you only if you've decided to go on the journey in the first place. So let's assume that you want communion with God. How then do you draw the sail?

HOW TO DRAW THE SAIL: THE MEANS OF ABIDING

For more than two thousand years, spiritual guides from vastly different traditions have emphasized the importance of spiritual exercises for spiritual health.[1] These exercises have been called various names, such as "spiritual disciplines" or "means of grace." In the last few decades, there has been a surge of interest in this subject. One of the writers spearheading this renewal has been Richard Foster, who defines spiritual disciplines this way: "God has given us the disciplines of the spiritual life as a means of receiving his grace. The disciplines allow us to place ourselves before God so that he can transform us."[2]

We are going to be looking at a handful of these disciplines, but it's important to underscore that these means, by themselves, do not change us. God is the one who changes us. These means put us in the place where God can work within us. They are ordinary means God has provided for us to experience his extraordinary grace. They are means of drawing the sail.

Some of us might feel suspicious about spiritual disciplines, seeing them as rote or mechanical or empty. And they can be. But union with Christ changes how we understand these means of grace. It makes you see them in ways you never have. When union with Christ becomes the lens through which we view these means, they are transformed from mechanical duties into living opportunities to come into the presence of the living Christ.

ABIDING BY DAILY MEDITATION

Psalm 1 says that the one who meditates on God's Word day and night will be blessed. And yet for many of us, feeling overtired and overscheduled already, reading the Bible can easily become one more thing we *should* be doing. "I just don't get anything out of it," we may lament. But union with Christ transforms how we read the Bible:

> The reader of the Bible comes to the text not as a stranger to Christ—who is the central subject of all Scripture—but as one who is actually connected to Christ by the Holy Spirit, as one who is really in the real presence of the risen Lord in the prayerful

reading of Scripture. Meditating on Scripture can and should be a real-time experience of communion with the living Christ.[3]

Do you approach the Bible with the expectation that the same Spirit who inspired these words once, long ago, is the same Spirit who is in you now, speaking to you and illuminating these words for you? There is a reason the Bible is called "living and active" (Heb. 4:12), because the living Christ is actively speaking through these words to those who are willing to listen to his voice (John 10:27).

This doesn't mean you always experience the feeling of God's presence. You can't control the wind! But it does mean you can always hoist the sail and come into his presence expecting to hear a word from him. The Bible's word for this practice of reading with attentive expectation is *meditation*. Eugene Peterson says meditating on God's Word is like what a dog does with a bone.[4] By prayer and through the Holy Spirit, you gnaw and chew on God's Word until it metabolizes and gets into your bloodstream. You take it in, and you expect it to nourish you.

This means that reading the Bible is not primarily like opening a "toolbox" for navigating life's problems (though it certainly does teach us about how to live). It is, rather, one of the essential means God has provided to communicate the wonder of his presence to us. Union with Christ is how the Bible comes alive. The Bible is no longer just words on a page, and the call to meditate on it is not simply a call of duty. This is bread for your journey. Jesus himself says, "Man shall not live by bread alone, but by every word that comes from the mouth of God" (Matt. 4:4). An awareness of the living Christ dwelling in you is how the Bible becomes a burning bush out of which God speaks to you.

ABIDING BY PERSISTING IN PRAYER

Mother Teresa once said that we learn to pray by praying.[5] But we're so busy and prayer feels so inefficient. And we have so many questions. Does prayer make a difference? Won't God do what God will do? Besides, who hasn't been disappointed in prayer? We've prayed fervently for something—nothing excessive, not a Lamborghini—something good: a restored marriage, a loved one to be healed, but it hasn't appeared to make a difference. Why keep praying?

Of all the questions surrounding prayer, I want us to focus on why God calls us to keep on praying and why persistence in prayer is essential to abiding in Christ. Jesus once told a parable "to the effect that they ought always to pray and not lose heart" (Luke 18:1). Why should we have to keep asking God for what he already knows we need? Perhaps the question is, do we know what we need?

Jesus asked, "What do you want me to do for you?" (Mark 10:51). This may not seem like a challenging question until you consider what writer Oscar Wilde once wrote: "When the gods wish to punish us they answer our prayers."[6] Can't you look back and think of some prayers you are glad God answered no to? We often don't know what is best for us.

Oswald Chambers once said, "The greatest enemy of the life of faith in God is not sin, but good choices which are not quite good enough. The good is always the enemy of the best."[7] Because God is better than anything we could be asking for, better even than life itself (Ps. 63:3–4), the call to persist in prayer is not for God's sake, but for ours—to train and purify our desires. Prayer is integral to abiding because the real point of prayer is not some*thing* but some*one*.[8]

Just as union with Christ changes how we read the Bible, it also changes how we pray. "The LORD is near to all who call on him" (Ps. 145:18), but for us to know God is near—nearer to us than we can imagine—we must call out to him. Prayer is to union with Christ what conversation is to marriage; it's how this union remains vital. If you never spoke to your spouse beyond "Good morning" and "Good night," then you would undoubtedly be drifting apart. You would not be experiencing the fullness of your union.

What wonder is prayer! Not only can we speak to the Creator of the universe, not only does he hear and use our prayers to accomplish his will, but our Father also *desires* to hear from his children. He desires to hear from us so much more than we desire to speak with him. The call to persist in prayer doesn't guarantee we will always get what we are praying for. But union with Christ does guarantee that God always hears our prayers. As Søren Kierkegaard put it, "This is our comfort because God answers every prayer, for either he gives what we pray for or something far better."[9] Union with Christ reminds us that the real reward of prayer is not what we're asking God for. The real reward of prayer is communion with God, made possible by our union with Christ (Heb. 4:16).

ABIDING BY WORSHIPPING TOGETHER

Another discipline by which we may draw the sail is the practice of gathering weekly in community to worship God (Heb. 10:24–25). In the Garden of Eden, God rested on the seventh day, not because he was tired, but to model for us the rhythm he has built into the

fabric of creation: one day in seven to rest and remember who God is
and who we are. The Sabbath is a gift God gives his people to commune with him in weekly worship together, "that by his example he
might woo humanity to its needed rest."[10]

Union with Christ changes how we worship. We can now come
to worship aware that Christ is present in us, that Christ is our high
priest who is *leading* us into his Father's presence (Heb. 8:1–2), and
that Christ is speaking through all the elements of the worship service, from beginning to end. This allows us to come into worship
expecting to hear from God, as opposed to evaluating the music or
the quality of the sermon.[11] You come to church, and instead of passively observing, you can actively ask, "God, what do you want to do
in me now? What do you want me to hear? How do you want my life
to look different as a result of being here?"

On some days, you may come to worship full of doubts and
fears, not really trusting that God is good or that you are loved. But
when you hear the voice of the person next to you singing of God's
goodness and care, not to mention a room full of voices, it strengthens your faith beyond what you can understand.

In addition, because God knows our faith is weak, he has given
us pictures to remind us of the gospel—the sacraments of baptism
and the Lord's Supper. Sacraments are *visible* signs of an *invisible*
reality.[12] And it is so sad, tragic even, that these signs of the church's
unity (Eph. 4:5; 1 Cor. 11:20) have more often than not been occasions for division.

One of the reasons we've said that union with Christ has been
eclipsed in our understanding today is because we live in a disenchanted world where the sense of God is vanishing from the earth. In

no part of the church's worship is this disenchantment more evident than in our view of the sacraments.

Many Protestants, perhaps out of fear of appearing too "Catholic," have moved away from seeing the sacraments as means of grace. But throughout the New Testament, baptism is described as a sign of our union with Christ (Col. 2:12; Rom. 6:4; Gal. 3:27). What is most important about baptism is not *how* (immersion or sprinkling?) or *whom* (children or adults?) but *what*. Baptism is a sign of our entrance into union with Christ.[13] It may look forward in hope or back in celebration, but anytime you see someone being baptized—if you are a Christian—it is a visible reminder of what is most true about your life. "Or don't you know that all of us who were baptized into Christ Jesus were baptized into his death?" (Rom. 6:3 NIV).

Likewise, the Lord's Supper is a sign of our ongoing union with Christ. In observing the Lord's Supper, we remember ("Do this in remembrance of me") in gratitude (Eucharist, as the Lord's Supper is sometimes called, means "giving thanks"), but these are perhaps secondary to what is more important. In taking the Lord's Supper, we commune with the living Christ and his body (1 Cor. 11:27). It is no accident that the observance of the Lord's Supper is most often called communion.

"The cup of blessing that we bless, is it not a *participation* in the blood of Christ? The bread that we break, is it not a *participation* in the body of Christ?" (1 Cor. 10:16). The Bible is saying that the Lord's Supper doesn't merely remind us of a gift. It *is* a gift. And that gift is nothing less than Christ himself. As Christ says, "This is my body, which is given for you" (Luke 22:19). What the signs of bread and wine (or juice) represent, they also present—the real spiritual presence of Christ.[14]

The Lord's Supper is a means of grace whereby Christ feeds our faith, nourishes our souls, and gladdens our hearts. He strengthens our union with him beyond what we can comprehend.

> Nothing remains but to break forth in wonder at this mystery … it is a secret too lofty for either my mind to comprehend or my words to declare. And to speak more plainly, I rather experience it than understand it.[15]

By injecting these gifts with deeper meaning and enchantment, union with Christ gives us something that is sorely needed today—a deeper appreciation of the place of the sacraments in worship. The mindset of union with Christ can revitalize your expectations and experience of gathering in community to worship.

ABIDING IN COMMUNITY

How can we abide in Christ if we don't abide in what the Bible calls "the body of Christ" (see 1 Cor. 12:24)? Union with Christ means being united not only to Christ but also to all others who are in him, and so abiding in him can't be separated from abiding in Christian community, as difficult as that can be at times. (The Christian community has been memorably compared to Noah's ark—the stench on the inside would be unbearable were it not for the alternative outside.)

But the Christian life was never meant to be lived alone. Even in paradise, when Adam had perfect communion with God, it was the Lord, not Adam, who said it was not good for Adam to be alone (Gen. 2:18). We were made for community. How could it be otherwise when we are created in the image of a God who is himself a community of three persons?

Dietrich Bonhoeffer describes one reason we need to abide in community:

> The Christian needs another Christian who speaks God's word to him. He needs him again and again when he becomes uncertain and discouraged. The Christ in his own heart is weaker than the Christ in the word of his brother; his own heart is uncertain, his brother's is sure.[16]

We are so prone to doubt the promises of the gospel; they are so grand and our faith is so weak, and the sins in our hearts rise up to condemn us. We need a community in which to confess our sins to one another (James 5:16) and to hear the gospel spoken over our lives by others. As we gather together, we meet one another as bearers of salvation. We need people we can call on when we are in great need or just feeling out of sorts. On this journey, as on any great quest, we need others to travel with us, so we can help one another, spur one another on, and carry one another's burdens.

In particular, we need spiritual friends.[17] We need friends to help us to see our blind spots. On our own, it can be easy to deceive ourselves. "But exhort one another every day, as long as it is called 'today,' that none of you may be hardened by the deceitfulness of sin" (Heb. 3:13). Almost the entire New Testament was written to groups of people—the "you" in your Bible in English might more accurately be translated as "y'all." We need community, to "exhort one another every day," to abide in Christ.

EXPECT THE DOLDRUMS

You might be thinking, *I've heard all this before. Read the Bible. Pray. Worship. Stay in community. And I've tried it. But it didn't work. They don't work.*

It is imperative to stress once again that these means of abiding are just that—means. If you don't see these means of abiding as ways of experiencing the freedom that is yours in Christ (Gal. 5:1) but rather as encumbrances on your life, then they will be just that— heavy yokes around your neck instead of ways to take on Christ's easy yoke (Matt. 11:29).

When the horizon of communion with God is lost, you can be doing all the right things for all the wrong reasons. You can be drawing the sail routinely and still be stuck. If you don't keep this great end before you, then you are bound to get discouraged and grow weary in these practices.

To extend the sailing metaphor we've drawn through these two chapters, consider the nautical term *doldrums*. The doldrums are an area near the equator where the water is especially warm and so the wind can die down suddenly, leaving a ship stranded for an extended period of time. The word has carried over into common usage to mean a period of listlessness, depression, or stagnation. Just as experienced sailors know to expect the doldrums, so those who want to grow in God's grace must know to expect the doldrums.

The doldrums are an important, even necessary, part of learning to abide. They protect us from the dangerous temptation of enthroning our experience of Christ over the real Christ. See, if you always got a high, or a spiritual surge, every time you drew the sail, it would be easy to shift into pursuing your own immediate gratification instead of pursuing Christ. It might become less about the horizon and more about another spiritual jolt. In the name of seeking God, you'd be using God to help you maintain a sense of control over your own life.

But precisely because it is the real God you are seeking, by definition this means you must give up your right to control him. You can't control the wind! You are utterly dependent on a power outside of you. Jesus says, "Apart from me you can do nothing" (John 15:5). It's a terrifying truth, but in order for it to become life giving to us, we have to be made aware, sometimes painfully so, that we can't coerce or control God by our own frantic maneuvering.

Think about how silly and pointless and exhausting it would be for someone to stand up in his sailboat and blow with all of his might onto a limp, hanging sail. How sad. But isn't that how many of us approach these means of grace—if we just try hard enough, we'll be bound to move? No wonder we get so easily flustered.

The doldrums train you to place your trust in God and not in your own frantic blowing. There will be, even must be, times when you draw the sail and nothing happens. You are doing everything "right." You are reading the living Word, but it does not seem alive. You are praying to the living God, but it seems like no one's listening. You are worshipping, but it just sounds like noise. You're doing all you know how to do, yet you are stuck.

The doldrums are there to remind you that it is the real God you are seeking. You must wait on him because he is God. He is not in our service. We are in his. Waiting on him means ... *waiting* on him. How else would we learn to wait? Waiting on God is critical to knowing God (Ps. 130:5–6) because it teaches us that we are not God.

In terms of a biblical picture, we can be like a tree planted by streams of living water, meditating day and night, and still be in a season with no visible fruit. Psalm 1 describes this tree, which "yields its fruit in its season" (v. 3), implying that there are other seasons when there is no fruit.

Every tree has seasons of winter, when it looks as though nothing is happening. It may almost look dead. But far below the surface where no one can see, the roots are forcing their way down deeper so that the tree can bear more fruit when spring comes again.

This means the most important periods of your communion with God will almost necessarily be those when you are "not getting anything out of it." The doldrums. The most important seasons of growth will often be the ones you feel the least growth. The doldrums. They are training you to put your trust in the wind. Waiting for the wind, and being out of control, forces us to let go of our cherished idol of instant gratification. "For God alone my soul waits in silence" (Ps. 62:1).

When you remember that these means are precisely that—means to an end; when you remember that you are not looking for an experience (which may or may not come) but communing with God, who is always there; when you remember that there will be doldrums, then you can be assured that the most important times of meditation and prayer, worship, and community may in fact be the times you enjoy them the least. Take heart.

THE IMPORTANCE OF HABITS—KEEP DRAWING THE SAIL

Abiding in Christ doesn't come naturally for us. We have to learn how to do it. We have said that abiding is an art, and like any art, abiding requires practice and discipline. Like any artist, you have to keep on practicing—continually, repeatedly, habitually—or you'll get rusty. Quickly.

When he was a young man, Jonathan Edwards made a list of seventy resolutions that he committed to read over at least once a week. My favorite is number twenty-five: "Resolved, to examine carefully what that one thing in me is which causes me in the least to doubt the love of God."[18]

Above his list of resolutions, Edwards wrote the words, "Being sensible that I am unable to do any thing without God's help, I do humbly entreat him, by his grace, to enable me to keep these Resolutions, so far as they are agreeable to his will."[19] There's the art of abiding—he is unable to do this without God, yet he is humbly asking God to enable him to *do* it.

Edwards knew he had to keep these resolutions in front of him every week. You might think, *I'm not Jonathan Edwards!* And that is precisely the point. If a man of his towering intellect and spiritual sensitivity needed a disciplined habit to remind himself of the truths of the gospel, how much more then do we?

Blaise Pascal was a seventeenth-century French mathematician and scientist. He was a genius (as a child, he discovered all the theorems of Euclid before he'd ever even heard of Euclid!), and some of his mathematical theorems are still studied today. Then when he was thirty-one, something life-altering happened to him. And we know this because eight years later, when he died an untimely death, a worn parchment was found sown into his coat. Written on it was the following testimony:

> The year of Grace 1654. Monday, 23 November
> From about half past ten in the evening until about
> half past midnight.
> FIRE! "God of Abraham, God of Isaac, God of
> Jacob,"
> not of philosophers and scholars.
> Certainty, certainty, heartfelt, joy, peace.
> God of Jesus Christ ...   ,
> My God and your God ...
> The world forgotten, and everything except God ...
> Joy, joy, joy, tears of joy ... *the fountain of living
> waters* ...
> Jesus Christ.
> Jesus Christ.
> Let me never be cut off from him![20]

Pascal kept this parchment on his person for eight years, moving it from coat to coat, so that it was literally next to his heart wherever he went. Pascal knew that while God would never forget him (Isa. 49:15), he was prone to forget God. So he sewed a reminder into his life, a daily tutorial to keep his union with Christ before him. And if Pascal, a genius, needed a reminder sewn into his coat, then how much more do we need to sew reminders into our lives?

I had a friend named Will. He went into the hospital one day with what he thought was a sinus infection. Less than a year later, he was dead at the age of thirty-three from a rare form of cancer. Over that year, we spoke often. He kept a rock in his pocket wherever he went. He said it was to remind him, when he got discouraged or afraid, that just as the edges of that rock had to be worn smooth, so the rough edges of his heart needed to be sanded down.

I tell you these stories not so you'll make resolutions or sew a piece of paper in your jacket or keep a rock in your pocket. The point is that each of these three found a way to make pursuing God a habit. They found a way to keep the promises of God "on your heart ... when you sit in your house, and when you walk by the way, and when you lie down, and when you rise" (Deut. 6:6–7). The point is to "take care lest you forget the LORD" (v. 12). Find a way that works for you. However you choose to do it, like Pascal we must find ways to sew reminders into our lives—daily and habitually—of our union with Christ.

We've emphasized over the course of this book that union with Christ means that you are united to the Savior in a living relationship. And like any relationship that you want to develop, you must invest time and choose to do certain things that magnify the priority of that relationship. That's how any relationship grows.

If the examples above haven't convinced you, consider that even Jesus set aside time to commune with God (Luke 4:42; 5:16; 6:12), and he was God's own son. How much more important, then, is it for us to set aside time—repeatedly and habitually—to cultivate the art of abiding?

Learning this art will require new habits. Don't be turned off by this or think this preparation somehow cancels out the spiritual vitality of the gospel. Don't get seduced into thinking, *If I have to try this hard, it must not be authentic.*

Anthony Trollope, the great nineteenth-century writer, who managed to be a prolific novelist (writing forty-seven novels) while also revolutionizing the British postal system, observed, "A small task, if it be really daily, will beat the labours of a spasmodic Hercules."[21] Trollope was saying that over the long run, the unglamorous habit of repetition sparks creativity and adds to productivity. "Inspiration is for amateurs," photographer and painter Chuck Close said, "the rest of us just show up and get to work."[22]

The myth of just sitting and waiting to be hit by inspiration, artistic or spiritual, is just that—a myth. Real artists, spiritual or otherwise, just show up and get to work.

There are no gospel prodigies. There's no one-and-done way to keep your union with Christ in front of you. You must draw the sail, repeatedly and habitually. Or you won't move.

Chapter 13

THE SECRET OF ABIDING

This little chapter contains a big idea. I've saved for last what's most important for the art of abiding, this secret of abiding. I don't mean secret in the sense of something hidden. I mean it in the sense that Paul does in Philippians 4:12, "I have learned the secret of facing plenty and hunger," that is, the unexpected, unfamiliar way.

A name you've seen repeated throughout this book is John Owen, and that's because he's one of the writers who has thought best and most about communion with God. In his book *Communion with God*, Owen makes a distinction between union with Christ and communion with God that remains so helpful for us today.

On the one hand, our *union* with Christ is fixed and unalterable. It does not rise and fall with our faith or the quality of our lives, with what we've done or failed to do. Our union with Christ is as certain as Christ's irrevocable love, which does not wax or wane. It is as sure as Christ's grip on our lives and his promise that nothing can snatch us from his hand (John 10:28).

On the other hand, our *communion* with God does change and vary. It *is* affected by our faith and what we choose to do or not do. To be clear, the love of God for us does not change, but our *experience* of his love does. Jesus says, "Whoever has my commandments and keeps them, he it is who loves me. And he who loves me will be loved by my Father, and I will love him and *manifest* myself to him" (John 14:21). Jesus is saying that the way we respond to God will affect our experience of him. If we trust God and obey him, then Jesus promises he will "*manifest*" himself to us. He will make himself more apparent. Jesus couldn't be clearer that we will know God better by obeying him more.[1]

Our response to God is not the root of his love; it is the fruit. But the fruit is where the nourishment drawn from the root manifests in sweetness and beauty. And the presence of fruit will give us greater assurance that our lives are rooted in him: "By this we know that we have come to know him, if we keep his commandments" (1 John 2:3–6).

Now *why* is this distinction between union and communion so important for us? Because we naturally fall into the trap of assessing the security of our union (*Does God really love me?*) on the strength of our communion (*How am I feeling? How am I doing?*). And we get seduced into thinking it's up to us to keep it up. Abiding then becomes a chore, a box to check, a bar to clear—"Read your Bible!" comes across like "Clean your room!" "Pray more" sounds like "Do more." It then becomes easy to feel frustrated and think, *But I'm not getting anything out of this. So why bother?*

Don't you see how this is like standing up in your sailboat and blowing on your own sail? Not only will you never move forward this way, not only will you exhaust yourself, but how could you ever rest?

How could you ever have any assurance that God loves you if the ground of your confidence is your own frantic blowing?

Thank God that the basis of our acceptance is found outside of us in our union with Christ! Christ is always faithful, even when we are not (2 Tim. 2:13). We change, but he never does. He is the same yesterday, today, and forever (Heb. 13:8). One of the Puritan writers put it memorably, "Your heart is not the compass Christ saileth by."[2]

UNION IS THE SECRET TO COMMUNION

Union is the secret to communion. Because only when you are absolutely "sure" and "certain" (see Heb. 11:1) that you are loved by God, that you are safe in Christ, will you want to pursue the one who already loves you best.

For example, when you don't read or pray, God is not like a disappointed schoolteacher, scolding you for failing to complete your assignment. Rather, God is your patient and loving Father. He desires communion with his child so much that Owen says nothing grieves God more than our "hard thoughts" about him, that is, our unwillingness to believe that God really is this tender and kind toward us. Why does nothing grieve God more? Because he knows "how unwilling is a child to come into the presence of an angry father."[3]

This is how much God desires communion with you, that what grieves him most is not our sin but our refusing to believe that he is so kind, and that he desires to be with us so much more than we do with him. If our soul only knew this, "it could not bear an hour's absence from him; whereas now, perhaps, it cannot watch with him one hour."[4] Owen is saying that embracing your union with Christ is what moves you into greater communion with God.

To draw together these chapters on abiding, your irrevocable union with Christ—this is the wind in your sails. And his unflagging grace is always blowing. He is not only the wind (this is where our metaphor fails); he is also the one who enables us to do our part to draw the sail, and he is the one who feeds and nourishes us for the journey. "Apart from me you can do nothing," including the work of abiding.

And to gather together the themes of the four basic questions we addressed in part 3: when you know that you are not your own (chapter 7); when you know that Christ sets the horizon for your life (chapter 8); when you know that pursuing him gives purpose to each new day, not in fear of what you lack, but in the freedom of what you already have (chapter 9); when you know that Christ not only sets the horizon and charts the path but is himself in the boat with you (chapter 10); and when you know that your heart is not the compass he sails by but rather his own constantly faithful heart, then the means of abiding become means of resting and refreshment.

Union with Christ is the secret to communion with God.

You are drawing near to the one who is already near, singing praises to him who is already singing over you (Zeph. 3:17). You are blowing on the embers of God's white-hot love for you so that the truth of it might catch fire that day. But most of all, you are consoled that even when you don't feel its warmth or see its light, the fire is still burning, inextinguishable (Luke 3:16; John 1:5).

Union with Christ makes the art of abiding a duty of delight.

Chapter 14

THE NECESSARY PATH OF ABIDING: SUFFERING

It's one thing to talk about continuing to "draw the sail" in the doldrums. It can be hard enough to press on when it feels as though the winds have stilled and you are unable to move. But how do you keep going on those days when it took all you had just to get out of bed? How do you remain in the vine (John 15:5) when the wind blows so hard that your life is turned upside down or when you feel knocked off your feet by an overpowering gust, disoriented by a storm, even lashed by a hurricane?

The author of Psalm 73 begins his song by saying, "Surely God is good to Israel ... But as for me ..." (NIV). When you feel like "God may be good in general, or good to others, but not to me," when God seems distant or against you, and doubt, distrust, and anger have dropped anchor in your heart—how do you abide in Christ then? How do you move toward God when you are disappointed in him?

The Bible is filled with calls to "not lose heart" (2 Cor. 4:1; Eph. 3:13; Ps. 27:14), which implies that we will sometimes feel as though we're about to or maybe that we already have (Ps. 40:12). And nothing can cause you to lose heart like suffering. But neither can anything lead you into God's heart like suffering can. If you let it, suffering can drive you "like a nail" into the heart of God.[1]

To return to our sailboat image, a storm, though terrifying, can propel you further and faster along than you ever imagined. You were totally disoriented and felt like you were going to die, but you woke up and discovered you had moved hundreds of miles in the night, far swifter than sunny days and smooth sailing could have ever propelled you. In the same way, the storms of life can lead you where you want to go, as long as communion with God is your horizon. Suffering can be a shortcut toward this destination. It's a shortcut no one would ever choose, but looking back, few would trade it for where it has brought them.

If you're in the midst of one of these storms right now, I hope that you'll find some encouragement among these pages. But I'm well aware that it's hard to read a book while sailing through a hurricane. What you need most is only to *know* the central claim of this book—you are not alone, Christ is with you, in you, and you are hidden in him.

But if your storms are still on the horizon or not yet in view, may I suggest that it can be most helpful to consider your theology of suffering *before* the need arises, such that your suffering is not amplified by confusion when it arrives. Just as sailors run emergency drills in fine weather to prepare for the storms to come, so you have the opportunity to prepare your heart by considering how and why God can use suffering in your life.

We certainly can't talk about being united to the person of Christ and skip over suffering. Each one of us has been marked, or will be marked, by suffering. Christ's life was marked by suffering as well. We can't talk about the means of abiding in Christ, about how to make union with Christ a daily and lifelong experience, and bypass the uncomfortable reality, the necessary path, of suffering.

What's the relationship between suffering and union with Christ?

Let's look first at how the biblical writers assume suffering is integral to knowing Christ. And then we'll look, much too briefly, at why suffering is a necessary means for those who want to know Christ and grow in intimacy with him.

UNION WITH THE SUFFERING CHRIST

Before we look at *why* suffering is integral to union with Christ, let's start by observing that the writers of Scripture assume that it is. We will look at three passages.

First, "I want to know Christ—yes, to know the power of his resurrection and participation in his sufferings, becoming like him in his death" (Phil. 3:10 NIV).

We talked in chapter 11 about the importance of the question, do you want to go on this journey in the first place? We said that the means of abiding will only compel you to the degree that you prize what they enable—communion with God. Can you say of yourself, with Paul, "I want to know Christ"?

Do you want to know Christ's power? The power of his resurrection is the power that overcame death. Who wouldn't want that power for their lives? And yet, we typically use power to make ourselves safe and comfortable. Christ's is a decidedly different kind of power. Paul says that the power of Christ is inseparable from participation in his sufferings, that the way to know Christ is the way of becoming like him in his death. Do you really want to know *this* Christ?

Our second passage comes from Romans: "The Spirit himself bears witness with our spirit that we are children of God, and if children, then heirs—heirs of God and fellow heirs with Christ, *provided we suffer with him* in order that we may also be glorified with him" (8:16–17).

Do you want to know in your spirit that you are an adopted child of God with all the rights and privileges of God's own Son, an heir of God, and a fellow heir with Christ? Why would we ever need to fear or envy again if we knew the riches of the inheritance that is ours? Any true follower of Christ will want this.

And yet, once again, Paul makes an important provision. You could hardly call it hidden in the fine print of the contract. It's right in front of us: "provided we suffer with him." This is the required path of living in Christ's family and sharing in his glory.

In a third passage, Jesus says, "If anyone would come after me, let him deny himself and take up his cross daily and follow me" (Luke 9:23).

The cross in the ancient Roman world was an instrument of torture and excruciating pain, a place of forced suffering. And yet, Jesus tells us that following him is inseparable from willingly (and daily) entering into suffering and pain.

We can see that the Bible assumes suffering is intrinsic to knowing Christ. But why?

WHY IS SUFFERING INTEGRAL TO ABIDING IN CHRIST?

These verses (and others like them) raise all kinds of difficult, even troubling, questions that deserve book-length treatments themselves.

Many of these questions have been ably addressed in other books. My immediate concern here is to touch on why suffering is integral to experiencing our union with Christ and why union with Christ is integral to experiencing suffering in a way that propels us further along rather than crippling us.

Remember how we summarized union with Christ back in chapter 2? Union with Christ means you are in Christ and Christ is in you. Both parts of this definition teach us about suffering, helping us see why suffering is part and parcel of the new life in Christ. They help us to see what suffering means and, just as importantly, what it doesn't mean.

Christ Is in You

If we are united to Christ, we are united to "a man of sorrows, ... acquainted with grief" (Isa. 53:3). We are united to a suffering servant. How could we expect not to suffer if we are united to one who suffered so much? The Bible dares to say of Christ that "he learned obedience through what he suffered" (Heb. 5:8). If God's own Son, who was perfect, had to *learn* obedience through what he suffered, how much more necessary must it be for us to learn to trust God through what we suffer? Jesus reminds us, "A servant is not greater than his master" (John 15:20).

Pain and suffering were not just something that happened to Jesus. Pain and suffering marked his life. "He was not only continuously afflicted, but his whole life was a perpetual cross."[2] That means the crucifixion isn't just something that happened to Jesus—the crucifixion is who Jesus is.

To know Jesus is to know his cross and to carry your own. Apart from carrying this cross, you cannot know this Savior, nor be united to him. The Christ in you is indeed triumphant and victorious, but, again, he is "a man of sorrows, ... acquainted with grief." Paul didn't just resolve to know Christ. He resolved to know "Christ and him crucified" (1 Cor. 2:2). Is this the Christ you know?

How is this helpful? Why is this good news? Think of the prevalence today of support groups—there are support groups for cancer patients, for parents who have lost children, for families of addicts. Why are these groups so manifold and helpful? Because great comfort can be found in the presence of others who have suffered in similar ways. When tragedy strikes, the most welcome comforters can be those who have experienced similar loss and pain. While all suffering is unique, because each person is, you want to be around someone who can sympathize and speak the language of your pain.

In Christ, we have with us one who has moved into our neighborhood, as it were. He is able to sympathize with us in every way because he too speaks the language of sorrow and loss. To be united to him and to know the comfort he brings must of necessity involve sharing in his sufferings (2 Cor. 1:3–5). If you want to be consoled by the comforts of the Christ who is in you, then suffering is the necessary door. To be saved is to be united to *this* Savior—the one who suffered and who still bears his scars.[3]

You Are in Christ

"So I ask you not to lose heart over what I am suffering," Paul says (Eph. 3:13), knowing how suffering—in our own lives or in others' around us—can cause us to lose heart. Suffering causes us to wonder whether God is really good. Is God really *with* me no matter what? Is God really *for* me no matter what? Then why is this happening?

Asking why does not reflect a lack of faith. David asked, "My God, why?" (Ps. 22:1), and of course Jesus took this psalm upon his own lips at his hour of greatest need (Mark 15:34).

In our pain, there is a temptation to prefer our own will above God's will for us, which is a temptation even our Lord faced (Luke 22:42). In our bewilderment, there is a temptation to turn away, to try to hide, or to seal off places in our hearts from a God we might be inclined to think is frowning at us or punishing us.

But if you know that you are "in Christ," and all the wonders that little phrase entails—that you are completely atoned for by Christ, covered by Christ, forgiven in Christ, washed clean in Christ—then you can be sure and certain that God loves you even though you may not know why he is allowing this suffering or what it will mean. It can't mean God is punishing you or condemning you since Christ already bore all the punishment and condemnation that our sins deserved, and he bore it completely, "once for all" (Heb. 10:10; Rom. 8:1).[4]

Moreover, knowing how much Christ suffered while he was sinless shows us that a life of trust and obedience, a life of striving to please God, does not exempt us or release us from a life of pain and suffering. *Why do bad things happen to good people?* The Bible doesn't give us an airtight answer to this. Instead, it gives us a perfect person to show us that no life, not even the best one, is exempt from pain and suffering.

Jesus lived a perfect life and terrible things still happened to him. Jesus was the only one who ever trusted and obeyed God perfectly, yet he nevertheless was made to walk the way of suffering unto death, leading George MacDonald to conclude, "The Son of God suffered unto death, not that men might not suffer, but that their sufferings might be like his."[5]

Why is remembering that you are "in Christ" so crucial to navigating suffering? Horatio Spafford was a prominent Chicago lawyer and follower of Christ in the mid-1800s. After his four daughters drowned in an Atlantic shipwreck, he wrote the now-famous hymn "It Is Well with My Soul."

> When peace, like a river, attendeth my way,
> When sorrows like sea billows roll;
> Whatever my lot, thou hast taught me to say,
> "It is well, it is well with my soul."
> My sin—O the bliss of this glorious thought!
> My sin, not in part, but the whole,
> Is nailed to the cross and I bear it no more;
> Praise the Lord, praise the Lord, O my soul![6]

Why, in his grief, does Spafford call to mind his own sin being "nailed to the cross"? In his book *Walking with God through Pain and Suffering*, Timothy Keller asks:

> What has that got to do with his four little girls who are dead? Everything! Do you know why? When things go wrong, one of the ways you lose your peace is that you think maybe you are being punished. But look at the cross! All the punishment fell on Jesus. [Or] you may think … maybe God doesn't care. But look at the cross![7]

The only way it can be "well with your soul" in the midst of agonizing personal trauma is if you know and are assured that you are covered "in Christ." This is why Spafford, as he processed his own grief, calls to mind the complete sufficiency of Christ's cross to bear the penalty of all his sins. This is how he doesn't succumb to the torment of thinking he is being punished or condemned for his own sins or that he has brought this suffering down on himself or on those he loves.

He writes this hymn of praise to a God who has lost a child as well. Spafford's loss was involuntary. But God voluntarily chose to give up his own Son for us all, on the cross, to deliver us (Gal. 1:4). Mindful of this bond of sorrow, Spafford allows his suffering to bring him nearer to God.

While some suffering can be the Lord's discipline to draw us back toward him (Heb. 12:5–11), it is not the Lord's punishment for us, if we are in Christ. Christ has borne the condemnation, "not in part, but the whole." And this storm may yet be God's instrument to remind us (or those around us) of our utter dependence on the grace of God. It is always true that we are completely dependent on the grace of God for our salvation. It is always true that we are not in control. It is always true that we need Christ more than we can imagine.

But we forget, don't we, how much we need the grace of God? Prosperity and comfort—the very gifts that God gives us in his gracious blessing—can cause us to forget the Lord (Deut. 8). Therefore, God uses suffering not to punish us but to cause us to remember the miracle of his grace and his abundant provision. God uses suffering to bring us back to himself, back to his own heart.

SUFFERING DRIVES US INTO THE HEART OF GOD

Suffering drives us into the heart of God because this is what is in God's heart—his suffering, still-scarred Son (Rev. 5:6). But thanks be to God, who causes the comfort of Christ to abound in our hearts as well (2 Cor. 1:5). If the means of grace we discussed in chapter 12 are the ordinary means of abiding in Christ, suffering is the extraordinary means God has provided for us to move toward communion with him.

But suffering also makes the art of abiding (believe and repent, again and again) and the ordinary means of abiding (prayer, meditation, worship, and community) as needful and essential to us as medicine is to someone who is ill. Suffering, like an illness, teaches us how much we need our medicine each day to become and remain healthy.

When he was older, my grandfather had to take a battery of pills first thing every morning and at night before bed. He didn't look forward to it. In fact, he loathed it. It was an unpleasant task and seemed to serve only to remind him of how much his once able body had broken down with age. Although he knew at one level that the pills were good for him, his feelings told him that this was an unpleasant and pointless task.

Like aging, suffering and pain are inevitable. The question is whether this pain will drive you *further in* to the heart of God or *further away* from the one who is "near to the brokenhearted" (Ps. 34:18).

When you know this Christ, when you experience the fellowship of sharing in his sufferings, when you meet him in this most unwanted and unlikely place, the ordinary means of abiding cease to feel like a burden to you (like taking your pills) and instead become a necessary way to choose health and healing (John 5:6). They become a valued part of remaining in the vine. They become something you look forward to and cherish as a way to mark your day (Ps. 55:17). They might even come to feel like a lifeline. For they are the means of coming in from the storm, into Christ's living presence, and of being strengthened and nourished for the day's journey by him.

In short, when we know our suffering can't mean God doesn't love us, suffering becomes a spur to "keep drawing the sail," keep drawing near to God, even when we are confused or disappointed and may feel like pulling away.

SUFFERING SEALS OUR UNION WITH CHRIST

Why is suffering so integral to our union with Christ? In truth, we have only scratched the surface of this question. It deserves its own book—what the cross of Christ has to say about the art of living. For now, it is sufficient to say, with the biblical writers, that suffering is integral "because Christ also suffered for you, leaving you an example, so that you might follow in his steps" (1 Pet. 2:21). The Christ who suffered is in you, and you are hidden in him. Suffering is therefore integral to our coming to know and enjoy life with God.

> But rejoice insofar as you share Christ's sufferings,
> that you may also rejoice and be glad when his
> glory is revealed. (1 Pet. 4:13)

We can choose to rejoice in our sufferings, not because we are masochistic or naive, but because we believe that the pain of having gone through this will make the joy of that day (when Christ's glory is revealed) even deeper and sweeter. We can be encouraged not only that joy will come in the morning (Ps. 30:5) but also that this suffering will lead to a joy that we otherwise could never have known had we not gone through this grief and shed these tears (Ps. 126:5–6).

These tears, each one of them, will be counted (Ps. 56:8). And each one of them will water and make soft the hard ground of our hearts. Each tear will fall like rain on the arid land and will one day produce a harvest of peace that could only have grown in this way.

CASTAWAY

In the movie *Selma*, Dr. Martin Luther King Jr. goes to comfort the grandfather of a boy who has been tragically murdered. This greatest of orators meets the old man at the morgue and says, with difficulty, "There are no words." When tragedy strikes and the hurricane of suffering threatens to undo us, we do not need a sermon or a how-to manual on getting through suffering. In the film, Dr. King goes on to say, "But I can tell you one thing for certain: God was the first to cry for your boy."[8] And this is what we too have in our suffering: God sees, God knows, and God is with us. If we are united to Christ, we have the real presence of Christ, the suffering servant, weeping with us and carrying us along. He understands, and he is near.

One day, you may find yourself washed up on the shore of a far country by a way you would have never wished to travel.

And yet you find this is not a place you want to leave. You realize it's the place you've always wanted to be, though you've never been here before. You never would have chosen the storms it took to bring you here. They were too hard, too painful, too overwhelming to ever choose them willfully. You'd never want to go through that again.

But now that these storms have brought you here, you can never go back to where you were, even if the days were sunlit and the waters smooth.

Chapter 15

EVERY DAY—UNION WITH THE COSMIC CHRIST

In deep disappointment I have wept over the laxity of the church.
But be assured that my tears have been tears of love. There can be
no deep disappointment where there is not deep love. Yes, I love the
church. How could I do otherwise? ... Yes, I see the church as the body
of Christ. But, oh! How we have blemished and scarred that body
through social neglect and through fear of being nonconformists.

"Letter from a Birmingham Jail," Dr. Martin Luther King Jr.

Union with Christ is cosmic in its scope. It stretches our horizons like nothing else. It adds "breadth and length and height and depth" (Eph. 3:18) to our daily lives. It rescues us from what sociologist Robert Bellah calls our "radical individualism"[1] and helps resolve some of the false choices that narrow our vision.

The problem with defining union with Christ as "you are in Christ and Christ is in you" is that it makes union with Christ sound as though it's all about "you." But in fact, one of the most rewarding aspects of union with Christ is that it reminds you it's *not* about you. To be in Christ, is, by definition, to be a part of something much bigger, more comprehensive, and more wonderful than you.

One of the regrets I have for this book is that I've not given more attention to the body of Christ, the church. I may thereby be perpetuating one of the very dangers union with Christ protects us from, this radical individualism that Bellah defines as "a powerful cultural fiction that we not only can, but must, make up our deepest beliefs in the isolation of our private selves."[2]

There is so much we could say about the cosmic and communal aspects of our union with Christ, but for now, let's just whet our imaginations. Union with Christ means we are part of a larger family, a broader mission, a longer story, a bigger world, and a deeper love.

WE ARE PART OF A LARGER FAMILY

Union with Christ is not just about you and Jesus. You are not the only one, after all, who is in Christ. When you are united to Christ, you are connected to the whole body of Christ in a bond that is even closer than the ties that bind you with your own flesh and blood. The New Testament talks about this new family in a way that has always been staggering and countercultural.

In John 17, Jesus prays, "Just as you, Father, are in me and I in you, [I ask] that they also may be in us ... I in them ... that they may become perfectly one" (vv. 21, 23). Jesus is praying that we might become in *practice* what we already are in *reality*. We are called to become one because we are already one in Christ. "For you *are* all one in Christ Jesus" (Gal. 3:28). Dietrich Bonhoeffer captures this mystery in his book *Life Together* when he writes, "Christian community is not an ideal we have to realize, but rather a reality created by God in Christ in which we may participate."[3]

Christ has already created this new reality. He "*has* made us both one" (Eph. 2:14). He has torn down the walls that so often divide us—of race, ethnicity, class, and gender. As Martin Luther King laments, we can live in denial of this reality. And sadly, we often do. But when we do, we are living in denial of who we now are in Christ. "Is Christ divided?" (1 Cor. 1:13). If not, then those of us in him should not be either. That's the logic of the New Testament.

The Most Diverse Family You'll Ever See

If Christ is your Savior, then all those who have ever known him, from across the centuries and around the globe, from every nation and people group, are your new brothers and sisters. This was the conviction underlying Dr. King's challenge to the white religious leaders of the South in his "Letter from a Birmingham Jail." In effect King was saying, "You claim to be part of Christ's body. Now live like it."

This call to be who we already are in Christ remains the hope for bringing Christ's church together today—not our friendships, not our common circumstances, but the reality of our union with Christ. As scholar D. A. Carson writes:

> The church itself is not made up of natural "friends."
> It is made up of natural enemies. What binds us
> together is not common education, common race,
> common income levels, common politics, com-
> mon nationality, common accents, common jobs,

or anything of the sort. Christians come together, not because they form a natural collocation, but because they have been saved by Jesus Christ.... In this light, they are a band of natural enemies who love one another for Jesus' sake.[4]

Union with Christ overturns what naturally comes to mind when we think of family. It explains why Jesus is pretty hard on what are sometimes called "traditional family values" (see Luke 14:26); it's because Jesus expects our commitment to him and our new family to trump our commitment to the family into which we were born (Mark 3:31–35). To be united to him is to be united to all those who are "in him," past, present, and future—a large family indeed.

It's a Package Deal

Union with Christ, therefore, gives much-needed breadth to our understanding of what salvation means, specifically whether it is a personal matter or a public concern. I have said union with Christ rescues us from false choices, and here is a prime example: Is your salvation an individual thing or a community thing? Is it about you, or is it about the church?

Some of us might lament that there is a low view of the church today, such that a large number of people who identity themselves as Christians are reluctant or unwilling to affiliate with a local church. This reluctance is not all that surprising, given the church's spotted reputation. But more is behind this phenomenon than merely bad press. Is it any wonder people don't treasure the church when the gospel is often presented solely in individual terms (*Christ died for you and forgives your sins so you can go to heaven*)?

Yes, God cares about each one of us. He leaves the ninety-nine and goes after the one (Luke 15:4). Yes, the gospel must become personal, so that you too can sing with Charles Wesley:

> Died He for me, who caused His pain? …
> Amazing love! How can it be,
> That Thou, my God, should'st die for me?[5]

But when we stop here, we make the fatal mistake of placing ourselves at the center of the gospel. And when we place ourselves (rather than Christ) at the center, does this not cater to what historian Christopher Lasch memorably called "the culture of narcissism"?[6] For is anything more narcissistic than to hear, "You are so loved by God that if you were the only person in the world, he would have died just for you?"[7]

This is a dangerous half truth, and like any half truth, it obscures something critical. You *are* so loved by God, but God *didn't* die just for you: "God so loved the *world*" (John 3:16), and God so loves the church, "which he bought with his own blood" (Acts 20:28 NIV). But when we make the gospel primarily about us as individuals and the benefits it brings us, is it so surprising that the church comes across as an unnecessary add-on, as excess baggage, as an easy target? Is it surprising that a common sentiment today is "Jesus, yes; church, no," as if you could have one and not the other?

You may be aware there is a debate going on in academic circles today about the relationship of salvation to the church. Specifically, the question debated is this: Did the biblical writers describe salvation primarily as a legal category having to do with an individual's standing before God, or did they mean it as primarily a social category having to do with the community of God's people?[8]

Union with Christ shows you that this is a false choice. If you are in Christ, then, by definition, you are a part of his body (1 Cor. 12:27). That's why the church historically (from the early church through the Reformation and even beyond) said things that sound strange, even offensive to our ears today, such as, "Outside of the church there is no salvation."[9] In their thinking, in line with the biblical writers, there was no separation. To love Christ means that you love his body, the church.

Union with Christ gives us what we know the American church is lacking: a high view of the church. So that without compromising the importance of individual conversion, we too might say with Dr. King, "Yes, I love the church. How could I do otherwise?"[10]

WE ARE PART OF A BROADER MISSION

What is the mission of the church? Is it primarily to *declare* the good news of what God has done in Christ? Or is it to *demonstrate* the new kingdom that Christ has inaugurated? Are we to be focused on proclaiming the gospel of grace? Or should we direct our energies toward manifesting the justice of God, especially to the poor and marginalized?[11] It's another false choice.

One of the sad story lines of twentieth-century American Christianity has been what historians have called the "Fundamentalist-Modernist Controversy" that drew battle lines over questions such as these. We are still living in the polarizing and politicized legacy of those divisions today, as if we *must* choose one and completely reject the other, as if it *must* be an either/or.

As we have seen throughout this book, union with Christ brings together in harmony voices that don't need to be pitted against one another. It gives us the ability to hold both of these voices together without compromising the distinct and vital place of each.

On the one hand, the gospel is news to be announced. Like newsboys on the corner, we are to declare "the gospel of the grace of God" (Acts 20:24), to proclaim what our King has done and point others to the door of possibility that has now been opened. You can be forgiven (Acts 2:38)! You can be rescued (Gal. 1:4), and you need to be (Rom. 5:9)! Christ died for our sins and was raised—this news is of "first importance" (1 Cor. 15:3). We can't ignore what we are saved *from* (1 Thess. 1:10). The cross of Christ is central and always needs to be part of our proclamation (1 Cor. 2:2).

Yet, at the same time, precisely because Christ is at the center— like a stone dropped into a pond—the effects of his gospel must ripple out to include what we were saved *for*. Christ himself calls it the "gospel of the kingdom" (Matt. 24:14). By his death, a whole new kingdom, a whole new way of life has opened. A new day has dawned for the whole world (Rom. 13:12).

And the church is charged to reflect the light of the risen Christ (Matt. 5:14), to shine like stars in the sky (Phil. 2:15), and to be agents of God's kingdom here on earth. We are Christ's ambassadors, called to represent his rule and reign in every sphere of creation. "You will be my witnesses," Jesus says (Acts 1:8). This is our primary identity as God's people—witnesses.

It's Not Your Party, but You're Invited

We don't usher in or build up the kingdom of God; we witness to it, with the cross before us as both our message and our means. It's not our party. We are not the guests of honor. But we are invited to participate in what Christ has done and what Christ is doing. And we do so in the humble confidence that the kingdom of God "is not," as one missionary statesman puts it, "a candle we kindle and carry, shielding its flame from the wind. It is the light that already shines on our radiant faces, turned toward that dawning glory that is already lighting up the Eastern sky with the promise of a new day."[12]

Union with Christ gives us much-needed breadth to understanding the church's mission.[13] It says that grace and justice, the cross of Christ and the kingdom of God, can no more be separated than Christ himself can be torn in two. If we insist on only one or pit one against the other, then we are dividing the heart of Christ, who so plainly cared about both (compare Luke 4:18 and Mark 10:45).[14]

Union with Christ is about being united to the heart of Christ. Accordingly, we must be both the declaration community *and* the demonstration community. If Christ cares about both, shouldn't his church? If we are united to him who is full of both grace and justice, how could we choose just one?

WE ARE PART OF A LONGER STORY

Tennessee Williams once described one of his characters as a "water plant,"[15] suggesting that she was rootless and dislocated, cut off from her history, and adrift. This displacement is a recurring theme in modern literature, and social theorists have increasingly commented on our growing sense of loneliness, especially as societies become more transient.[16] This feeling of being unmoored, of being disconnected from our roots, might explain the proliferation of websites and television shows that help to trace one's ancestry. We long to be connected to something greater than ourselves.

Union with Christ connects you to a history far longer than you could ever trace on a family tree. It stretches from eternity past to eternity future and puts everything in between into a fresh perspective.

It tells you that God's love for you stretches back before creation. "He chose us in him before the foundation of the world" (Eph. 1:4). It tells you that in the fullness of time, God sent forth his Son to secure our redemption with his blood (v. 7). Jesus Christ is our Savior. It was his sacrificial death and resurrection that objectively accomplished our salvation. When the twentieth-century theologian Karl Barth was asked, "When were you saved?" he famously answered, "It happened one afternoon in AD 34 when Jesus died on the cross."[17]

And yet, if you are "in Christ," there was a time when you were "without Christ" (see Eph. 2:12). The possibility of being connected to him is rooted in a history that predates you. But that seed must take root in the soil of your time-bound life (1 Pet. 1:23). The seed comes to fruition when we respond to God in faith. By faith, Christ's finished work in the past is applied to our lives in the present by the Holy Spirit, who gives us the eyes of faith to see who Jesus is and what he has done for us (Acts 26:18). The Holy Spirit is the bond who connects us to Christ today. And once Christ's life is connected to yours, nothing, not even death, can separate you from him (Rom. 8:38–39). He is yours and you are his forever.

This means that all the events of our lives—from before our birth to beyond our death—find their meaning and coherence only as they are related to Christ. Every fact of our lives is to be interpreted in light of our union with Christ. Every trial, every suffering, every gift, and every blessing—everything that happens to us takes place within this canvas. In every problem we face or mystery we confront, Christ is the clue who alone can make sense of our lives. "In him all things hold together" (Col. 1:17), and not just for us individually.

Christ, the Clue to History

For all creation, Christ is the origin, the creator, and the sustainer (Heb. 1:2; John 1:3). He is the intended destiny of all things. "All things were created *through* him and *for* him" (Col. 1:16). He is "the first and the last" (Rev 1:17), the "Alpha and the Omega" (v. 8). Scholar Richard Bauckham says that when the Bible calls Jesus the Alpha and the Omega, it is not only equating Jesus with God. It is saying that Jesus precedes and originates all things. He is "the only source and goal of all things."[18] And we are united to him!

Union with Christ not only puts in perspective each event of your own life, but his life puts in perspective every event of history. This is why writer Lesslie Newbigin calls Christ "the clue to history."[19] He is saying that every detail of world history, from every time and culture, finds its meaning and significance in Christ. Such a statement sounds outlandish, even offensive, to our modern pluralistic sensibilities. And yet, that is the assumption of the biblical writers (Eph. 1:10–11; Isa. 40:15).

This does raise some troubling questions. If Christ is the clue to history, much of history is dark, even terrifying. As we saw in our last chapter, you can't talk about union with Christ and not take into account human suffering. To say that Christ is the clue to history is not to say that everything that happens in history is good, or that terrible, unjust things don't come to pass. It is to say that only in Christ can all things work together for good (Rom. 8:28) and find not only a resolution but also a joyful ending.

How many times have you read a story of someone who endured some terrible suffering and, years later, said, "Though I never would have chosen this, I wouldn't trade it now for anything, because of what it has turned into in my life"? If that is the perspective that a few years or decades can give, imagine pulling back your perspective to eternity. You are united to him who is ruling and over-ruling over all the details of history. So today you can be encouraged, knowing that Christ, who sees "the end from the beginning" (Isa. 46:10), has united your story to his own.

Union with Christ gives you a new perspective, one that enables you to say, "But this I know, Christ is still ruling in the midst of this. And he will use even this terrible thing for his Father's glory and for the good of those who love him."

WE ARE ENGAGED IN A BIGGER WORLD

Our age has mixed feelings when it comes to the supernatural. On the one hand, the dominant voice in higher learning today is the materialist. A materialist is one who believes that physical matter is the fundamental, indeed the only, reality and that scientific, biological explanations are sufficient to describe human experience. On the other hand, in popular culture—just look at movies and television—attention to the supernatural and interest in spirituality appear to be everywhere.

But it's not just the culture at large that has ambivalent feelings about the spiritual realm. People of faith, despite our professed belief in the supernatural, struggle with compartmentalizing the spiritual truths we hear about from the real world in which we live. The temptation always looms to draw a hard line between the sacred and the secular, to separate our spiritual life from our earthly life. In fact, philosopher Charles Taylor says this line of demarcation characterizes our time, which he calls "a Secular Age."[20]

But Jesus and the New Testament writers draw no such dividing lines. They assume that heaven and earth interpenetrate one another as part of one seamless tapestry. On three occasions, Jesus refers to Satan as "the ruler of this world" (e.g., John 16:11). And Paul calls him "the prince of the power of the air" (Eph. 2:2) and reminds his readers that "we wrestle not against flesh and blood, but against principalities, against powers" (6:12 KJV). This isn't the place to spell out exactly what these powers and principalities are, or what the "rulers or authorities" (Col. 1:16) encompass, but suffice it to say that the biblical writers assume there are invisible but real spiritual powers diffused throughout our world, influencing not just individuals but also institutions and governments, indeed, the very structures that make up our world.[21] The Bible assumes that the stage on which history is being played out is cosmic, containing visible *and* invisible realities.

For example, throughout the book of Revelation, there is a correspondence between an unseen spiritual war and the visible conflicts on earth. The happenings on earth are understood in terms of an ongoing spiritual battle between the victorious Christ and the spiritual powers that still challenge his reign and rule.

All this may sound fantastical to us, yet it is not too hard to imagine that behind some of the injustice and evil we see today, behind unjust and tyrannical regimes, behind sex trafficking and the pornography industry, behind totalitarian oppression, persistent racism, child soldiers, and horrific evil stand not only a few isolated bad seeds but real, albeit invisible, powers of darkness. You can dismiss this as primitive and superstitious, the relic of an outworn mythology. But as poet Charles Baudelaire once said, "This is the devil's greatest trick, convincing people he doesn't exist."[22]

How Do These Invisible Powers Relate to Our Daily Union with Christ?

When Jesus was crucified, it's true that he was dying for the sins of the world (1 John 2:2). But more was happening than this. In Colossians 2:15, Paul gives one of the most vivid pictures in Scripture of what was also happening at the crucifixion: "He disarmed the rulers and authorities and put them to open shame, by triumphing over them in him."

These "rulers and authorities" are spiritual powers that oppose God's rule. On the cross, the Bible is saying, Jesus put them to shame. That is, he exposed their pretense, their false claims to authority, by "triumphing over them." Paul draws on the image of a victorious Roman general leading a triumphal procession of prisoners who are compelled to submit against their wills to a power they cannot resist.[23] What was happening when Christ was hanging on the cross? Commentator F. F. Bruce puts it eloquently:

> As he was suspended there, bound hand and foot
> to the wood in apparent weakness, [the powers

> and principalities] imagined they had him at their
> mercy, and flung themselves on him with hostile
> intent. But, far from suffering their attack without
> resistance, he grappled with them and mastered
> them, stripping them of the armor in which they
> trusted, and held them aloft in his outstretched
> hands, displaying to the universe their helplessness
> and his own unvanquished strength.[24]

The cross of Christ is the victory of God (oh, strange victory!) over all the powers of this world that pretend to be absolute. "Nothing now is absolute except God as he is known in Jesus Christ; everything else is relativized."[25] This means Christ is not just your individual savior, who came to save you from your individual sins and then whisk you away from this world. Rather, Jesus is the King of all creation, who in the most unlikely place and in the most unlikely fashion, unmasked, disarmed, and defeated these opposing powers with his own bleeding hands. By death, he defeated death and "the one who has the power of death" (Heb. 2:14; 1 John 3:8).

This means that all the structures that are so important to our daily lives—our families, our careers, our companies, our nation—all of these authorities that demand our devotion have been put in their place, their subordinate place, "that in everything [Christ] might be preeminent" (Col. 1:18). And "he must reign until he has put all his enemies under his feet" (1 Cor. 15:25).

Today, the battle rages on. The rivals to Christ's supremacy have been decisively defeated but not yet destroyed. In Christ, as Christ's body, we engage these powers, seen and unseen, in the humble confidence that we are united to our King. He must win the battle, and he will. And one day he will return as King, to complete the new creation his own resurrection has begun. It has begun.

For now, he has not left us to our own resources. It's easy to look at our lives and to complain about what we haven't been given or murmur over what's going wrong or what we are missing. Yet, united to this Christ, how could we ever become cynical or feel that we have not been given enough? "For all things are yours … the world or life or death or the present or the future—all are yours, and you are Christ's" (1 Cor. 3:21–23). Sinclair Ferguson comments, "That gives union to Christ a very important practical dimension. It is not to be thought of primarily as a subjective experience which encourages us to look in and down. Rather it is something which lifts us up and out."[26]

WE ARE LOVED WITH A DEEPER LOVE

Head spinning yet? Back in time, forward in time, around the world, things high above and things dark and shadowy. Poet Robert Frost once said, "I have it in me so much nearer home / To scare myself with my own desert places."[27] Yet even into these dark crevices of the human heart, Christ reaches. Union with Christ assures us there is no depth to which humanity can go that God's love cannot reach and redeem. The King James Version of Psalm 139 puts it beautifully:

> Whither shall I go from thy spirit? or whither shall
> I flee from thy presence?
> If I ascend up into heaven, thou art there: if I make
> my bed in hell, behold, thou art there.

As we look at ourselves, we may see only failure or disgrace, but this is neither the whole truth nor the final truth about who we are in Christ. Jesus sees into the very depths of our shame and pours his love into these broken places.

God in Christ reaches all the way down into the depths of the human experience and pulls us all the way up into his very life (John 14:23; 17:23). It is "staggering, but it is the case."[28] This doesn't mean that we become divine in the sense that God's essence is infused into ours. It means that we are called "into the divine family."[29] We don't become something more than human. We become fully human when God joins his life to ours.

The highest good of human life, indeed the purpose of creation and redemption, is communion with God. By rooting and grounding our lives in something so much greater than ourselves, God convinces us, beyond our ability to comprehend, that we are loved in a way "that surpasses knowledge" (Eph. 3:19).

We have communion with all three persons of the Trinity, each in turn; and each in turn cares for us and ministers to us. This is how union with the cosmic Christ becomes an everyday reality—as the Father, Son, and Holy Spirit impress these truths on our hearts and minds even as we labor to be brought near.[30]

We have communion with the love of God the Father. Perhaps you don't have trouble believing that Jesus loves you, but God the Father remains a shadowy figure, distant and dark. Adding to this distance, sometimes we speak as if Jesus had to die to convince or coerce his Father into loving us, as if the Father were unwilling. But this is a tragic misunderstanding of God's heart. It is only because God the Father loved us first, while we were yet his enemies, that he was willing to deliver up his only Son for us (Rom. 8:32). Such is the love of God the Father, with whom we now have communion. What heights of love!

We have communion with the grace of our Lord Jesus Christ, who is full of "grace upon grace" (John 1:16). Jesus, the only child of God by nature, is yet not ashamed to welcome us into his family by adoption through his blood. Our communion with God the Father is made possible by the grace of our Lord Jesus, who is our mediator (1 Tim. 2:5) and who never grows tired of us or weary of dispensing his grace. What depths of peace!

And we have communion with the Holy Spirit, our comforter and advocate. In the courtroom of our conscience, when the voice of our own heart rises up to condemn us (1 John 3:20), the Spirit of God bears witness with ours that we are God's children (Rom. 8:16) and gives us, beyond what words alone could, certainty of our salvation by pointing us back to our Savior (John 16:14). The Spirit subjectively assures us of what is objectively true. What blessed assurance!

LARGER, BROADER, LONGER, BIGGER, DEEPER

If I've made it sound as though union with Christ touches on everything God has given us in the gospel, well, that's because it does. Union with Christ is cosmic in its scope, and we have only peeked through the telescope at its unfathomable expanses.

The Christ who is the head of this new family; who has inaugurated this new mission; who is the clue to understanding the story of your own life and also of all history; who has decisively defeated all challengers to his power and authority; the Christ before whom everything is relativized—we are united to this Christ. And through him we have been called up into God's own life. Isn't it fitting, then, that our heads should spin?

When you consider the cosmic dimensions of our union with Christ, can we do anything but break out in wonder and praise? "Oh, the depth of the riches and wisdom and knowledge of God!" (Rom. 11:33).

Over and against a shallow emotionalism that reduces the things of God only to how they impact us individually, but also over and against an arid intellectualism that reduces the things of God to abstract doctrines of cold assent, union with Christ brings together what we so desperately need today: the highest theology and the deepest spirituality. Union with Christ holds together God and life like nothing else can because it shows us that these are inseparable.

Union with Christ shows us truth is not an abstract idea to be understood. Truth is a Person to whom we are united and in whom our lives are rooted and grounded in love. This is what it means to be saved—to be united to him who is grace and truth, justice and peace.

Final Word

A PRAYER FOR UNION WITH CHRIST

For this reason I bow my knees before the Father, from whom every family in heaven and on earth is named, that according to the riches of his glory he may grant you to be strengthened with power through his Spirit in your inner being, so that Christ may dwell in your hearts through faith—that you, being rooted and grounded in love, may have strength to comprehend with all the saints what is the breadth and length and height and depth, and to know the love of Christ that surpasses knowledge, that you may be filled with all the fullness of God.

Ephesians 3:14–19

DO YOU KNOW WHAT YOU KNOW?

The prayer above is well known and well loved, so much so that it can be easy to miss what is so unusual about it. Paul prays, "That Christ may dwell in your hearts" (3:17). And yet, the letter to the Ephesians is addressed to those who already know Christ (1:1). Elsewhere Paul makes it clear that a follower of Jesus is, by definition, one in whom

Christ dwells (Rom. 8:9). So why does he ask for Christ to dwell in their hearts? Why does Paul pray for what must already be the case?

Ephesians 3 is a prayer for what preacher Martyn Lloyd-Jones once called "experiential knowledge."[1] To return to the theme we touched on in the introduction to this book, it's one thing to know the truth, but it's another thing altogether for this truth to come alive, capture our imaginations, and change our lives. Our imagination must be renewed by the reality of our union with Christ.

To bring our book around full circle, this is a prayer that acknowledges the *gap* between the inheritance we've been given and our present experience of how we see ourselves (filled with all the fullness of God, really?). This is a prayer for the gap to be closed, or at least narrowed, that we may *know* the riches of our glorious inheritance, that we may *know* "the love of Christ that surpasses knowledge," that we "may be filled with all the fullness of God."

This is no small request! Paul does pray for strength and power to comprehend it, after all. But nevertheless, he prays. Not for the supersaints, not for only the most deeply committed or those furthest along. Paul prays for all of his readers, for the names with which we began this book, for Melissa and Thom, for Lucy and Bill, for you and for me. He prays that we might *know* our union with Christ in all its cosmic dimensions—its "breadth and length and height and depth." This is a prayer that we might experience what we believe.

In light of all we have touched on in this book, "every spiritual blessing" that has been given to you "in Christ" (Eph. 1:3) and the glorious inheritance that is yours in him (v. 18), it must be asked: Do you know the riches of your inheritance?

DO YOU KNOW THE RICHES OF WHAT YOU HAVE?

Imagine you inherited a bank account with $100 million in it, bequeathed to you by someone who loved you dearly. You are aware of this treasure. You have been given a deposit guaranteeing your inheritance (Eph. 1:14). You receive weekly statements reminding you of your substantial balance (that is, you go to church). But suppose you have never drawn down on this fortune. You remain in dire poverty, living paycheck to paycheck. From one point of view, you are exceedingly wealthy, but insofar as how you live, you remain poor. You know you are wealthy beyond imagining, but you don't really *know* your wealth.

If your reluctance to draw on your inheritance were born of a true modesty, it might be commendable. But perhaps it stems from a refusal to accept such a lavish gift: "Oh no, I don't deserve anything like that. That would be too much. I'll just keep the life I have." Or maybe it stems from fear or an unwillingness to risk, or even begin to imagine how, and how much, your life can change. "I'll just remain as I am, thank you."

Does this not describe how so many of us are living?

It's like living in a trailer while millions of dollars worth of oil course underneath the land you own. Untapped. All this time untold riches have been right under our noses, but most of us keep on living the life we know. Even if we aren't particularly happy with it, at least it's familiar. We modestly decline rather than embrace a risk-filled, unknown future.

The children of Israel, wandering in the wilderness, yearned to return to Egypt. They actually preferred the idea of returning to slavery (Num. 11:5) because the Promised Land ahead was unknown and terrifying to them (Deut. 1:28). But unlike those children of God who went before us, our promised land, our horizon, is known (Heb. 11:12–16). What they sought and looked forward to, a better country, a heavenly one—the door to this city has now been opened to us.

On this journey, we walk along the narrow road, taking the hard, uphill way. Yet we do not labor under the threat or suspicion that God is disappointed in us or that we must arrive before he will embrace us. He is near, closer to us than any other relationship we have, closer than we can imagine. God is with us—that is his name. And so, like a child learning to pedal his own bicycle, we press on, day after day, pedal by pedal, in faith and repentance, confident that our Father is not only with us but also for us. *He's got you.* We can move forward on this journey in confidence and joy to take hold of that for which Christ Jesus has already taken hold of us.

Along the way, Paul prays for us because he is all too aware that it is one thing to have this inheritance but another thing altogether to live out of it so that it changes the substance of our daily lives.

Paul isn't praying for Christ to be present with you. If you are a Christian, Christ already is. He is praying for you to know of yourself "I am one in whom Christ Jesus dwells." He is praying for your awareness of your union with Christ. He is praying that you would *know* what you know—for the gap to be narrowed—until the day when faith becomes sight and we see him, face to face, who has already, all this time, been there beside us.

Until that day, how can we possibly participate in these heavenly realities as we walk around in our mundane lives of grocery shopping, bill paying, traffic jams, and CAT scans? That's been the driving question of this book. It will take some imagination—not to call to mind what is unreal, but to set your mind on what is real yet unseen.

> What no eye has seen, nor ear heard,
> nor the heart of man imagined,
> what God has prepared for those who love him.
> (1 Cor. 2:9)

My hope is that, as we recover union with Christ—the depth and the wonder of it, the mystery and beauty of it—we will recover something greater than we could ever understand. For while it is beyond our understanding (it "surpasses knowledge," Paul says), it is not beyond our possessing.

ACKNOWLEDGMENTS

This book is the product of a long conversation, and I have had many conversation partners beyond those mentioned in the endnotes, though I am deeply indebted to them and grateful to be walking in the path others have blazed.

My hope is that this book will find an audience among those who don't normally read books on theology, as it was written to return union with Christ to prominence in the place it most belongs, in the lives of so-called ordinary men and women. But it is also my hope that union with Christ will capture the imaginations of the formative voices of pastors and teachers, so as to change the conversation at large going forward as to *what is the gospel* and *how do we talk about salvation*.

I'd like to thank my almost-daily sounding board, men of generous spirit, sharp minds, and pastoral hearts. Sons of thunder Ben Milner and Peter, his brother; Russ Hightower and Chris Ziegler. Paul Cagle and Patrick O'Mara, who know where the bodies are buried.

The scholars who have graciously lent their time and expertise to reading and improving portions of this manuscript, Dick Gaffin and Adam Neder and Brian Gregor. And the pastors who have done the same, Stephen Phelan and Eric Youngblood. And to Skip Ryan and Mike Milton, who have taught me about success.

John Ortberg, who went out of his way to invest in someone he had never met. The people of David C Cook who encouraged and invested in a first-time author. Tim Keller, whose fingerprints are all over this book. And Joe Novenson, whose fingerprints are all over my life.

To the staff and Session and people of Pacific Crossroads Church, most especially Chris, John and Julie, Paul and Jeremy, Melissa, Milla, Alex and Grace, and other friends from our community who gave their time and feedback: Tyler, Thom, Allen, Jamaal, Shannon, Francis, and Stephen Kim, my advocate. Chris Chown, my spiritual friend and research assistant.

To my family, Glen and Carole, Dave and Sheela, Paul and Sally. Hannah. To my big sister, Caroline, who is always looking out for her little brother with a penny loafer in hand. To my mom, an English teacher who gave me a love of words and who has read about ninety-eight versions of most of these chapters. Thanks, Mom. I'm done. To Jack, Emi Bea, and Will, who lent their parents to this project and kept us laughing all along the way.

And to the one to whom this book is not only dedicated but who sacrificed more than anyone will ever know, the big-city girl who married the small-town boy. "You have been such light to me that other women have been your shadows." Not only my editor but the one most responsible for any beautiful sentence in this book. My best friend, my Beatrice, my wife. Tomorrow the sun will shine again, Morgen.

NOTES

INTRODUCTION

1. G. K. Chesterton, "Ethics of Elfland," *Orthodoxy* (Chicago: Moody Classics, 2009), 82.

2. Chesterton, *Orthodoxy*, 82.

3. Albert Einstein, quoted in "What Life Means to Einstein: An Interview by George Sylvester Viereck," *Saturday Evening Post*, October 26, 1929.

4. Walter Brueggemann, *Interpretation and Obedience: From Faithful Reading to Faithful Living* (Minneapolis: Fortress, 1991), 199.

5. It's not a perfect analogy, and here's one place the analogy breaks down: while physical DNA is with you from birth and you have no control over it or choice in the matter, the spiritual DNA of the Holy Spirit is given to you at a certain point in your life when God regenerates your heart and you respond in faith.

6. J. I. Packer, *Knowing God* (Downers Grove, IL: InterVarsity, 1993), 218.

7. John Calvin, *Institutes of the Christian Religion*, ed. John T. McNeill, trans. Ford Lewis Battles (Philadelphia: Westminster, 1960), 3.1.1.

8. C. S. Lewis, *Surprised by Joy* (New York: Harcourt Brace Jovanovich, 1984), 181.

CHAPTER 1: LIVING IN THE GAP

1. *Tender Mercies*, directed by Bruce Beresford (1983; Santa Monica, CA: Lionsgate, 2009), DVD.

2. "The Writer's Almanac," email, January 1, 2016.

3. John Newton, "Thoughts upon the African Slave Trade," accessed February 29, 2016, http://thriceholy.net/Texts/African.html.

4. Ernest Hemingway, *The Sun Also Rises* (New York: Simon & Schuster, 1954), 251.

5. T. S. Eliot, "East Coker," *The Four Quartets* (San Diego: Harvest, 1971), 29.

6. John Calvin, *Institutes of the Christian Religion*, ed. John T. McNeill, trans. Ford Lewis Battles (Philadelphia: Westminster, 1960), 3.11.10.

7. Calvin, *Institutes*, 3.11.10.

8. Jonathan Edwards, *The Works of Jonathan Edwards*, vol. 2, ed. Patrick H. Alexander (Peabody, MA: Hendrickson, 1998), Kindle location 89700.

9. Thomas Goodwin, *Of Christ the Mediator*, cited in *A Puritan Theology: Doctrine for Life*, ed. Joel R. Beeke and Mark Jones (Grand Rapids, MI: Reformation Heritage Books, 2012), 483.

10. Robert Letham, *Union with Christ in Scripture, History, and Theology* (Phillipsburg, NJ: P&R, 2001), 1.

11. Lane G. Tipton, "Union with Christ and Justification," in *Justified in Christ: God's Plan for Us in Justification*, ed. K. Scott Oliphint (Fearn, Scotland: Mentor, 2007), 34.

12. Robert Reymond, *A New Systematic Theology of the Christian Faith*, 2nd ed. (Nashville: Thomas Nelson, 2010), dccclix.

13. J. Todd Billings, *Union with Christ* (Grand Rapids, MI: Baker Academic, 2011), 1.

14. J. I. Packer, *A Quest for Godliness: The Puritan Vision of the Christian Life* (Wheaton, IL: Crossway Books, 1990), 202.

15. Marcus Peter Johnson, *One with Christ: An Evangelical Theology of Salvation* (Wheaton, IL: Crossway Books, 2013), 29.

16. John Murray, *Redemption Accomplished and Applied* (Grand Rapids, MI: Eerdmans, 1955), 161.

17. Calvin, *Institutes*, 3.11.10.

18. John Owen, *Communion with the Triune God*, ed. Kelly M. Kapic and Justin Taylor (Wheaton, IL: Crossway Books, 2007), 123.

19. John Owen, quoted in *Puritan Theology*, ed. Beeke and Jones, 112.

20. John Owen, *An Exposition of the Epistle to the Hebrews*, in *The Works of John Owen*, vol. 20 (Edinburgh: Banner of Truth, 1991), 148, cited in *Puritan Theology*, ed. Beeke and Jones, 483.

21. John Owen wrote, "'The grace of our Lord Jesus Christ be with you all.' Yea, [Paul] makes these two, 'Grace be with you,' and, 'The Lord Jesus be with you' to be equivalent expressions." As quoted by Sinclair Ferguson, who added that this may be one of Owen's most important theological insights: "Grace is, ultimately, personal. Grace is Jesus Christ; Jesus Christ is God's grace. For grace is not substantial in the sense of being a quality or entity that can be abstracted from the person of the Savior." Ferguson, *The Trinitarian Devotion of John Owen* (Lake Mary, FL: Reformation Trust, 2014), Kindle location 801.

22. C. S. Lewis, *The Last Battle* (New York: Collier, 1986), 163. Others have pointed out how central the theme of union with Christ is to the writing of C. S. Lewis (see Leanne Payne's book *Real Presence*). This might explain why the notion of union with Christ is even vaguely familiar to many Christians, because it was so central for one of the twentieth century's most significant Christian authors.

CHAPTER 2: UNION WITH CHRIST: WHAT IS IT?

1. John Calvin, *Commentary on Ephesians*, chap. V.32, cited in Marcus Peter Johnson, *One with Christ: An Evangelical Theology of Salvation* (Wheaton, IL: Crossway Books, 2013), 49.

2. Richard Longenecker, *Word Biblical Commentary: Galatians* (Dallas: Word Books, 1990), 159.

3. Herman Ridderbos, *Paul: An Outline of His Theology* (Grand Rapids, MI: Eerdmans, 1997), 38.

4. The Son of God assumed our full human nature to redeem our full human nature. Jesus was "born of woman" (Gal. 4:4) "in the likeness of sinful flesh" (Rom. 8:3). He was tempted in every way as we are, so that he is able to sympathize with us, and yet he was without sin (Heb. 4:15). Though he was innocent, he "gave himself for our sins" (Gal. 1:4) and died in our place (1

Pet. 3:18) to deliver us from the power of death (Heb. 2:14). He was raised for us (Rom. 4:25) that we too might pass from death to life (John 11:25). He "ascended far above all the heavens" (Eph. 4:10), where he sits "at the right hand of God" (Col. 3:1) and "lives to make intercession for [us]" (Heb. 7:25), as our "high priest forever" (Heb. 6:20).

5. Charles Wesley, "Christ the Lord Is Risen Today," in *Trinity Hymnal* (Atlanta: Great Commission, 1990), 277.

6. Sinclair Ferguson, *The Holy Spirit* (Downers Grove, IL: InterVarsity, 1996), 71.

7. John Murray, *Redemption Accomplished and Applied* (Grand Rapids, MI: Eerdmans, 1955), 172.

8. John Calvin, *Institutes of the Christian Religion*, ed. John T. McNeill, trans. Ford Lewis Battles (Philadelphia: Westminster, 1960), 3.11.10. *Mysticism* is a notoriously vague word in the history of Christian spirituality, but we shouldn't let the abuses of this word prevent us from being staggered by the mystery of our union with Christ. For this reason, even these most careful of theologians, Murray and Calvin, do not hesitate to use the word *mysticism*. See chapter 6 for a fuller treatment.

9. Special thanks to my friend Paul Kim for this helpful analogy.

10. C. S. Lewis, *Letters to an American Lady*, ed. Clyde S. Kilby (Grand Rapids, MI: Eerdmans, 1967), 36–37.

11. Flannery O'Connor, *The Habit of Being* (New York: Noonday, 1995), 477.

12. To address concerns some readers may have about where I stand on the "New Perspective" on justification: I hold to the traditional Protestant understanding of justification as a legal, forensic, declarative verdict, the imputation of our sins to Christ and the imputation of his righteousness to us by faith. My interest in union with Christ is not to open the door to a concession on justification. My concern is that the desire to protect a historic understanding of justification has led to an overcorrection, and subsequently to our letting go of the overriding importance of union with Christ as the *ground* of both justification and sanctification. Such that union with Christ, if it is mentioned at all, gets reduced to some aspect of what happens *after* salvation. It gets reduced to an aspect of Christian experience, rather than the foundation of it. Consequently, our focus has shifted to understanding the mechanics of Christ's work, often divorced from Christ's person. Doctrine can then become abstract, something to be understood and mastered. This is perhaps why some seem to love theology more

than we love people, even more than we love God, because we concentrate on wanting others to understand the work of Christ, as opposed to emphasizing that Christ's work always flows out of what is even more basic than our understanding of it, that is, our actual communion with God through the person of Christ. Theology is important, even vital. This book is all about theology. And yet, it is not our theology, or the presumed accuracy of it, that saves us. It is the perfect Christ who saves us, not our imperfect theology or our imperfect faith. For more on this idea, see Marcus Peter Johnson's important book, *One with Christ*, pages 52–53.

13. While many have made this point, see especially James B. Torrance, *Worship, Community and the Triune Grace of God* (Downers Grove, IL: InterVarsity, 1996), 34.

CHAPTER 3: WHY WE NEED IT: TWO SONGS PLAYING IN OUR HEADS

1. See Jay Parini, *The Last Station: A Novel of Tolstoy's Final Year* (New York: Knopf Doubleday, 2010).

2. See the book *unChristian* by David Kinnaman and Gabe Lyons, full of research about perceptions of the church today. "One of the surprising insights from our research is that the growing hostility toward Christians is very much a reflection of what outsiders feel they receive from believers. They say their aggression simply matches the oversized opinions and egos of Christians. One outsider put it this way: 'Most people I meet assume that *Christian* means very conservative, entrenched in their thinking, antigay, antichoice, angry, violent, illogical, empire builders; they want to convert everyone, and they generally cannot live peacefully with anyone who doesn't believe what they believe'" ([Grand Rapids, MI: Baker Books, 2007], 26).

3. Brennan Manning, *All Is Grace: A Ragamuffin Memoir* (Colorado Springs: David C Cook, 2011), 192–94. This quote is from a later book, but it distills the essence of the controlling idea in Manning's earlier works.

4. This was a theme Nouwen returned to over and over in his works—receiving the love of God, letting yourself be loved by God, being the beloved. As he put it, "The question is not 'How am I to know God?' but 'How am I to let myself be known by God?' And, finally, the question is not 'How am I to love God?' but 'How am I to let myself be loved by God?' God is looking into the distance for me, trying to find me, and longing to bring me home." *The Return of the Prodigal Son* (New York: Image Doubleday, 1994), 106.

5. See Kenneth E. Bailey's book *The Cross and the Prodigal*, which highlights the significance of the father running toward his son.

6. Tobias Wolff, *Old School* (New York: Vintage, 2004), 195.

7. For a masterful extended treatment of this story, see Timothy Keller's *The Prodigal God*.

8. Dietrich Bonhoeffer, *The Cost of Discipleship* (New York: Collier-Macmillan, 1963), 45, 47, 55, 60.

9. Bonhoeffer, *Cost of Discipleship*, 55. This might offend some sensibilities, so it's worth quoting John Calvin also at this point. "For when [repentance] is rightly understood it will better appear how man is justified by faith alone, and simple pardon; nevertheless actual holiness of life, so to speak, is not separated from free imputation of righteousness." *Institutes of the Christian Religion*, ed. John T. McNeill, trans. Ford Lewis Battles (Philadelphia: Westminster, 1960), 3.3.1. He's saying there is no justification without sanctification.

10. Manning, *All Is Grace*, 194.

11. Bonhoeffer, *Cost of Discipleship*, 58.

12. Bonhoeffer, *Cost of Discipleship*, 55.

13. Dallas Willard, *The Great Omission: Rediscovering Jesus' Essential Teachings on Discipleship* (San Francisco: HarperOne, 2006), 226.

14. Dallas Willard, *The Divine Conspiracy: Rediscovering Our Hidden Life in God* (San Francisco: HarperSanFrancisco, 1998), 41.

15. Willard, *Divine Conspiracy*, 37.

16. Willard, *Divine Conspiracy*, 301.

17. It is striking that the twentieth-century theologian Karl Barth lists sloth alongside pride as the deadliest of the deadly sins.

18. "Indeed, we shall not say that, properly speaking, God is known where there is no religion or piety." Calvin, *Institutes*, 1.2.1. Calvin here and elsewhere insists that piety—real life correspondence to God's character—is inseparable from any true knowledge of God.

19. I'm deliberately referring to two books in conversation with each other: *Radical* by David Platt and *Ordinary* by Michael Horton. This conversation is an example of the tension between these two songs that the church is facing today.

20. Bonhoeffer, *Cost of Discipleship*, 74, 76.

21. Calvin, *Institutes*, 3.11.10.

22. Calvin, *Institutes*, 3.11.6.

23. Calvin, *Commentary on John 6*, "They sought in Christ something other than Christ himself," cited in Julie Canlis's essay, "Sonship, Identity and Transformation," in *Sanctification: Explorations in Theology and Practice* (Downers Grove, IL: InterVarsity, 2014), Kindle location 3731.

24. Paraphrased from Calvin, *Institutes*, 3.11.6 in Richard B. Gaffin, "Justification and Union with Christ," in *A Theological Guide to Calvin's Institutes: Essays and Analysis*, ed. David W. Hall and Peter A. Lillback (Phillipsburg, NJ: P&R, 2008), 268.

25. Leo Tolstoy, *My Religion*, quoted in *Religion from Tolstoy to Camus*, ed. Walter Kaufmann (New Brunswick: Transaction, 1961), 45.

26. Quoted in Phillip Yancey, *The Jesus I Never Knew* (Grand Rapids, MI: Zondervan, 2002), 138.

27. Quoted in Yancey, *Jesus I Never Knew*, 139.

28. See www.fightthenewdrug.org.

29. Let's take an example of a socially approved medicating agent: work. The addiction cycle runs like this:

Step 1: Pain, anxiety, feelings of inferiority. These are an inescapable part of life.

Step 2: Medicating agent—we seek to salve our pain through, in this example, working hard or doing a good job to validate ourselves.

Step 3: Temporary relief—praise! Reward! Accolades and achievement! It works, temporarily …

Step 4: Negative consequences—but your relationships suffer from your overwork. Or your body starts to give out from the stress.

Step 5: Shame/guilt—Why am I doing this? Why am I working so hard? Why am I neglecting what I know is more important, my relationships? Which only makes you feel worse and leads you back to step 1.

And the hook is set. You become stuck in a circular pattern of negative reinforcement. You know you're addicted when you seek to medicate yourself with the very substance that sent you spiraling downward in the first place. For more on this cycle, see Robert Hemfelt and Richard Fowler, *Serenity: A Companion for Twelve Step Recovery* (Nashville: Thomas Nelson, 2010), 22–23.

30. Here I'm speaking generally about all idols that might enslave us, but there are certainly some addictions that require the help of a supportive recovery community in order to overcome.

CHAPTER 4: UNION WITH CHRIST IN THE BIBLE

1. Sandra Richter, *The Epic of Eden: A Christian Entry into the Old Testament* (Downers Grove, IL: IVP Academic, 2008), 18.

2. Richter, *Epic of Eden*, 15.

3. Richard B. Hays and N. T. Wright have done a great service to New Testament scholarship by highlighting the narrative substructure of the New Testament, understanding it as the culmination of Israel's story.

4. A great complement to Richter's book is Greg Beale's *The Temple and the Mission of God*. Beale and Richter together show how at its heart the temple has always been about the presence of God. "Let them make me a sanctuary, that I may dwell in their midst" (Exod. 25:8). They show how the iconography of the temple (cherubim, palm trees, flowers and fruit, rivers and gold) as it unfolds through the Bible always looks back to the Garden of Eden even as it always looks ahead to the New Jerusalem.

5. Luke 24:27; Gen. 12:3; 2 Sam. 7:12–13; 2 Cor. 1:20; John 5:39.

6. Matt. 3:15; Gal. 3:13; Ps. 23:1; John 10:11; John 1:29; Heb. 2:14; 1 John 3:8.

7. 1 Cor. 15:3; 1 Cor. 2:2; 1 Pet. 1:19.

8. Jonathan Edwards writes, "What is it which chiefly makes you desire to go to heaven when you die? … Is the main reason, that you may be with God, have communion with Him, and be conformed to Him? That you may see God and enjoy Him there? Is this the consideration which keeps your hearts, and your desires, and your expectations toward heaven? … Could you be content to stand in no child-like relation to God, enjoying no gracious intercourse with Him, having no right to be acknowledged by Him as His children? Or would such a life as this, though in ever so great earthly prosperity, be esteemed by you a miserable life?" in "God the Best Portion of the Christian," in *The Works of Jonathan Edwards*, vols. 1–2 (Edinburgh: Banner of Truth, 2011), Kindle locations 59215–59219, 59240–59241.

9. If you're interested in reading more about this theme, John Walton's books are a great place to start, in particular *The Lost World of Genesis One* and *Ancient Near Eastern Thought and the Old Testament*.

10. "The Pauline theme of union with Christ has risen to prominence in the current world of New Testament scholarship." Constantine Campbell, *Paul and Union with Christ* (Grand Rapids, MI: Zondervan, 2012), 31. Of particular interest has been the relationship of union with Christ and justification, with some seeming to think that union with Christ has made justification (as understood by the Protestant reformers) less central or important, or that it has made the imputation of Christ's righteousness unnecessary. That's not my conviction. We don't have to choose between justification and union with Christ. We can hold on to justification as a forensic, onetime legal declaration and, at the same time, have a robust understanding of the importance of union with Christ. Nor am I interested in parsing out whether union with Christ is the grounds of justification or if, on the other hand, justification is that which makes union possible. That remains a hot topic among some Reformed theologians. What I hope all sides can agree on is that union with Christ is important, has too long been neglected, and needs to be restored and reemphasized. For further reading on the importance of union with Christ to the apostle Paul, see Richard B. Gaffin Jr., *By Faith, Not by Sight: Paul and the Order of Salvation* (Phillipsburg, NJ: P&R, 2013).

11. Campbell, *Paul and Union with Christ*, 441.

12. Lewis B. Smedes, *Union with Christ: A Biblical View of the New Life in Jesus Christ* (Grand Rapids, MI: Eerdmans, 1983), 55.

13. Nicolaus Cabasilas, *Life in Christ*, trans. Margaret I. Lisney (London: Janus, 1995), 5, cited in Robert Letham, *Union with Christ: In Scripture, History, and Theology* (Phillipsburg, NJ: P&R, 2011), 99.

14. Dallas Willard quotes I. Howard Marshall, saying that over the course of sixteen years he recalled hearing only two sermons on the kingdom of God, and commented, "I find this silence rather surprising because it is universally agreed by New Testament scholars that the central theme of the teaching of Jesus was the Kingdom of God." Cited in *The Divine Conspiracy: Rediscovering Our Hidden Life in God* (San Francisco: HarperSanFrancisco, 1998), 59.

15. Tony Lane, quoted in Robert Letham, *Union with Christ: In Scripture, History, and Theology* (Phillipsburg, NJ: P&R, 2011), 7. That's not a perfect analogy because electricity is an impersonal force, but the implication is striking: unless we are connected to Christ, personally and vitally, all that he has done for us remains without power or value to us.

16. We'll look more at how our union with Christ changes our experience of reading the Bible in chapter 12.

17. To take a striking example, a preacher I respect for his unwavering commitment to grace is Paul Zahl. He says in his book *Grace in Practice*, "Grace ... comes under criticism in three of the larger letters of the New Testament: Hebrews, James and Second Peter" (Grand Rapids, MI: Eerdmans, 2007), 51. He continues, "Hebrews damages grace ... it is therefore at odds with the theology expressed almost everywhere else in the New Testament." He adds, "James comes to a different conclusion [from Paul] ... these positions are incompatible" (52–53). I'll provide one more example: "I am saying," Zahl says, "that the canon within the canon of grace covers just about all, but not absolutely all, of the biblical data ... are there exceptions to this? Yes but these are obvious exceptions. They stand out because of their inconsistency" (55). We need preachers like Zahl, who preach God's grace in the way it is meant, to shock our sensibilities. And yet, he presents a clear example of a *false choice* between Paul and James, or between Jesus and Hebrews. He assumes that we have to choose. What I appreciate about Zahl is that he has the courage and consistency to be honest about his convictions. Other writers and speakers, who might implicitly follow the same line of thought, would never be so bold, but this is how we may in practice still read the Bible. We turn down the warnings, for example, of Hebrews because we are not sure how to square them with God's grace. We just might not be as honest about our underlying convictions as Zahl. This book will argue that because of union with Christ you are not forced to make these false choices.

18. James 1:6–8; cf. 1:26; 2:9. It is fascinating that James never mentions the crucifixion or the resurrection of Jesus, even though they were obviously pivotal in his own life (1 Cor. 15:7). What could explain James not mentioning what is central to the faith? Only if he assumes his readers have already heard the good news and now he is explicating for them what a life of integrity, one that is not "double-minded," looks like (James 1:8). If you are in Christ, then this is the life to which Christ calls you. Examine yourself. But if you are in Christ, this is the life Christ can now give you. The union with Christ that James assumes (you couldn't be accused of adultery—James 4:4—unless you were married to Christ) thus allows you to read James at full volume, as opposed to James being "incompatible" with the apostle Paul. You can say the same thing for 1 John or Amos or Isaiah or any of the Old Testament prophets. For example, without turning down the warnings of Amos 5 or Isaiah 1, if you truly know God (Hos. 6:1–3), then your life will be marked by authentic worship, a concern to do good, and a love of justice. And if it doesn't look like this, then you don't truly know God. What God commands, God enables by dwelling within—if indeed he does.

CHAPTER 5: UNION WITH CHRIST IN THE HISTORIC TRADITION

1. "I know the place; it may perhaps be superstitious, but, whenever I go to Oxford, I cannot help running to the spot where Jesus Christ first revealed Himself to me, and gave me the new birth." Whitefield continues, "I read a little further, and discovered that they who know anything of religion know it is a vital union with the Son of God—Christ formed in the heart. O what a ray of divine life did then break in upon my soul! ... From that moment God has been carrying on His blessed work in my soul." Quoted in L. Tyerman, *The Life of the Rev. George Whitefield*, vol. 1 (New York: Anson D. F. Randolph, 1877), 27.

2. Henry Scougal, *The Life of God in the Soul of Man* (Mansfield Centre, CT: Martino, 2011), 30.

3. I'm not a professional theologian by training, only a pastoral one by trade, so professionals in each of these fields covered will have to forgive my oversimplifications.

4. Hans Boersma, *Heavenly Participation: The Weaving of a Sacramental Tapestry* (Grand Rapids, MI: Eerdmans, 2011), Kindle locations 39–40.

5. Robert Reymond, *A New Systematic Theology of the Christian Faith*, 2nd ed. (Nashville: Thomas Nelson, 2010), dccclix.

6. For further reading, see William B. Evans, *Imputation and Impartation* (Eugene, OR: Wipf & Stock, 2008), where he traces the development of and different understandings of union with Christ in the Reformed tradition.

7. Irenaeus, *Against Heresies*, bk. 3, chap. 19, par. 1, quoted in Donald Fairbairn, *Life in the Trinity: An Introduction to Theology with the Help of the Church Fathers* (Downers Grove, IL: InterVarsity, 2009), Kindle locations 794–97. Emphasis added.

8. Athanasius, *On Incarnation*, par. 54, cited in Fairbairn, *Life in the Trinity*, Kindle location 350.

9. Saint Augustine of Hippo, *The Trinity, XIII.12* (Hyde Park, NY: New City, 1991), 354.

10. Fairbairn, *Life in the Trinity*, 6–7. Fairbairn's book is particularly helpful in demonstrating that the early church often talked about the gospel in ways we have lost hold of today. I am indebted to Marcus Peter Johnson for directing me toward Fairbairn's work on this subject.

11. Charles Williams, *Descent of the Dove* (Oxford: Oxford University Press, 1939), 28.

12. Williams, *Descent of the Dove*, 28.

13. At the conclusion of his book *Participation in Christ: An Entry into Karl Barth's Church "Dogmatics,"* Adam Neder shows there is a great diversity and breadth in how the words *theosis* or *deification* have been and can be understood and makes a strong and welcome case for the widespread recovery of this language across theological traditions, East and West (Louisville: Westminster John Knox, 2009).

14. Calvin references Bernard second in frequency only to Augustine, and these are the only two writers that he almost always cites approvingly. See Dennis E. Tamburello, *Union with Christ: John Calvin and the Mysticism of St. Bernard* (Louisville: Westminster John Knox, 1994).

15. Like the early church fathers, Bernard frequently equated the Holy Spirit's presence as a kiss on the believer's life.

16. Bernard of Clairvaux, "Sermon 2.II.3," in *Classics of Western Spirituality, Bernard of Clairvaux: Selected Works* (New York: Paulist, 1987), 217.

17. Martin Luther, *Luther's Works, Vol. 31: Career of the Reformer*, ed. J. J. Pelikan, H. C. Oswald, and H. T. Lehmann (Philadelphia: Fortress, 1999), 351.

18. In recent years, Lutheran scholars in Finland have argued for the recognition of a more central place of union with Christ in Luther's theology. See Carl E. Braaten and Robert W. Jenson, eds., *Union with Christ: The New Finnish Interpretation of Luther* (Grand Rapids, MI: Eerdmans, 1998). I am not convinced by the Finnish School's claim that it's the *center* of his theology, but it does seem indisputable that union with Christ was important to Luther. For more on union with Christ in Luther and Calvin, see Marcus Peter Johnson, *One with Christ: An Evangelical Theology of Salvation* (Wheaton, IL: Crossway Books, 2013), 51–57.

19. And apparently, I was not alone in my surprise. "What was shocking to me," writes theologian Marcus Peter Johnson, "was the way in which Calvin spoke of salvation." Johnson, *One with Christ*, 11. I read Johnson's book while writing this one and felt like I had discovered a kindred spirit, as he shares my passion for recovering union with Christ. If you want a sampling of great historical quotes on the subject or a detailed look at how union with Christ frames "the order of salvation," you should most certainly read Johnson's book.

20. John Calvin, *Institutes of the Christian Religion*, ed. John T. McNeill, trans. Ford Lewis Battles (Philadelphia: Westminster, 1960), 3.11.11.

21. Calvin, *Institutes*, 3.11.10.

22. Calvin, *Institutes*, 3.1.1.

23. One of the best quotes on the significance of union with Christ in all of Calvin's writings is: "When we see that the whole sum of our salvation and every single part of it, are comprehended in Christ, we must beware of deriving the minutest portion of it from any other quarter. If we seek salvation, we are taught by the very name of Jesus that he possesses it. If we seek any other gifts of the Spirit, we shall find them in his unction; strength in his government; purity in his conception; indulgence in his nativity, in which he was made like us in all respects, in order that he might learn to sympathize with us. If we seek redemption, we shall find it in his passion; acquittal in his condemnation; remission of the curse in his cross; satisfaction in his sacrifice; purification in his blood; reconciliation in his descent into hell; mortification of the flesh in his sepulcher; newness of life in his resurrection; immortality also in his resurrection; the inheritance of a celestial kingdom in his entrance into heaven; protection, security, and the abundant supply of all blessings, in his kingdom; secure anticipation of judgment in the power of judging committed to him. In fine, since in him all kinds of blessings are treasured up, let us draw a full supply from him, and none from any other quarter." Calvin, *Institutes*, 2.16.19.

24. B. B. Warfield, "On Calvin as a Theologian," Third Millennium Ministries, accessed March 22, 2016, www.thirdmill.org/newfiles/bb_warfield/Warfield .Calvin.pdf.

25. J. I. Packer, *A Quest for Godliness: The Puritan Vision of the Christian Life* (Wheaton, IL: Crossway Books, 1990), 201.

26. R. Tudor Jones, quoted in John Jefferson Davis, *Meditation and Communion with God: Contemplating Scripture in an Age of Distraction* (Downers Grove, IL: IVP Academic, 2012), 46.

27. Thomas Goodwin, *Of Christ the Mediator*, cited in *A Puritan Theology: Doctrine for Life*, ed. Joel R. Beeke and Mark Jones (Grand Rapids, MI: Reformation Heritage Books, 2012), 483.

28. "As the bifurcation of union with Christ became complete, the theme itself also become superfluous as an umbrella concept unifying justification and sanctification. To speak of a federal or legal union with Christ is simply to describe justification without remainder. Likewise, to speak of a vital union is to speak of sanctification. To the extent that the theme of union with Christ remains present in the successors of Hodge and Berkhof, it is largely

vestigial ... The religious implications of this federal trajectory should also be carefully noted ... the bifurcation of forensic and transformatory categories made it virtually impossible to grasp the essential unity of salvation, and the Christian is left with an unstable dialectic tending toward legalism one moment, and antinomianism the next." William Evans, *Imputation and Impartation: Union with Christ in American Reformed Theology* (Eugene, OR: Wipf & Stock, 2008), 237.

29. B. B. Warfield, *Faith and Life: "Conferences" in the Oratory of Princeton Seminary* (London: Longmans, Green, and Co., 1916), 422–23.

30. John Murray, *Redemption Accomplished and Applied* (Grand Rapids, MI: Eerdmans, 1955), 161.

31. Sinclair Ferguson, *The Holy Spirit* (Downers Grove, IL: InterVarsity, 1996), 100.

32. Reymond, *New Systematic Theology*, dccclix.

33. John Owen, *An Exposition of the Epistle to the Hebrews*, in *The Works of John Owen* (Edinburgh: Banner of Truth, 1991), 20:148, cited in *A Puritan Theology*, ed. Beeke and Jones, 483.

34. Sinclair Ferguson, *The Trinitarian Devotion of John Owen* (Lake Mary, FL: Reformation Trust, 2014), 64.

35. See John Owen, *Communion with the Triune God*, ed. Kelly M. Kapic and Justin Taylor (Wheaton, IL: Crossway Books, 2007).

36. Jonathan Edwards, quoted in George M. Marsden, *Jonathan Edwards: A Life* (New Haven, CT: Yale University Press, 2003), 463.

37. Edwards, quoted in Marsden, *Jonathan Edwards*, 463.

38. Michael J. McClymond and Gerald R. McDermott, *The Theology of Jonathan Edwards* (Oxford: Oxford University Press, 2012), 38.

39. For a full-length development of this theme, see John Piper, *God Is the Gospel: Meditations on God's Love as the Gift of Himself* (Wheaton, IL: Crossway Books, 2005).

40. Edwards, quoted in Marsden, *Jonathan Edwards*, 463.

41. McClymond and McDermott, *Theology*, 8.

42. *The Works of Jonathan Edwards*, vols. 1–2 (Edinburgh: Banner of Truth, 2011), Kindle location 89700.

43. Karl Barth, *Church Dogmatics*, IV 3.2., quoted in Neder, *Participation*, Kindle location 68.

44. Neder, *Participation*, Kindle location 72.

45. T. F. Torrance, *Incarnation: The Person and Life of Christ* (Downers Grove, IL: IVP Academic, 2008).

46. See above all Bonhoeffer's *Ethics*.

47. C. S. Lewis, *Mere Christianity*, IV.4 (London: Fount Paperbacks, 1982), 149–50.

48. See Timothy Ware, *The Orthodox Church: An Introduction to Eastern Christianity* (New York: Penguin Books, 1997).

49. See Julie Canlis, *Calvin's Ladder: A Spiritual Theology of Ascent and Ascension* (Grand Rapids, MI: Eerdmans, 2010); Michael S. Horton, *Covenant and Salvation* (Louisville: Westminster John Knox, 2007); and Bruce L. McCormack, ed., *Justification in Perspective: Historical Developments and Contemporary Challenges* (Grand Rapids, MI: Baker Academic, 2006).

50. See Constantine Campbell, *Paul and Union with Christ: An Exegetical and Theological Study* (Grand Rapids, MI: Zondervan, 2012).

CHAPTER 6: WHATEVER HAPPENED TO UNION WITH CHRIST?

1. Alan Lightman, *The Accidental Universe: The World You Thought You Knew* (New York: Vintage Books, 2013), 15.

2. John Murray, *Redemption Accomplished and Applied* (Grand Rapids, MI: Eerdmans, 1955), 161, 170.

3. Kevin DeYoung, *The Hole in Our Holiness: Filling the Gap between Gospel Passion and the Pursuit of Godliness* (Wheaton, IL: Crossway Books, 2012), Kindle location 1379.

4. B. F. Westcott, quoted in Lewis B. Smedes, *Union with Christ: A Biblical View of the New Life in Jesus Christ* (Grand Rapids, MI: Eerdmans, 1983), 58.

5. Smedes, *Union with Christ*, 59.

6. Gerard Manley Hopkins, "God's Grandeur," Poetry Foundation, accessed March 23, 2016, www.poetryfoundation.org/poem/173660.

7. G. K. Chesterton, *Orthodoxy: The Romance of Faith* (Chicago: Moody, 2009), 81, 89.

8. Charles Taylor, *A Secular Age* (Cambridge, MA: Belknap, 2007), 25.

9. Taylor, *Secular Age*, 542.

10. Taylor, *Secular Age*, 27. For helpful summaries of Charles Taylor, see James K. A. Smith's *How (Not) to Be Secular* (Grand Rapids, MI: Eerdmans, 2014) and Timothy Keller's *Walking with God through Pain and Suffering* (New York: Dutton, 2013), 53–54.

11. Against the strident insistence that faith and science are incompatible (espoused by Richard Dawkins), see, among others, Francis S. Collins, *The Language of God: A Scientist Presents Evidence for Belief* (New York: Free Press, 2006).

12. Steven Jay Gould, "The Meaning of Life," *Life*, December 1988.

13. Chesterton, *Orthodoxy*, 36.

14. Shakespeare, *Hamlet*, 1.5.166–67, Shakespeare Online, accessed March 23, 2016, http://shakespeare-online.com/plays/hamlet_1_5.html.

15. MMPI Newsom, Archer, Trumbetta, and Gottesman 2003, cited in Jean M. Twenge, et al., "Egos Inflating Over Time: A Cross-Temporal Meta-Analysis of the Narcissistic Personality Inventory," Research Gate, August 2008, www.researchgate.net/publication/5342670_Egos_Inflating_Over_Time_A _Cross-Temporal_Meta-Analysis_of_the_Narcissistic_Personality_Inventory.

16. John Calvin, *Institutes of the Christian Religion*, ed. John T. McNeill, trans. Ford Lewis Battles (Philadelphia: Westminster, 1960), 3.1.1–2.

17. Sinclair Ferguson, *The Holy Spirit* (Downers Grove, IL: InterVarsity, 1996), 72.

18. J. I. Packer, *Keep in Step with the Spirit* (Tarrytown, NY: Revell, 1984), 66.

19. Frederick Dale Bruner, *The Holy Spirit: Shy Member of the Trinity* (Eugene, OR: Wipf & Stock, 2001).

20. Richard F. Lovelace, *Dynamics of Spiritual Life* (Downers Grove, IL: InterVarsity, 1979), 131.

21. Ferguson, *Holy Spirit*, 12.

22. Conversely, a deeper understanding of union with Christ will necessarily lead to a deeper experience of the Holy Spirit, and holds potential to bring these camps together and guard each from error.

23. Hans Boersma, *Heavenly Participation: The Weaving of a Sacramental Tapestry* (Grand Rapids, MI: Eerdmans, 2011), 3.

24. Murray, *Redemption*, 166.

25. D. A. Carson, quoted in Marcus Peter Johnson, *One with Christ: An Evangelical Theology of Salvation* (Wheaton, IL: Crossway Books, 2013), 47.

26. Murray, *Redemption*, 172.

27. D. A. Carson adds, "Moreover, the word *spirituality* today is often 'such an ill-defined, amorphous entity that it covers all kinds of phenomenon an earlier generation of Christians ... would have dismissed as error, even as 'paganism' or 'heathenism.'" Quoted in Klaus Issler, *Wasting Time with God: A Christian Spirituality of Friendship with God* (Downers Grove, IL: InterVarsity, 2001), Kindle location 212.

28. Augustine, quoted in Boersma, *Heavenly Participation*, Kindle location 38.

29. DeYoung, *Hole in Our Holiness*, Kindle location 1379.

30. This is a point J. Todd Billings stresses in his excellent book *Union with Christ: Reframing Theology and Ministry for the Church* (Grand Rapids, MI: Baker Academic, 2011).

31. J. R. R. Tolkien, "On Fairy Stories," in *Tree and Leaf* (New York: HarperCollins, 2001), 69. Special thanks to Timothy Keller for drawing my attention to this essay.

32. C. S. Lewis, *The Weight of Glory* (London: Collier Macmillan, 1980), 18.

33. Tolkien, "On Fairy Stories," 71–72.

34. Lewis, *Weight of Glory*, 16–17.

CHAPTER 7: A NEW IDENTITY: WHO AM I?

1. Ralph Ellison, interviewed by Alfred Chester and Vilma Howard, *Paris Review*, www.theparisreview.org/interviews/5053/the-art-of-fiction-no-8-ralph-ellison.

2. F. Scott Fitzgerald, *The Great Gatsby* (New York: Collier Books, 1992), 71.

3. *Rocky*, directed by John G. Avildsen (1976), quoted at IMDB, accessed March 23, 2016, www.imdb.com/title/tt0075148/quotes.

4. I first read this idea in Lewis B. Smedes, *Union with Christ: A Biblical View of the New Life in Jesus Christ* (Grand Rapids, MI: Eerdmans, 1983),

109. Smedes writes, "Christian self-understanding is found outside of the Christian."

5. Epictetus famously put it, "Men are disturbed not by things, but by the view which they take of them."

6. Carol Dweck, *Mindset: The New Psychology of Success* (New York: Random, 2008), 15. "Your mindset is all about your beliefs," writes Professor Dweck in her bestseller. "Your beliefs are the key to your happiness," she adds. Dweck says she wrote her book out of a concern for her students, most of whom assumed their mindsets were fixed. "But your mindset is all about your beliefs and your beliefs can change." Here is a bestseller, written by a renowned social scientist from a secular perspective, but saying something very similar to the apostle Paul in the New Testament.

7. *Frozen*, directed by Chris Buck and Jennifer Lee (Burbank, CA: Walt Disney Animation Studios, 2013).

8. David Brooks, *The Road to Character* (New York: Random, 2015), Kindle location 244.

9. Charles Taylor, *The Ethics of Authenticity* (Cambridge, MA: Harvard University Press, 1991), 23.

10. Dale S. Kuehne, *Sex and the iWorld: Rethinking Relationship Beyond an Age of Individualism* (Grand Rapids, MI: Baker Academic, 2009), 32.

11. Robert N. Bellah, et al., *Habits of the Heart: Individualism and Commitment in American Life* (Berkeley, CA: University of California Press, 1985), 27.

12. Kanye West, quoted in Ann Oldenburg, "Bruce Jenner: Kanye's Wise Words Helped Kim Accept Transition," *USA Today*, April 24, 2015, http://entertainthis .usatoday.com/2015/04/24/bruce-jenner-kanyes-wise-words-helped-kim -accept-transition/.

13. Barry Schwartz, "The Paradox of Choice," TED, July 2005, www.ted.com /talks/barry_schwartz_on_the_paradox_of_choice/transcript?language=en.

14. Planned Parenthood v. Casey, 505 U.S. 833 (Justices Kennedy, Souter, and O'Connor).

15. Alain Ehrenberg, *The Weariness of the Self: Diagnosing the History of Depression in the Contemporary Age* (Montreal: McGill-Queen's University Press, 2009), back cover copy.

16. Schwartz, "Paradox," www.ted.com/talks/barry_schwartz_on_the_paradox _of_choice/transcript?language=en.

17. Ellison, *Paris Review*, www.theparisreview.org/interviews/5053/the-art-of-fiction -no-8-ralph-ellison. Jonathan Franzen's novel *Freedom* makes a similar point that the freedom we so casually speak about and so easily champion often brings with it shackles that we didn't foresee.

18. W. H. Auden, "In Memory of W. B. Yeats," section 1.

19. J. Todd Billings, *Union with Christ: Reframing Theology and Ministry for the Church* (Grand Rapids, MI: Baker Academic, 2011), 15.

20. Billings, "Salvation as Adoption in Christ," chapter 1 in *Union with Christ*.

21. See Martin Luther, *On Christian Liberty*: "Faith … unites the soul with Christ as a bride is united with her bridegroom … It follows that everything they have they hold in common, the good as well as the evil. Accordingly the believing soul can boast of and glory in whatever Christ has as though it were its own, and whatever the soul has Christ claims as his own." *Luther's Works, Vol. 31: Career of the Reformer I*, ed. J. J. Pelikan, H. C. Oswald, and H. T. Lehmann (Philadelphia: Fortress, 1999), 351.

22. Thanks to my friend and colleague Paul Kim for this illustration.

23. Schwartz, "Paradox," www.ted.com/talks/ barry_schwartz_on_the_paradox_of_choice/transcript?language=en.

24. The phrase "center and circumference" is from Smedes, *Union with Christ*, xii.

25. Ralph Ellison, *Invisible Man* (New York: Knopf Doubleday, 2010), 243.

26. J. I. Packer, *Knowing God* (Downers Grove, IL: InterVarsity, 1993) 202, 206.

27. Dietrich Bonhoeffer, *Letters and Papers from Prison* (New York: Collier Macmillan, 1972), 348.

28. Victor Hugo, *Les Misérables*, trans. Charles E. Wilbour (New York: Modern Library, 1992), 96–97.

29. Quoted in *Seeing through the Eye: Malcolm Muggeridge on Faith*, ed. Cecil Kuhne (San Francisco: Ignatius, 2005), 5.

30. We need a different J. C. than Jiminy Cricket to help us, and I don't think the coincidence is incidental.

31. "Americans in Paris," *This American Life*, WBEZ, July 28, 2000, www.thisamericanlife.org/radio-archives/episode/165/americans-in-paris.

CHAPTER 8: A NEW HORIZON: WHERE AM I HEADED?

1. Walker Percy, quoted in Diogenes Allen, *Spiritual Theology: The Theology of Yesterday for Spiritual Help Today* (Cambridge, MA: Cowley, 1997), Kindle locations 285–88.

2. Walker Percy, "The Holiness of the Ordinary," *Signposts in a Strange Land* (New York: Noonday, 1991), 369.

3. Friedrich Nietzsche, *Twilight of the Idols*, 1.12.

4. Walter Brueggemann, *Genesis*, Interpretation: A Bible Commentary for Teaching and Preaching (Atlanta: John Knox, 1982), 32.

5. See Anthony A. Hoekema's *Created in God's Image* (Grand Rapids, MI: Eerdmans, 1994) for a good historical, theological survey.

6. J. Richard Middleton, *The Liberating Image: The Imago Dei in Genesis 1* (Grand Rapids, MI: Brazos, 2005), 109–10.

7. Middleton, *Liberating Image*, 104.

8. Middleton calls it "a genuine democratization of ancient Near Eastern royal ideology," *Liberating Image*, 121. He's saying that here we find the seeds of the democratic ideal we so cherish today—that all men and women are created equal.

9. In calling us "image of God," Middleton concludes, it "must be acknowledged as one of the most daring acts of theological imagination within Scripture … [It] crystallize[s] the central Israelite insight about being human in a term typically applied only to idols, kings, and priests—and thereby profoundly affected the worldview and theological imagination of generations of biblical readers," *Liberating Image*, 231.

10. C. S. Lewis, *The Weight of Glory* (New York: Macmillan, 1980), 19.

11. Carl R. Rogers, "Reinhold Niebuhr's *The Self and the Dramas of History*: A Criticism," *Pastoral Psychology* 9 (June 1958): 17, cited in Hoekema, *Created in God's Image*, 105.

12. Joel Lovell, "George Saunders's Advice to Graduates," 6th Floor, July 31, 2013, http://6thfloor.blogs.nytimes.com/2013/07/31/george-saunderss-advice-to-graduates/?_r=1.

13. Illustration from Derek Tidball, "Holiness: Restoring God's Image," in *Sanctification: Explorations in Theology and Practice*, ed. Kelly M. Kapic (Downers Grove, IL: InterVarsity, 2014), Kindle locations 273–86.

14. Dante Alighieri, *Purgatorio*, XVII.104–5, trans. Allen Mandelbaum (New York: Bantam Classics, 1984), 157.

15. For a recent treatment of the contemporary significance of Dante's poem, see Rod Dreher, *How Dante Can Save Your Life: The Life-Changing Wisdom of History's Greatest Poem* (New York: Regan Arts, 2015), Kindle location 77.

16. Peter Kreeft, *Christianity for Modern Pagans: Pascal's Pensées Edited, Outlined, and Explained* (San Francisco: Ignatius, 1993), 313–14.

17. Pascal, quoted in Kreeft, *Christianity*, 313.

18. Karl Barth, quoted in Adam Neder, *Participation in Christ: An Entry into Karl Barth's Church "Dogmatics"* (Louisville: Westminster John Knox, 2009), Kindle locations 582–83.

19. Kevin DeYoung puts it this way: "God does want you to be the real you. He does want you to be true to yourself. But the 'you' he's talking about is the 'you' that you are by grace, not by nature." *The Hole in Our Holiness: Filling the Gap between Gospel Passion and the Pursuit of Godliness* (Wheaton, IL: Crossway Books, 2012), 100.

20. P. T. O'Brien, quoted in Tidball, "Holiness," Kindle locations 346–47.

21. John Calvin, *Hebrews and 1 and 2 Peter*, Calvin's New Testament Commentaries (Grand Rapids, MI: William B. Eerdmans, 1994), 330.

22. Walker Percy, "Diagnosing the Modern Malaise," *Signposts in a Strange Land* (New York: Noonday, 1991), 213.

23. D. Martyn Lloyd-Jones, *Spiritual Depression: Its Causes and Cures* (Grand Rapids, MI: William B. Eerdmans, 1965), 75.

24. Leanne Payne, *The Healing Presence: Curing the Soul through Union with Christ* (Grand Rapids, MI: Baker, 1995), 12.

25. C. S. Lewis, *The Problem of Pain* (New York: Collier Macmillan, 1962), 42–43.

CHAPTER 9: A NEW PURPOSE: WHAT AM I HERE FOR?

1. Søren Kierkegaard, *Papers and Journals: A Selection* (New York: Penguin, 1996), 295.

2. Walker Percy, "Diagnosing the Modern Malaise," *Signposts in a Strange Land* (New York: Noonday, 1991), 213.

3. Widely attributed to Luther (unspecified). Luther also wrote in his *Preface to Romans*, "Faith cannot help doing good works constantly.... Anyone who does not do good works in this manner is an unbeliever.... Thus, it is just as impossible to separate faith and works as it is to separate heat and light from fire!" And Calvin, in his *Antidote to the Council of Trent*, "I wish the reader to understand that as often as we mention faith alone in this question, we are not thinking of a dead faith, which worketh not by love, but holding faith to be the only cause of justification. (Galatians 5:6; Romans 3:22.) It is therefore faith alone which justifies, and yet the faith which justifies is not alone: just as it is the heat alone of the sun which warms the earth, and yet in the sun it is not alone, because it is constantly conjoined with light."

4. J. I. Packer, *Rediscovering Holiness: Know the Fullness of Life with God* (Ventura, CA: Gospel Light, 2009), 33.

5. This is the Scripture verse on the cover of one of the first Christian books I ever read in college, *The Pursuit of Holiness* by Jerry Bridges (Colorado Springs: NavPress, 1990). For other classic works on the call of holiness for the Christian life, see *Holiness* by J. C. Ryle, *The Holiness of God* by R. C. Sproul, and more recently, *The Hole in Our Holiness* by Kevin DeYoung.

6. "Forgiven Knightley," *Sun*, accessed March 24, 2016, www.thesun.co.uk/sol /homepage/showbiz/bizarre/4285973/Atheist-actress-Keira-Knightley-wishes -she-believed-in-God.html.

7. Dana Dirksen, "What Were Adam and Eve Like When God Made Them?," *Questions with Answers Vol. 1: God and Creation* © 2006 Songs for Saplings.

8. *The Works of Jonathan Edwards*, vols. 1–2 (Edinburgh: Banner of Truth, 2011), Kindle locations 28482–84.

9. *Collected Writings of John Murray, Vol. 2: Systematic Theology* (Edinburgh: Banner of Truth, 1977), 277.

10. J. C. Ryle, quoted in Kevin DeYoung, *The Hole in Our Holiness: Filling the Gap between Gospel Passion and the Pursuit of Godliness* (Wheaton, IL: Crossway Books, 2012), 11.

11. Augustus Toplady, "Rock of Ages, Cleft for Me," *Trinity Hymnal* (Atlanta: Great Commission, 1990), 499.

12. Herman Bavinck, quoted in G. C. Berkouwer, *Faith and Sanctification* (Grand Rapids, MI: Eerdmans, 1980), 22.

13. Walter Marshall, *The Gospel Mystery of Sanctification: Growing in Holiness by Living in Union with Christ* (Eugene, OR: Wipf & Stock, 2005), 10.

14. Pindar, *Pythian 2*, line 72.

15. Jerry Bridges, *The Pursuit of Holiness* (Colorado Springs: NavPress, 1990), 14.

16. Both Sinclair Ferguson (*The Holy Spirit* [Downers Grove, IL: InterVarsity, 1996], 105) and Kevin DeYoung (*Hole in Our Holiness*, 104) reference the power of union with Christ as an aid against temptation.

17. Romano Guardini, *The Mystery of Grace*, in *Prayers from Theology*, posted on The Christocentric Life, June 25, 2011, http://christocentriclife.blogspot.com/2011/06/mystery-of-grace-by-romano-guardini.html.

18. *Letters of Samuel Rutherford* (Carlisle, PA: Puritan Paperbacks, 2006), 167.

CHAPTER 10: A NEW HOPE: WHAT CAN I HOPE FOR?

1. Sherry Turkle, *Alone Together: Why We Expect More from Technology and Less from Each Other* (New York: Basic Books, 2011), 11.

2. Thomas Wolfe, "God's Lonely Man," in *The Hills Beyond* (New York: Plume/New American Library, 1982), 146.

3. There are a few excellent treatments on the continuing importance of the ascension out there. Elyse Fitzpatrick's *The Continuing Importance of the Incarnation*. Gerrit Dawson's *Jesus Ascended* is well worth your time. For more advanced treatments, see T. F. Torrance's *Atonement*, Julie Canlis's *Calvin's Ladder*, and Douglas Farrow's *Ascension and Ecclesia*.

4. The Apostle's Creed.

5. That God created "the heavens and the earth" (Gen. 1:1) demands that we think differently about how the whole cosmos is, so to speak, put together. But heaven and earth are not simply two different locations. They are two different dimensions of God's creation beyond what we can see or observe. "Certainly the church, just because it believes that God in Christ has given himself to creation as its *Lord,* has something unique to say about the way creation is ordered." Douglas Farrow, *Ascension and Ecclesia* (Grand Rapids, MI: Eerdmans, 1999), x.

6. N. T. Wright, *Simply Jesus: A New Vision of Who He Was, What He Did, and Why He Matters* (New York: HarperCollins, 2011), 196.

7. J. I. Packer, *Knowing God* (Downers Grove, IL: InterVarsity, 1993), 102. Packer actually uses this illustration as an example of a mistaken understanding of the gift of God's wisdom—that it would be a mistake to expect God to ever take us up into the control room to let us see how everything fits together.

8. Philip Yancey, *The Jesus I Never Knew* (Grand Rapids, MI: Zondervan, 1995), 229.

9. Ian McEwan, *Atonement* (New York: Anchor Books, 2007), 479.

10. 1 Pet. 3:22; Eph. 1:20–21, Mark 14:62.

11. James B. Torrance, *Worship, Community and the Triune God of Grace* (Downers Grove, IL: IVP Academic, 1996), 47–50.

12. See Heb. 2:17; 1 Tim. 2:5; Isa. 49:16; Heb. 9:12, 22; Heb. 7:27; John 1:29; Heb. 9:26; Mark 15:38.

13. John Owen, whom I've referenced several times in this book, wrote a great deal about the priesthood of Christ. "The Lord underwent the punishment due to our sins in the judgment of God, and according to the sentence of the law; for how did God make our sins to meet on him, how did he bear them, if he did not suffer the penalty due to them, or if he underwent some other inconvenience, but not the exact demerit of sin?" *The Priesthood of Christ: Its Necessity and Nature* (Fearn, Scotland: Christian Heritage, 2010), 17.

14. C. S. Lewis, *Mere Christianity* (Glasgow: Collins Fount Paperbacks, 1982), 123.

15. The Heidelberg Catechism says it this way: "Q. 49. What benefit do we receive from Christ's ascension into heaven? First, that He is our Advocate in the presence of His Father in heaven. Second, that we have our flesh in heaven as a sure pledge, that He as the Head, will also take us, His members, up to Himself. Third, that He sends us His Spirit as an earnest, by whose power we seek those things which are above, where Christ sits at the right hand of God, and not things on the earth."

16. As described in Barbara Brown Taylor, "The Day We Were Left Behind," *Christianity Today*, May 18, 1998, www.christianitytoday.com/ct/1998/may18/8t6046.html. Julie Canlis, in her book on the importance of the ascension for the theology of John Calvin, adds, "For Calvin, the ladder is Christ—not in the facile explanation that 'Christ is the way,' but that our ascent is profoundly bound up in Christ's ascension, by our *participation in his descent* … His ascent is our path and goal. His narrative has become our own." *Calvin's Ladder* (Grand Rapids, MI: Eerdmans, 2010), 50–51.

17. Gerrit Scott Dawson, *Jesus Ascended* (Phillipsburg, NJ: P&R, 2004), 7. Of the books on the ascension I mentioned earlier, Dawson's has been the most helpful to me. And I am indebted to him for pointing me toward several of the early church references in this chapter.

18. Elyse M. Fitzpatrick, *Found in Him: The Joy of the Incarnation and Our Union with Christ* (Wheaton, IL: Crossway Books, 2013), 44.

19. See Taylor, "The Day We Were Left Behind," www.christianitytoday.com/ct /1998/may18/8t6046.html.

20. "Let us remember how far the secret power of the Holy Spirit towers above all our senses, and how foolish it is to wish to measure his immeasurableness by our measure. What, then, our mind does not comprehend, let faith conceive: that the Spirit truly unites things separated in space." John Calvin, *Institutes*, 4.17.10.

21. Robert Hass, "Privilege of Being," in *Human Wishes* (New York: Ecco, 1989), 69–70.

CHAPTER 11: THE ART OF ABIDING

1. A favorite reminder of Dallas Willard (*The Great Omission: Rediscovering Jesus' Essential Teachings on Discipleship* [San Francisco: HarperOne, 2006], 61). Martin Luther also writes, "What Augustine says is true, 'He who has created you without you will not save you without you.' Works are necessary to salvation, but they do not cause salvation, because faith alone gives life." Quoted by Bernhard Lohse in *Martin Luther's Theology* (Minneapolis: Fortress, 1999), 265.

2. Walter Meller, *Village Homilies* (London: W. Skeffington and Son, 1878), 182.

3. Quoted in Marcus Peter Johnson, *One with Christ: An Evangelical Theology of Salvation* (Wheaton, IL: Crossway Books, 2013), 49.

4. John Owen, *Overcoming Sin and Temptation*, ed. Kelly M. Kapic and Justin Taylor (Wheaton, IL: Crossway Books, 2006), 332.

5. *The Works of Jonathan Edwards*, vols. 1–2 (Edinburgh: Banner of Truth, 2011), Kindle location 67575.

6. We can hold on to him only because Christ first holds on to us, a point we will stress in the next chapter (2 Tim. 2:13).

7. David Brooks, *The Road to Character* (New York: Random, 2015), Kindle location 5044. Though Brooks is not writing specifically of the Christian life, but of character development in general, his question is still pertinent.

8. Christina Rossetti, "Up-hill," in *Rosetti: Everyman's Library Pocket Poets* (New York: Knopf, 1993), 248.

9. Quoted in Alister E. McGrath, *T. F. Torrance: An Intellectual Biography* (London: T & T Clark, 1999), 74.

10. Thanks to Bill Bright for the image of spiritual breathing.

11. Oswald Chambers, *My Utmost for His Highest*, "June 14."

12. Robert Robinson, "Come, Thou Fount of Every Blessing," in *Trinity Hymnal* (Atlanta: Great Commission, 1990), 457.

13. An oft-quoted summary of the *Rule of St. Benedict*.

CHAPTER 12: THE MEANS OF ABIDING

1. The importance of spiritual exercises is not unique to the Christian tradition. For example, the Stoic philosopher Seneca trained his pupils to examine at the end of each day their behavior and attitudes for that day—where they failed to live up to their Stoic ideals.

2. Richard J. Foster, *Celebration of Discipline: The Path to Spiritual Growth* (San Francisco: HarperSanFrancisco, 1978), 7.

3. John Jefferson Davis, *Meditation and Communion with God: Contemplating Scripture in an Age of Distraction* (Downers Grove, IL: InterVarsity, 2012), Kindle locations 723–27.

4. Eugene Peterson, *Eat This Book: A Conversation in the Art of Spiritual Reading* (Grand Rapids, MI: William B. Eerdmans, 2006), 4.

5. Mother Teresa, *The Joy in Loving: A Guide to Daily Living* (New York: Penguin, 2000), 108.

6. Oscar Wilde, *An Ideal Husband*.

7. Oswald Chambers, *My Utmost for His Highest*, "May 25."

8. See Jerry Sittser, *When God Doesn't Answer Your Prayer* (Grand Rapids, MI: Zondervan, 2007), esp. ch. 4.

9. Charles E. Moore, ed., *Provocations: Spiritual Writings of Kierkegaard* (Maryknoll, NY: Orbis, 2009), 349.

10. Robert Rayburn, "Should Christians Observe the Sabbath?" *Presbyterion* 10 (Spring–Fall 1984), 74.

11. For more on how union with Christ transforms our experience of worship, see James B. Torrance's *Worship, Community and the Triune God.* I understand it's a loaded thought, that Christ is our worship leader. It deserves a fuller treatment, and Torrance's book is a good place to whet your imagination.

12. Augustine defined sacraments as "a visible form of an invisible grace," quoted in Leonard Vander Zee, *Christ, Baptism and the Lord's Supper* (Downers Grove, IL: IVP Academic, 2004), 29.

13. Westminster Confession of Faith, 28.1: "Baptism is a sacrament of the New Testament, ordained by Jesus Christ, not only for the solemn admission of the party baptized into the visible Church; but also, to be unto him a sign and seal of the covenant of grace, of his ingrafting into Christ, of regeneration, of remission of sins, and of his giving up unto God, through Jesus Christ, to walk in newness of life. Which sacrament is, by Christ's own appointment, to be continued in His Church until the end of the world."

14. This too is an expansive subject that deserves more than an endnote. For a good primer on the place of the sacraments in the church's life, see Vander Zee's *Christ, Baptism and the Lord's Supper.* Or, for a more technical treatment, Keith Mathison's *Given for You.* Or, for the most interested, Brian Gerrish's *Grace and Gratitude.* The Reformation debates concerning the Lord's Supper almost all assumed Christ was present in the sacrament. The question was always *how*? How is Christ present? This question divided Catholics and Luther and Calvin and Ulrich Zwingli. But even Zwingli himself (whose name is associated with the "memorialist" position) was not a memorialist in the sense of believing the signs were completely divorced from the reality they represented. On this point, Luther, Calvin, and the Catholic Church agreed—the elements were not simply bare remembrances. Each camp believed Christ was truly present. Their question was *how*, and why it mattered. Our aversion to the real spiritual power of the Lord's Supper today—as an ongoing means of grace—has much less to do with our biblical fidelity and much more to do with our Enlightenment worldview.

15. Calvin, *Institutes*, 4.17.7, 4.17.32.

16. Dietrich Bonhoeffer, *Life Together* (New York: Harper & Brothers, 1954), 23.

17. See Wesley Hill's book, *Spiritual Friendship* (Grand Rapids, MI: Brazos, 2015).

18. *The Works of Jonathan Edwards*, vols. 1–2 (Edinburgh: Banner of Truth, 2011), Kindle locations 1582–84.

19. *Works of Jonathan Edwards*, vols. 1–2, Kindle locations 1545–47.

20. Blaise Pascal, *Pensées* (New York: Penguin Books, 1995), 285–86.

21. Anthony Trollope, *An Autobiography* (New York: Dodd, Mean, 1912), 105.

22. Chuck Close, quoted in Mason Currey, *Daily Rituals: How Artists Work* (New York: Alfred A. Knopf, 2014), 64. Currey's book is a delightful sampling that I'd recommend to any one interested in how daily rituals can foster creativity.

CHAPTER 13: THE SECRET OF ABIDING

1. "All right knowledge of God is born of obedience," writes John Calvin, *Institutes*, I.6.2, echoing Jesus's statement in John 14. For more on this idea, see John Owen, *Communion with the Triune God*, ed. Kelly M. Kapic and Justin Taylor (Wheaton, IL: Crossway Books, 2007), 21. For a contemporary gloss on this idea, see Kevin DeYoung, *The Hole in Our Holiness: Filling the Gap between Gospel Passion and the Pursuit of Godliness* (Wheaton, IL: Crossway Books, 2012), 124–31.

2. Samuel Rutherford, letter to Earlston, younger, June 16, 1637, in *Letters of Samuel Rutherford* (Carlisle, PA: Puritan Paperbacks, 2006), 87.

3. John Owen, *Communion with God*, from *The Essential Works of John Owen*, Kindle locations 42928–29.

4. Owen, *Communion*, Kindle locations 42865–66.

CHAPTER 14: THE NECESSARY PATH OF ABIDING: SUFFERING

1. Timothy Keller, *Walking with God through Pain and Suffering* (New York: Dutton, 2013), 30.

2. John Calvin, *The Golden Booklet of the True Christian Life* (Grand Rapids, MI: Baker Books, 2004), 48.

3. If Jesus is the perfect embodiment of the image of God—what God intends humanity to be—and Jesus's life was oriented toward a cross, and this cross

was necessary for him and necessary for us, then it's a provocative question: What does the cross of Jesus have to tell us about what it means to be human? What does the cross tell us about the art of living?

4. Yes, the Lord *may* be using suffering to discipline us (Heb. 12:3–11), but the author of Hebrews is clear to say that this discipline is a reflection of our Father's love, not a punishment for sin that needs atoning for (10:10).

5. George Macdonald, *Unspoken Sermons*, First Series, quoted in C. S. Lewis, *The Problem of Pain* (New York: Collier Macmillan, 1962), 7.

6. Horatio G. Spafford, "It Is Well with My Soul," in *Trinity Hymnal* (Atlanta: Great Commission, 1990), 691.

7. Keller, *Walking with God*, 312.

8. *Selma*, directed by Ava DuVernay (London: Cloud Eight, 2014).

CHAPTER 15: EVERY DAY—UNION WITH THE COSMIC CHRIST

1. Robert N. Bellah, et al., *Habits of the Heart: Individualism and Commitment in American Life* (Berkeley, CA: University of California Press, 1985), 21.

2. Bellah, *Habits*, 65.

3. Dietrich Bonhoeffer, *Life Together* (Minneapolis: Fortress, 2015), 13.

4. D. A. Carson, *Love in Hard Places* (Wheaton, IL: Crossway Books, 2002), 61.

5. Charles Wesley, "And Can It Be That I Should Gain," in *Trinity Hymnal* (Atlanta: Great Commission, 1990), 455.

6. Christopher Lasch, *The Culture of Narcissism: American Life in an Age of Diminishing Expectations* (New York: W. W. Norton, 1979).

7. A popular way of personalizing the distinctness of Christ's love. To be certain, the gospel must be personal (Gal. 2:20), but it can never remain private.

8. Once again I'm talking about the "New Perspective on Paul" and its challenge to the traditional Protestant understanding of justification. Is justification primarily a soteriological category, how one "gets into" the people of God? Or is it primarily an ecclesiological category, who's "in" the people of God? Five hundred years before modern scholars began to argue that ecclesiology and soteriology were inseparable, John Calvin made the very same argument, and without compromising justification as a legal, forensic category. At the same

time, Calvin has the highest view of the church and could agree that "outside of the church there is no salvation," because for him, to be in Christ was inseparable from being part of Christ's body, the church.

9. See the Westminster Confession of Faith 25.2: "The visible church ... is the kingdom of the Lord Jesus Christ, the house and family of God, out of which there is no ordinary possibility of salvation."

10. For a much richer treatment of why this is a false dichotomy, see *Exploring Ecclesiology* by Brad Harper and Paul Louis Metzger.

11. For an example of the false choice we may be presented with today, here's a representative quote from a recent book on the mission of the church: "We know this sounds heartless, but it's true: it simply was not Jesus's driving ambition to heal the sick and meet the needs of the poor, as much as he cared for them. He was sent into the world to save people from condemnation (John 3:17), that he might be lifted up so believers could have eternal life (3:14–15)."

12. Lesslie Newbigin, *The Open Secret: An Introduction to the Theology of Mission*, rev. ed. (Grand Rapids, MI: W. B. Eerdmans, 1995), 63–64.

13. Without compromising one bit that the gospel is "good news" to be announced. We don't add to the gospel or complete it in any way. We proclaim it. And we adorn it with the quality of our lives and the concern of our hearts (see Titus 2:10).

14. See Calvin, *Institutes*, 3.11.6: "Christ cannot be torn into parts, so these two which we perceive in him together and conjointly are inseparable."

15. Tennessee Williams, *Small Craft Warnings*, Act II, in *The Theatre of Tennessee Williams: The Milk Train Doesn't Stop Here Anymore* ... (New York: New Directions, 1990), 284.

16. See Robert D. Putnam, *Bowling Alone: The Collapse and Revival of American Community* (New York: Simon & Schuster, 2001).

17. Quoted in Ralph C. Wood, "In Defense of Disbelief," *First Things*, October 1998.

18. Richard Bauckham, *The Theology of the Book of Revelation* (Cambridge, UK: Cambridge University Press, 1993), 58.

19. Lesslie Newbigin, *The Gospel in a Pluralist Society* (Grand Rapids, MI: Eerdmans, 1989), 103.

20. Charles Taylor, *A Secular Age* (Cambridge, MA: Belknap Harvard, 2007).

21. This is one of the more exciting and provocative fields of twentieth-century New Testament scholarship. See G. B. Caird's *Principalities and Powers*, Walter Wink's *The Powers* (three volumes), Marva Dawn's *Powers, Weakness, and the Tabernacling of God* (Grand Rapids, MI: Eerdmans, 2001), and Lesslie Newbigin's *The Gospel in a Pluralist Society* (Grand Rapids, MI: Eerdmans, 1989). Newbigin sums up, "The principalities and powers are real. They are invisible … [but] they meet us as embodied in visible and tangible realities—people, nations, and institutions. And they are powerful … they are created in Christ and for Christ; their true end is to serve him … but they become powers for evil when they attempt to usurp the place which belongs to Christ alone…. They are at the heart of our business as Christians" (207–8). "If we dismiss this as merely outworn mythology, we shall be incapable of grasping the central message of the New Testament" (210). Marva Dawn quotes Thomas R. Yoder Neufeld, who says, "[The powers'] demonic character rests … in their capacity to control the imaginations and behaviors of human beings, individually and communally" (2).

22. Drawing on the work of G. B. Caird, Lesslie Newbigin says that one of the best places in the New Testament to observe how these powers conspire in the world is to ask the question, who killed Jesus? There were various visible historic forces: religious leaders, such as Caiaphas; political leaders, such as Pontius Pilate and Herod; social forces, including the mob who yelled, "Crucify him." Are they *solely* to blame? Paul wrote to the church at Corinth some twenty-five years later, "The rulers of this age, who are doomed to pass away … crucified the Lord of glory" (1 Cor. 2:6, 8). It's clear Paul isn't talking about Herod and Pilate. They have already passed away. He is not just talking about an individual called Herod or Pilate. He is talking about something working behind the scenes in and through these officeholders—a very real power embodied in and exercised by human beings but not identical with them. It's not that these human actors don't have responsibility, but it is to say that Caiaphas, Herod, and Pilate were not just a few wicked men. They were acting as temporary agents, of something more fundamental and more enduring than their own individual opinions. This is not to say that all structures are evil, but that all things were created by Christ and for Christ, including these powers and principalities and that they can be taken captive by spiritual powers and become agents of rebellion. See "Principalities, Powers, and People," ch. 16 in *The Gospel in a Pluralist Society* (Grand Rapids, MI: Eerdmans, 1989). John Stott adds, "That social, political, judicial and

economic structures can become demonic is evident to anybody that has considered that the state, which in Romans 13 is the minister of God, in Revelation 13 has become an ally of the devil." *The Message of Ephesians* (Downers Grove, IL: InterVarsity, 1979), 274.

23. N. T. Wright adds, "The cross was not the defeat of *Christ* at the hands of the *powers*; it was the defeat of the powers at the hands—yes, the bleeding hands—of Christ." *Following Jesus: Biblical Reflections on Discipleship* (Grand Rapids, MI: Eerdmans, 1994), 19.

24. F. F. Bruce, *The Epistles to the Colossians, to Philemon, and to the Ephesians* (Grand Rapids, MI: William B. Eerdmans, 1984), 111.

25. Newbigin, *Gospel in a Pluralist Society*, 208.

26. Sinclair Ferguson, *The Christian Life: A Doctrinal Introduction* (Edinburgh: Banner of Truth, 2013), 101.

27. Robert Frost, "Desert Places," in *The Poetry of Robert Frost* (New York: Owl Book, Henry Holt, 1979), 296.

28. John Murray, *Redemption Accomplished and Applied* (Grand Rapids, MI: Eerdmans, 1955), 168.

29. Jonathan Edwards. "There was, [as] it were, an eternal society or family in the Godhead, in the Trinity of persons. It seems to be God's design to admit the church into the divine family as his son's wife." Quoted in Brad Harper and Paul Louis Metzger, *Exploring Ecclesiology: An Evangelical and Ecumenical Introduction* (Grand Rapids, MI: Brazos, 2009), 37.

30. For John Owen, this is the structure of his masterwork *Communion with God*. Owen divides his book between communion with each member of the Trinity and uses 2 Corinthians 13:14 as his launching point: "The grace of the Lord Jesus Christ, and the love of God, and the communion of the Holy Ghost, *be* with you all" (KJV).

FINAL WORD: A PRAYER FOR UNION WITH CHRIST

1. D. Martyn Lloyd-Jones, *The Unsearchable Riches of Christ: An Exposition of Ephesians 3:1–21* (Grand Rapids, MI: Baker, 1980), 6.